Privatising Power Cuts?

Ownership and Reform of State Electricity Boards in India

The Author

Dr. Joël Ruet, alumni from Ecole des Mines, Paris, is Fellow at the London School of Economics and teaches in Jawaharlal Nehru University, New Delhi. He has been the Head Economist and Director of Centre de Sciences Humaines, New Delhi.

He has specialised in the study of economic reforms of the infrastructure and urban sectors in India, on which he has published extensively in academic journals, edited volumes, as well as books he has coordinated.

He sits in several Indo-French bilateral committees, and has been consulted on reforms by several Government of India committees and electricity regulatory commissions of State governments in India. He has contributed or coordinated several research reports to the French Government.

He currently is the co-ordinator of two Indo-European research networks, on integrated management of water and urban governance in Indian cities.

Privatising Power Cuts?

Ownership and Reform of State Electricity Boards in India

Joël Ruet

Published by Academic Foundation
in association with
Centre de Sciences Humaines,
New Delhi

Academic Foundation
NEW DELHI

First published in 2005 by

Academic Foundation
4772-73 / 23 Bharat Ram Road, (23 Ansari Road), Darya Ganj, New Delhi - 110 002 (India).
Phones : 23245001 / 02 / 03 / 04. Fax : +91-11-23245005. E-mail : academic@vsnl.com
www : academicfoundation.com

Published in association with :
Centre de Sciences Humaines,
New Delhi

Privatising Power Cuts ?
Ownership and Reform of State Electricity Boards in India
by Joël Ruet

ISBN 81-7188-416-4

Designed and typeset by Italics India, New Delhi.
Printed and bound in India.

Contents

...CONTD. ...

List of Tables

List of Boxes and Figures

BOXES

...CONTD. ...

FIGURES

Foreword

Subject and Problematic

The present book is about the reforms in the power sector in India, and more specifically about those in the State Electricity Boards (SEBs). It is based on field work and in-depth interviews, studies and training carried out at various times within the SEBs themselves which covered a total period of seven months spread over two years. It involved interviewing nearly 200 people belonging to SEBs, ministries, governmental agencies, regulatory commissions, private groups, multilateral agencies etc., ranging from meter readers to Power Secretaries in seven States (Andhra Pradesh, Delhi, Haryana, Kerala, Orissa, Punjab, Rajasthan). These States have been selected for reasons not only of economic diversity, but also of political choices towards reforms. By early 2001, SEBs as a whole faced an average 50 per cent level of technical plus non-technical losses, and they collectively owe around $ 5 billion to the Government of India undertakings. This is accelerating, since they face a yearly deficit of an equivalent size. Given this relative failure of current reforms, the book focuses on two issues, first a practical concern on participating in the current round of reforms and second, a more academic concern on the characterisation of the functioning and nature of the Indian state. These issues are:

(i) What are the structural factors (weight and type of procedures, forms of budgetary and hierarchical power etc.) in the organisation and the decision-making process within the SEBs leading to or reinforcing the problems faced by the power sector, or strengthening them? Once these elements are identified, what is their internal consistency, what is the rationality at stake in SEBs?

On this the argument follows the French tradition of non-neo-classical analysis of the economics of the public sector and the three lines of analysis of Simon and March and also takes a position on the New Institutional Economics, following Coase, North and Williamson and others which have influenced the Bretton Woods kind of reform.

(ii) How to reverse the internal rationality of SEBs to implement a reform which would have some chances of success, and what is the impact of current reforms in this respect?

Here the book takes a position on the command economy literature following Kornai, who had a substantial influence on Indian planning and others on property rights, linking up with the current state of Chinese reforms, but the author keeps on coming back to the Indian case.

These two questions are the subject of the book. Its first part studies the organisational nature of SEBs. It gives an alternate and non-classical explanation for their inefficiency. The second part highlights the limits of the reforms engaged further to these classical analyses, and proposes a reform better adapted to the organisational nature of SEBs. As far as the nature and rationality of SEBs are concerned, the book suggests that the latter are not "inefficient enterprises" but actual administrations, whose nature is to simultaneously pursue objectives that are heterogeneous to each other and irreconciliable through sole economic criteria.

Decision making, therefore, cannot rely on sole cost benefit analysis, and the SEBs are by nature alien to the question of the productive efficiency.

The book argues that reforms aiming at improving the efficiency cannot succeed if *in fine* they are only based on monetary incentives. They have to be based on a radical transformation of the organisational nature of SEBs, called "enterprisation". The latter is defined as the tranforming of an administration into a full-fledged enterprise, a point which is not reached through the current so-called 'structural' reforms. The process of this transformation is detailed in the book for paving the way to practical implementation.

The book takes the position that there is misuse of traditional economic concepts and categories to analyse SEBs, which has some dramatic consequences in the proposed reform agenda. Economic concepts derived from the concept of cost can hence not describe the functioning of SEBs, which is articulated on procedural rationality only. Cost cannot be identified *ex-post,* since it cannot be related to any decision, which by nature does not consider any cost, in an information system that does not take cost into account. Cost can neither be used *ex-ante,* as already discussed. Hence, cost is neither a category that circumscribes decisions, nor a category that explains them, nor relates them to each other. The category of cost is neither explicative nor predictive in a SEB. The concept of cost, and further, all the derived concepts, do not apply for SEBs' analysis. In particular, the book shows that the diagnosis of inefficiency is inadequate if solely based on concepts of soft budget constraint or of inefficient allocation of property rights. Indeed, these analyses rely on behavioural hypothesis in which the agents: (i) identify costs, (ii) have the discretionary power to base their decisions on them, and (iii) actually behave as such. These two approaches do not apply for SEBs, respectively because the decisions do not rely on budgets, and because property rights over or in SEBs are not defined. This latter aspect deserves to be studied in detail.

Ruet's study permits him to discuss the privatisation schemes proposed by the World Bank. Certainly, privatisation "enterprises", in the sense that the process that prepares it necessarily includes the specifying and setting up of property rights externally to the entity to privatise (specifying of rules on the appropriation of financial flows, on the control rights). The private enterpreneur, naturally considering financial incentives, will then achieve the internal allocation of property rights. However, a big difficulty has to be overcome in this scheme. Privatisation implies a bidding process, including the monetary evaluation of the SEB. But this is quite impossible technically in an un-enterprised SEB. Indeed, if the preparatory phase consists in setting up property rights (among others through giving guarantees on the non-discretionary intervention of the State), then on one hand, the evaluation of the credibility of these guarantees is uneasy, and on the other hand, the estimation of the value that can generate the use of these rights does not exist. The privatisation of an SEB that is not previously enterprised can then lead to an under-bidding, if each investor takes a premium, as happened in Orissa. Over and above this, the absence of structured information induces an asymetry of information among the various investors. For this reason, there is a risk not to select the most efficient investor in the long run. The concept of enterprisation can then be used to indicate and refine the guarantees to give, and the book provides a clear mathematical model on that issue, helping specifying the efficiency parameters to take into account in the decision to privatise or not.

Contemporary Relevance

The book has contemporary relevance given the policy stance to review the Electricity Act. It is obvious that the issues Ruet raises cannot be papered over and any legislation which attempts to do so will be fragile. Some instances describe this fragility in addition to Ruet's more elaborate analysis.

As far as the regulating bodies and high-level governing institutions are concerned, recently, there has been a sharp attack by a group which was led by the Principal of the Administrative Staff College of India (ASCI). After the good professional studies released for public discussion by the Central Electricity Regulatory Commission under Dr. S.L. Rao, a professional economist, including a Discussion Paper on the principles of tariff fixation there has been little worthwhile work and in fact a number of State-level Commissions have acted in a fairly non-transparent manner. The whole question of the structuring and manning of these bodies has been opened up for debate.

In this context I may be permitted a brief personal intervention. As Minister of Power, the worst kind of pressures I could see were in appointments. Together with my Secretary, who later took premature retirement from the IAS and became Principal of the ASCI mentioned above, I appointed the Member Planning Commission M.N. Srinavasan, the no nonsense former Chairman of Atomic Energy Commission, as the Chairman of an Advisory Committee to the Minister on senior appointments in the Power parastatals. The individuals appointed then implemented some of the largest expansions of capacity in power generation and transmission at lowest costs. This transparent appointing procedure was introduced after quite some introspection in The Electricity Regulatory Commissions Bill, 1997 introduced by me in the Eleventh Lok Sabha on August 14, 1997 (India, Lok Sabha, 1997, Gazette of India, 1997). Fairly high standards of professional competence were also laid down. This provision was removed in later legislation and the selection processes for such appointments are now again chaired by political persons with the unedifying spectacle in some cases of Secretaries to the Government openly lobbying for post retirement perks in this form. The management of regulation and appointment to high level governing institutions is obviously an issue of the highest importance and needs to be discussed openly and transparently. I am indeed happy that the Prime Minister of India heading the UPA Government is emphasising 'professionalism' as the only criteria for appointments. I hope the new Electricity Act amendments being thought of, and other such rules of appointments to high level governing and security bodies, will enforce such provisions. There will be opposition from those who look for post retirement perks from political beneficiaries, but these will have to be resisted.

As far as India and non-renewable resource scarcities is concerned and the long-term issues, it is useful to begin with the kind of problematiques the sustainable development framework studies bring out. The 'business as usual scenarios' bring out unsustainable outcomes. For example:

Projections for the Year 2020

Population	1330 million
Urban Population	**Low:** 465 million **High:** 590 million
Slum Population	**Low:** 85 million **High:** 130 million
Solid Waste Disposal	100 to 110 million tonnes
Demand for Coal for Power Generation	**Low:** 817 million tonnes **High:** 2016 million tonnes
Cropping Intensity	More than 1.5
Net Area Sown	Constant at 141 million hectares since the nineties
Irrigation Intensity	Around 1.75
Water Shortage	Around 10% to 25% between the years 2020/50
Noise Levels	Twice the norms in trend forecast
Air Pollution	Two to two and a half times the norms in trend forecast

Source: Y.K. Alagh, UNU/IAS, 2000.

It has been argued that "The sharp breaks in many indicators and unmanageable problematiques emerging in major environmental concern areas is self-evident. Solid waste disposal levels of more than 100 million tonnes, slum population of around 100 million persons, acute water shortages and air and noise pollution of a severe kind, all manifest themselves. The serious environmental implications of burning poor quality coal are apparent underlining the critical energy situation in the country. The glaring magnitudes indicate the long-haul for improving the living standards in the country. This also brings into sharp focus the hazards of following an unbridled consumerist path both at the global and national levels." (Y.K. Alagh, UNU/IAS, 2000). It is interesting that in a recent attempt "India Vision 2020", the Planning Commission has, as I have argued—used very genteel energy forecasts.

Hydel shares fall in a big way by 2020 and Nuclear share, at present much higher than the 97 base level they take doesn't rise much from the present. This is both in the BAU and BCS scenarios. Then coal demand is kept at half a million tonnes, only by massive imports of oil and gas. As an afterthought after the projections, they add on even larger renewables, but it is well known that there is a limit to such a strategy, however much we push it and even the 5 per cent renewables provision in the BCS scenario is tough although worth aiming at."

Alagh, *op. cit.*, has used work by the late J.P. Maggo, who collaborated with him in the India 2020 study and which is close to recent French-Swiss models, summarised below which clearly bring out the need for public policy initiatives in the energy sector, rather than relying on a private profitability dominated strategy alone. This will require some firm decisions. Water and energy are concerns one will have to battle with and again technology and networking with communities will be the answers one will have to find (See Alagh, 2000 for Best Practices).

The fragility of reform rules in India is also very clear. There were unfortunately very few rule based incentives for producers, transmitters and distributors of electricity in India, to assure increased supply at competitively determined efficiency costs and with reasonable quality. The system of cost plus pricing was built into the Electricity Act and works out a rate of return on the cost of electricity to serve. It is only now that the Electricity Act is being amended with a new legislation which has been tabled in Parliament as the Electricity Bill. A detailed study of the Gujarat Electricity Board that if unplanned shutdowns at the unit level could be reduced, substantial savings would emerge (Alagh, Shah and Shah, 1991). Examining the record of each generator, the study found that the major hours of shutdown were on account of tube failures. If the GEB could implement the systems approach to maintenance of tubes, the cost of production of electricity would go down on account of three reasons—reduction in energy input per unit of output, overhead costs distributed over larger volumes of production and larger revenue sales from the same capacity. The study estimated this saving at 40 paise per unit if GEB could achieve the maintenance norms set by the NTPC. When the study was done this was around a third of the actual cost of producing electricity.

The tariff setting principles after the liberalisation policy in 1991 ignored this aspect. In the initial phase the Government announced "counter guarantees" for specific projects, which was an amazingly anti-efficiency principle of incentive setting and will always act as a bottleneck towards genuine reform in the power sector as we will see later. Here the Government agreed to buy power based on unit level capital and current costs. If electricity was not demanded "deemed generation benefits" would be given to the producer. When tariff principles were finally enunciated for the Independent Power Producers, they were all cost based—separately for thermal and hydel producers. As is well known cost plus pricing systems have built in pressures for escalation and worse still, do not give incentives for technical improvements. For example, the Gujarat study had worked out that beginning with a saving of around 10 paise in the unit cost to serve power, the savings could go up to 52 paise per unit.

The estimates of actual cost in the Nineties showed that the average cost of generation varied from 19 p/kwh to 115 p/kwh for hydel stations and 79 p/kwh to 288 p/kwh for thermal stations. The average costs went up as follows for hydro and thermal stations:

(*p/kwh*)

Item	*1992/93*	*1996/97*	*% Increase*
Fuel	33	47	42
Power Purchase	36	57	58
Establishment	20	24	20
Total	**129**	**187**	**45**

The Planning Commission estimates given above, for normative costs for Indian coal *versus* imported naphtha were as follows (to give an idea of cheaper and expensive options):

(*p/kwh*)

Fuel Type/Location	*Delhi*	*Gandhar*	*Vizag*	*Cuddalore*	*Ib Valley*
Indian Coal	199	209	177	213	158
Imported Naphtha	246	219	219	223	229

Now it is quite obvious that normative costs of new plants can compare favourably with the actual cost of electricity to serve, even when their capital charges are much higher. The issue of efficiency pricing has, therefore, serious implications for the economy. There are two implications to discuss. First, in very limited fields efficiency pricing is being tried in spite of considerable opposition from power producers who want to stick to guaranteed returns. This is particularly so in the transmission and distribution sectors. Second, in Indian reform it was clear by the mid-nineties that if pricing and incentive systems fostering efficiency are not there, as a transition strategy, other systems have to be developed.

Some Examples Using Pricing Incentives in the Short Run

There were very marginal incentives for competition and efficiency in the short run working of electricity systems in India. One such system was developed in response to the need to transmit power across grids in India. In 1996/97, electricity growth in India, was only 3.7 per cent. This growth was minus 8 per cent in April 97 and 2.85 in May 97. With special efforts it went up from 7 to 8 per cent from June to October 1997. In November 1997, demand in the Northern, Eastern and Western region started slackening. In spite of full reservoirs a number of States backed down hydel generation. Energy deficits, as high as 12 to 14 per cent, went down to 6 to 8 per cent. Large generating units like Rihand, Badarpur, Kahalgaon, Talcher, thermal units of DVC and in the State sector, plants like Bhatinda, Ropar, Kota, Kolaghat and Titagarh had to back down. But the Southern Grid was still having large deficits. The United Front Government decided to approve a National Grid and a Power Trading Corporation. But this would take time. In the short run it was decided to explore all possible methods of transmitting more power to the South. First the Power Grids Chandrapur Ramagundam HVDC line was targetted for completion. Then back to back arrangements were worked out by the CEA.

Interestingly once the technical feasibilities were worked out, the economics became a bottleneck. The Eastern Region SEBs as also the Central parastatals with excess capacity, wanted full cost reimbursements. Now if your PLF is low, overhead costs per unit would be high. Some units wanted Rs. 6/kwh of electricity. Inefficient rules never make sense. Here were units willing to shut down but would not supply at marginal cost, the first rule for profit making. Government forced through an "availability" tariff, in spite of publicly stated objections including by Central parastatals. This tariff works on opportunity cost efficiency principles and so power from unutilised capacities would be rationally priced. In January 1998, 2 million units of electricity went from the Eastern coal belt to Kerala.

The progress on the side of capital markets for the power sector reform has been good. In 1996 the Minister was not able to introduce the regulatory body bill in Parliament. It was introduced in August 1997 (The present author was Minister then). The successor Minister first got this implemented as an Ordinance, but later on, unfortunately, giving up some critical clauses on rural tariff discipline and on mandatory reform, got it passed as law. Unfortunately, because experience in piloting the Transmission Bill, which went through the crucial Committee stage in 1997 was that with discussion and some give and take it was possible to get legislation through multi-party acceptance.

There is now a definite private market for power projects in India and MoP is actively pursuing it. The policy for competitive bidding, the Power Trading Corporation, which makes the availability tariff happen and the Coelho Committee on distribution led to The Electricity Act, 2003. We have gone at some length to state the development of the market to make the point that non-arbitrary rules take time to develop and implement, but once they are on line, individual firm or plant level rules and negotiations become redundant. We have developed the system as in India, but other South Asian countries have similar rule based systems now.

The counter guarantee projects moved slower, because Government would have to shell out cash with default, but other large if not larger projects made progress, because of the rule based systems. The Finance Ministry has became more liberal, but many of the counter guarantee projects were stuck, but GoI can do little. However, other projects moved faster, India was getting better terms.

ICBs (International Competitive Bids) are now encouraged and there are tariff and bidding schedules in all South Asian countries. So from "counter guarantees" which is a negotiated contract for each project, the sub-continent went to competitive bidding for power capacity creation. However, the power generation capacity industry is intensively competitive. Some countries offer better terms than those available in 'bids'. If other countries were willing to negotiate easier terms with India, it was considered silly to say no on "competitiveness" terms. In 1997, the Government set up the Bhagwati Committee and the expert group which identified mega projects, and this has been continued. This was the originator of the mega project policy under which a group of eminent persons negotiates special offers made to India for Governments consideration.

While the "availability tariff" for power transmission and trade is accepted by now, the question of a rational price for power generation is still a vexed issue. It has been recently pointed out that "One of the first activities of the Central Electricity Regulatory Commission on its establishment was to bring about a Consultation Paper on Bulk Electricity Tariff in September, 1999" (GoI, CERC, 2003, p.5).

That paper discussed alternatives and opted for a Long Run Marginal Cost Principle (LRMC) for electricity generation and the availability tariff (AT) for transmission. The AT we have discussed and is now an operative rule. We may now discuss LRMC *versus* firm or producer level rules. At any moment of time, given the vintage problem, a number of technologies can co-exist for electricity pricing with the same set of product prices and there is no prior reason to expect least cost and efficient technologies, then available, to prevail. At the same time the great opportunities for efficient structural adjustments have to be seen to lie at the enterprise or plant level. The task has to be seen as the harmonisation of economic policies with markets in a manner such that enterprises follow policy goals. This should be transparent and without firm or plant level intervention or in other words be rule based. Otherwise it will provide a base for corruption and arbitrariness.

To return to the level of the plant, an example helps again. A long range marginal cost schedule (LRMC) based on expansion possibilities for each plant, can be built up to introduce the new technology for the generator. Suppose this gives a modal price Pc. Pc would involve lower working capital costs than historical plants, but fixed capital requirements would be higher, although in most cases, still lower than a green field investment (For methods of computation, See Alagh, 1991).

The CERC correctly suggested that a LRMC price does not always mean accepting "high cost" options. Those who argue that by fixing incentives at an individual firm level, they do better are wrong. Take for example the following statement.

"The question then arises is: whether the concept of depreciation should relate to the economic value of the asset, which would mean the replacement cost of the asset, or of a corresponding asset whose services if evaluated as on date would constitute an element of the cost of the service. This would mean moving away from the historical cost and also broadening the concept of depreciation to provide for substantial amounts which could help in capacity addition in the form of new plants or new lines/bays, etc. On the other hand if this approach is adopted, the tariff would certainly increase from the present level. If such an approach is adopted, perhaps a detailed accounting system would also be required to be laid down under which the amounts collected from depreciation are credited to a separate Depreciation Fund which should be frozen for purposes other than the capacity creation" (Discussion Paper, GoI, CERC, June 2003, p.38).

This amazing statement showing ignorance of elementary economic and policy theory, arises, since the CERC don't have a professional economist any more. It also shows that the bureaucracy has a war economy mind set. We neurotically keep on coming back to the bad cost plus so called "fair rules", which uninformed politicos and bureaucrats love for the powers they give them on individual economic agents, and reformers and economists hate for the same reason. Fifteen years ago in Committees we had chaired, we set down the path in fertiliser and sugar that we should give up individual unit level price fixation, move over to a "group" in the case of fertilisers and a few "zones" for sugar and then after a reasonable adjustment period, move to a zoneless, groupless world of a long range marginal cost pricing rule, with a suitable tariff rate to regulate imports. Every few years an expert committee repeats the rule. We pay respects to it and move back. In rural Ahmedabad, the author worries if it is stupidity or vested interest, but the consequences are the same. The LRMC rule was used to move from firm level upto economy level rules for two-thirds of Indian industry in the late eighties. The CERC raises these naïve questions in 2003. Ruet gets at the roots of these kind of irrationalities.

The Ministry of Power, after piloting a path breaking Electricity Act is suggesting a cost plus pricing rule. In another part of the country the State-level power pricing regulator has not even done the cost calculations properly and wants the farmer to pay more, presumably as an act of good "faith". As of the moment the police and farmers are taking it out on each other. I feel particularly bad because I thought as Power Minister, we had moved away from all this. Way back in 1997, the Electricity Transmission Bill was stuck in the Parliamentary Standing Committee. We supported its Chairman Shri Jagmohan to get a near unanimous report. The vision of a market for power was now in draft law and the Coelho Committee spelt it out. The Cabinet decided to set up a Power Trading Corporation and a National Electricity Grid. At the end of 1997 and early 1998, started the large scale transmission of power across the land. Soon with back to back arrangements and the high voltage transmission lines in position, we were flinging power from almost a 1000 MW power capacity, literally from Kashmir to Kanya Kumari. But we soon discovered that pricing was a bottleneck. If you don't generate power, because in your region demand is low, you add on a high "overhead cost" of low capacity use to the one who solves your capacity use problem by buying from you. Disregard of simple economic rules leads to crazy outcomes. Power plants in the eastern region wanted Rs. 6 a unit from the South, for selling power which really cost them Rs. 2. We "solved" the problem then and I publically argued for an "availability tariff" based on the principle of efficiency avoidable cost. It is with this principle that the Maharashtra Electricity Regulator refused to grant cost plus prices to Enron for interstate sale of power.

The Central Electricity Regulatory Commission in its Discussion Paper on Electricity Pricing at the time when it was headed by an outstanding professional (1993), alas no more (2003), had suggested two principles for pricing—a long range marginal cost price for generation and an availability tariff for transmission. The first essentially means that a generator gets the efficiency price to the economy and latter that trade takes place at the least cost possible to the economy. Both are workable. For, an extra unit of electricity can come from rehabilitating an existing unit or a new technology, where capital costs are higher, but then energy costs will be lower on account of efficiency and the pricing principle takes it into account. The principle is workable, for we used it to chart out the transition to rule based policies for industries which were decontrolled from the mid-eighties and at least I have always made the calculations transparent. Also we can then tell the farmer that he is paying the real cost of energy to the economy rather than lining the coats of some fat cat. If we want him to pay less that will be a real subsidy and for some time cross subsidies are inevitable. Also these rules keep *babus* and *netas* from cosying up to one firm. Perhaps that is why they are ignored. The Electricity Bill cannot function without transparent rules.

There is, however, no prior reason to expect that Pc would equal the going market price if modern technology policy literature and theory is a guide and if taken as a guide may not permit such modernisation anyway. Now if a particular country is going to produce a commodity with real costs which will be higher than a long term international price trend, it has failed. The real world, however, in many cases consists of marginal cases. In such cases a "technological economic policy" would use tax reliefs, import tariffs, pricing policies and incremental incentives for internalising technology. The interesting point was that kind of policy regime got considerable attention in the policy debates of the early nineties at the global level. By this time the growth debilitating aspect of a Bretton Woods structural reform was documented showing negative growth for over a decade and alternatives models of globalisation were being discussed. The Indian example was seen as a counterfactual. Lance Taylor in a fairly widely quoted paper described an MPS (Multifaceted Price System) as a "transition from an administered towards a market regime" (L. Taylor, MIT, 1991, p.7). He gave the Polish and Indian examples of "it's homely virtues are perhaps becoming more evident" (*Ibid.*, p.7) and the Indians for transitional regimes "developing effective multi-tiered pricing systems for their nationalised firms and even in agriculture (Alagh, 1991)" (Taylor, *Ibid.*, p.38: the reference in Taylor here is to Y.K. Alagh, 1991, WIDER). Taylor in his review of the post socialist transition from a global development economics point of view was basically arguing that the Indians had switched industry successfully from firm level controls to an industry level efficiency policy, linked with economy level strategic objectives. "The Theory of a Multi-Faceted Price System" advocated the Indian and the present authors perception that in the transitional stage, dual pricing, threat of imports and set-off could all be used, for limited periods of time, in such a policy regime. Policy then has a level playing objective, so that the transition to a global economy, is knowledge based and without avoidable human costs.

Joel Ruet's book is required reading for policy reform in India.

— YOGINDER K. ALAGH*

* Vice Chairman, Sardar Patel Institute of Economic and Social Research, Ahmedabad; former Vice Chancellor, Jawaharlal Nehru University (JNU) New Delhi; former Minister of Power, Government of India.

Acknowledgements

This book has emerged out of a series of discussions on the State, as well as, out of repeated field investigations; in other words, people and places.

Its *problématique* first took shape throughout discussions, readings and seminars, with the researchers of CERNA (Centre of Industrial Economics, Ecole des Mines, Paris) : François Lévêque, to whom I owe the 'choice of India', Matthieu Glachant, Olivier Bomsel, Gilles le Blanc, around the concept of 'enterprisation', as well as, for a perspective on socialisms and post-socialism, Christian von Hirschhausen, from the DIW, Berlin, Jean-François Huchet then in the CEFC, Hong Kong, and Xavier Richet, from University Paris III.

Problematising feeds itself with critique, and, from this perspective, "critique is rare therefore precious", Jean-Michel Glachant once told me, who kept providing me this precious immaterial, both at a personal level, as well as, through the laboratory ATOM, University Panthéon-Sorbonne, and later the Jean Monnet Research Group. Other timely critiques were Jean-Marie Chevalier, whose expertise in energy completed a cycle that had opened a few years ago, from a seminar on Indian SEBs he had organised in Paris, as well as, Dominique Finon with whom a (traveling) ongoing dialogue emerged from an early meeting in Grenoble, or Carine Staropoli. Ultimately, this work could find a rigorous, as well as, precise disciplinary framework, thanks to Thierry Weil, who gave me the happiness to be one of the early readers of his *Introduction à la lecture de James March,* and thereby made me discover a vast and fascinating field of the economics of organisations. At many a times, I reverted to Gilbert Etienne, with whom our discussions on our respective 'Indias', whether in his Geneva house or in Delhi taxis, always vest a colourful flavour.

The Indian academia and decision-making circles have warmly and all-heartedly opened their debates to me in a manner that but a few countries would have done, as early as the very initial field works. At the intersection of the two worlds, Yoginder Alagh (former Vice-Chancellor, Jawaharlal Nehru University, and former Minister Govt. of India), has ensured me with his continuous support, open speaking, and friendship. At thc same boarder of decision-making and academia, S.L. Rao and Sanjeev Ahluwalia (respectively, formerly Chairman and Secretary of the first Central Electricity Regulatory Commission) have offered a regular critique for my work, assorted with a clear understanding of the European and French State systems and academia, that is, with a clear understanding of where I was speaking from, and where from I departed from it to start speaking 'from India'.

Central to my insertion in the substance of SEBs, were the openness and the passionate work of S.Y. Quraishi, (former Power Secretary, Govt. of Haryana), who opened me in large the doors of the Haryana Electricity Board, who literally made me part of its 'staff' for six months, and with whom the working sessions, in-between our respective meetings, have ranged from Ambassador cars, Guest houses, to shared lunches at the Haryana Secretariat, to the Chandigarh evenings, as well as, Djamal Mostefai from the World Bank, whose contacts have made me enter several networks, and who has been my very first while constant 'rare and precious' critique, extended by his successor, Lucio Monari.

A long series of talks, seminars, discussions, debates, articles, were initiated at India International Centre and then at many institutes. The list is long, and by now it includes many friends, but I wish to really thank Balveer Arora (JNU Delhi), who has been quite instrumental in making this book published, Manmohan Agrawal, Dipankar Gupta, Amitabh Kundu, Dipankar Sengupta, Ramprasad Sengupta (JNU Delhi), Rajeev Bhargava (Delhi University), Sebastian Morris, P.R. Shukla, Siddharth Sinha (IIM Ahmedabad), R.K. Mishra (IPE, Hyderabad), Usha Ramachandra (ASCI Hyderabad), V. Ranganathan (IIM Bangalore), Anupam Rastogi (IDFC), U. Sankar, M.A. Kalam, S. Janakarajan (Chennai), Prem Kalra (IIT Kanpur), Kanchan Chopra and Pushpam Kumar (IEG, Delhi), S.K.N. Nair (NCAER, Delhi), D.V. Ramana (XIM Bhubaneshwar). Last but not least, Hari Vasudevan (Jamia Millia, Delhi), who, since a long discussion in Calcutta, which then repeatedly deepened in its multiple variances, has made me realise the very 'Indo-Frenchness' of my work... as well as provided me with many more research subjects that I will ever be able to handle. Yet another 'Indias'...

Beyond the shores of India, presentations made in conferences of International Society of New Institutional Economics, International Association for Study of Common Property, or at Department of Applied Economics, Cambridge UK, have helped me getting my ideas crisper, and I thank particularly David Newbery, Michael Pollitt and Tooraj Jamasb (Cambridge) for this.

Understanding the intricacies of the Indian State was made possible through interactions with its practitioners, and I thank P. Abraham, Ajay Dua, Arvind Jhadav, Ajay Shankar, Jiji Thomson, Rajiv Datt (respectively former Secretary, former Joint Secretary, Joint Secretaries, Director Reforms, Director Finance, Ministry of Power, Govt. of India), for their time, availability and early readings of my work.

Ideas have emerged from field, and in that respect, for a French to work in India has raised specific issues, but has always been gratifying. The first field investigation was conducted with Thomas Eymond-Laritaz, and keeps a particular flavour. Generally, the availability, the interest, the welcoming of the quasi-totality of the civil servants, officers and practitioners I have met and interviewed, leaves in me the nostalgic vision of a certain India. I have intruded their world to distillate it and reify it into a book. They were not deemed to find or recognise themselves in it, but still, their efforts to make me share their work, at times in the intimacy of their homes, their dialectical openness to 'my' final result, their adaptation to my time and space constraints, have not been spared. It would be impossible to do justice to all of them for they have been a few hundreds. A few names, however, among which secretaries, engineers, officers, who have collectively given me the clues to the whole system, sometimes extended a beginning of a geographically improbable friendship: in Chandigarh, R.K. Jain, Ranjit Issar, P.K. Das, Sanjay Gupta, S.S. Dhillon; in Sonipat, S.K. Handa, N.K. Devgon; in Hyderabad, Anil Kutty; in Bhubaneshwar, D.K. Roy; in Balasore, Mr Mukherji; in Jaipur, Mr Hingar; in Delhi Jiji Thomson, Rajiv Bhardwaj. Unfair selection also partly based on the frequency of my solicitations, more than on the sole quality of welcome, always excellent; how many times have I been offered to "stay a bit longer"? A few others, like Leena Srivastava, Gaurav Bhatiani (TERI), Anil Patnayak (AES), P. Neogi (NPC), Md. Zakaria Siddiqui, who has been, during his M.Phil, a constant relay in Kerala, without forgetting the *humour décalé* and direct talk of Rajendra Shrivastav (EDF).

A book, especially written in English by a French, calls for unending re-writings. Over years, and considering some early pieces or reports that have been precursors to this book, Babli Motraf Sarai, Uma Krishnan, Padma Natarajan, Attreyee Roy Chowdhury, Priya Vari Sen, Jayna Kothari, Shilpa Ekka, and Sona Kapila have been inducted in this task, which I think they have collectively performed in an admirable manner, given the original version. Such an 'Indo-French' book is also about a series of institutions. CERNA, of course, but also the Research Branch of the French Public Company, EDF, as well as the French Ministry of Research, had been the initial support of my PhD, already on SEBs. A great pluri-disciplinary working space has also been the Centre de Sciences Humaines, in New Delhi. A few names would comprise Frédéric Jouve (EDF), Christiane Lapier, Véronique Dubarry, Césaria Ferreira (CERNA), Emmanuel Bon, Bruno Dorin, Girish Kumar, François Leclercq, Stéphanie Tawa-Lama, Evelyne Thivet-Rispal, Prathik Malhotra, Anne Vaugier-Chatterjee, Marie-Hélène Zérah, Jasmine Zerinini (CSH), not forgeting Frédéric Grare, whose enthusiasm has served as a constant, emulating, base for keeping in time with deadlines as well as disseminating ideas in the public debate. As far as the latter is concerned, as already mentioned, India International Centre has played a big role in this, and I wish to specially thank Premola Ghosh for the work she does there. My publishers obviously deserve a special mention in that same respect, and I thank Sanu Kapila and Rituraj Kapila for the faith they have put in this subject.

Finally, Saroj Giri, Anandita Sharma, Helder de Oliveira, have, already a few years ago, collectively constituted my "Gateway to India", soon followed by others who will forgive my concision here, who all deserve my faithful thanks for this. It has so happened that for me the antichamber of India has been Egypt, and, among many rememberings, Ghuislaine Alleaume and François Ireton keep all my sympathy for they have hosted a bit of the redaction of the early versions of this manuscript in CEDEJ, in Cairo.

Ultimately, the 'archeology' of this work, derives from two friends who have given me access to the taste and tools of understanding the world. On the one hand, already long ago, in Dakar, Souleymane M'Bodj has let me discover the diversity of the world, and this work owes a lot to him. Equally, as stated in the poem by the Alexandrian Cavafy, *celui qui dit non* (the one who says no), one materialises a wish, otherwise it is not. Pierre-Noël Giraud, along with his friendship, has given me the tools for an understanding, allowing me becoming *celui qui dit oui*, the one who says yes.

Acronyms

ABT	Availability-Based Tariff
ADB	Asian Development Bank
APSEB	Andhra Pradesh State Electricity Board
APTransco	Andhra Pradesh Transmission Corporation
BATF	Bangalore Agenda Task Force
BRPL	BSES Rajdhani Power Ltd (South West Electricity Distribution Company, Delhi)
BSES	Bombay Suburban Electric Supply
BYPL	BSES Yamuna Power Ltd (Central East Electricity Distribution Company, Delhi)
CE	Chief Engineer
CEA	Central Electricity Authority
CERC	Central Electricity Regulatory Commission
CESC	Calcutta Electric Supply Company
Cesco	Central Distribution Company (Orissa)
Crore	An Indian unit ; equal to ten million
DERC	Delhi Electricity Regulatory Commission
DHBVN	Dakshan Bijli Vitran Nigam (Southern Haryana Electricity Supply Corporation)
DVB	Delhi Vidyut (electricity) Board
EDF	Electricité de France
ERC	Electricity Regulatory Commission
GDP	Gross Domestic Product

GEB	Gujarat State Electricity Board
GNP	Gross National Product
GoI	Government of India
GRIDCO	Grid Corporation (Orissa)
GW	Giga-Watt
HERC	Haryana Electricity Regulatory Commission
HPERC	Himachal Pradesh Electricity Regulatory Commission
HSEB	Haryana State Electricity Board
HV	High Voltage
HVDC	High Voltage Direct Current
HVPN	Haryana Vidyut Prasaran Nigam (Haryana Electricity Corporation)
Hz	Hertz
IIR	India Infrastructure Report
IPP	Independent Power Producer
JE	Junior Engineer
KESCO	Kanpur Electric Supply Corporation
KSEB	Kerala State Electricity Board
kWh	kilo-Watt-hour
Lakh	An Indian unit; equal to a hundred thousand
LV	Low Voltage
MD	Managing Director
MERC	Maharashtra Electricity Regulatory Commission
MoU	Memorandum of Understanding
MPERC	Madhya Pradesh Electricity Regulatory Commission
MV	Medium Voltage
MW	Mega-Watt
MYT	Multi-Year Tariff
NDPL	North Delhi Power Limited
Nesco	North Distribution Company (Orissa)

NHPC	National Hydro Power Corporation
NPC	Nuclear Power Corporation
NTPC	National Thermal Power Corporation
OERC	Orissa Electricity Regulatory Commission
OHPC	Orissa Hydro Power Corporation
PFC	Power Finance Corporation
PLF	Plant Load Factor
PR	Property Right
PSEB	Punjab State Electricity Board
RoR	Rate of Return
Rs	Rupees
S&V	Shleifer & Vishny
SBC	Soft Budget Constraint
SDO	Sub Divisional Officer
SE	Superintending Engineer
SEB	State Electricity Board
SERC	State Electricity Regulatory Commission
SOE	State Owned Enterprise
Southco	Southern Distribution Company (Orissa)
T&D	Transmission & Distribution
TEC	Tata Electricity Company
TWh	Tera-Watt-hour
UHBVN	Uttar Haryana Bijli Vitran Nigam (Northern Haryana Electricity Supply Corporation)
UN	United Nations
UPERC	Uttar Pradesh Electricity Regulatory Commission
UPJVNL	Uttar Pradesh Jal Vidyut Nigam Ltd (Uttar Pradesh Hydro Power Corporation)
UPPCL	Uttar Pradesh Power Corporation Ltd
UPRVUNL	Uttar Pradesh Rajya Vidyut Utpadan Nigam Ltd (Uttar Pradesh State Electricity Generation Corporation).

UPSEB	Uttar Pradesh State Electricity Board
WBERC	West Bengal Electricity Regulatory Commission
Wesco	Western Distribution Company (Orissa)
Xen	Executive Engineer

Introduction

Public Accountancy, Non-Integrated Information, Procedural Rationality and the State at 'Paper Work'

Through the *détour* of the reforms in the power sector in India, this book deals with the Indian State. For, to support a sound theory, the analysis of the State has to initially situate itself on more established grounds than the 'thin air of ideology', the real State at work is carefully studied here through one of its most emblematic sectors of activity: power. The focus is more specifically on State Electricity Boards (SEBs), the organisations responsible for generation, transmission and distribution of electricity in each of the States of India. The link between the generality of the State and the particularity of the power sector is actually ensured through what lies at the core of the book's analysis: the *administrative* nature of the SEBs. That is, SEBs cannot be analysed in isolation from the State, just like the functioning of the State can no longer be fully understood when its administrations are analytically encapsulated in a separate black-box.

The book is based on field work and in-depth interviews, as also studies carried out, at times within the SEBs themselves. This first step spread over two years, the pre-requisite condition to say something new in this much debated field. This preliminary study had examined the reforms in seven States (Andhra Pradesh, Delhi, Haryana, Kerala, Orissa, Punjab, Rajasthan), selected for reasons of economic diversity and political choices towards reforms[1]. Andhra

1. At the moment of the first field investigations, in July 1998, the States of Orissa, Haryana, and Andhra Pradesh were looking for a quick reform, to lead to the privatisation of the distribution of electricity, under the auspices of the World Bank. Punjab and Delhi were anti-reform; Rajasthan was looking for a light reform. From that time, changes have occurred. At mid-2001, Haryana has slowed down reform further to a change in its Government in 1999, Delhi has committed to reform, and Orissa had already privatised the distribution. By 2004, only Delhi with its privatisation in 2002, shows a substantial move compared to the late 1990s.

Pradesh, Haryana[2], Orissa, have been visited regularly from 1998 to 2000, and further followed-up since then with regular visits to field. The research involved interviewing nearly 200 people belonging to SEBs, ministries, governmental agencies, regulatory commissions, private groups, multilateral agencies etc., ranging from Meter Readers to Power Secretaries in the States, and a former Minister of the Government of India. This was followed till 2004 by a series of case studies, as well as, direct interaction in both public debate arena and expertise, either in the Indian or international academic world, or in the framework of Indo-French bilateral dialogue, or again various experts groups and discussions along the draft Electricity Bill 2001, Electricity Act, 2003, N.K. Singh Committee, 2004 debates. There have been as many opportunities to test and discuss the ideas presented in this book, on the characterisation and reforms of the developmental State in emerging countries. Though this is not the focus of this book, through the study of reforms in Ivory Coast (in 1997), Sudan (in 2002), Egypt (with a regular focus since 1999), and Pakistan (in 2004), I have had the opportunity to validate and reflect on the framework I propose in this current book.

In short, the book aims at answering practical questions of industrial economics analysis such as the impact of de-integration on the functioning of the SEBs, the impact of the creation of regulatory commissions, their privatisation when it so happens. Based on critical analysis of the proposed reforms, it puts forward practical propositions on reforming the SEBs.

Beyond this sectoral look, it goes further, and gives an alternative consistent analysis of the impact of measures widely professed and used as tools for the re-designing of the Indian State. It goes especially beyond the usually advocated '1991 crisis' reasons given for the reform of the State, underlining its structural causes. Finally, for stylisation feeds and supports theory, this book aims at contributing to a theory of the Indian State.

---

2. With the support of the then Power Secretary of the Government of Haryana, the author of this book had even been formally attached to the Harayana SEB over a period of six months in 1999.

The Problem: Limits of Existing Analyses and Genesis of an Organisational Approach

Each SEB directly depends on the Government of its respective State. The SEBs are at the heart of the Indian power system which supplies electricity to a billion people. The system, however, supplies it in an ever worsening manner since, even if the absolute level of generation rises, it is not able to keep up with the social and economic demand of the second most populated country of the planet, aiming at becoming a world economic power. This growing relative penury is taking place in a power sector which is also one of the first vectors of social redistribution, on account of the existence of cross subsidies between consumers and net subsidies paid by the State Governments. Electricity in India is still largely a good of primary necessity and/or an input with non-guaranteed availability, and not a service. This explains the economic and political importance of the debate on electricity, which does not see a single day pass by without a national or an influential regional daily publishing an article on the issue, often on the first page. There is a crisis of production as the gap between demand and supply increases; a crisis of maintenance and functioning as power cuts generalise to the point of becoming endemic. There is also a financial crisis as the SEBs generalise their arrears of payments to large branches of the public sphere. There is ultimately a confidence crisis as the Union Government and also the few private investors demand more and more financial guarantees to the SEBs, as the industrialists turn to captive generation, and a political crisis as parties win or loose elections on this issue. These different aspects of the crisis have developed and matured altogether and are the symptom of the exhaustion of a whole system, a whole vision of the State.

If this structural analysis is correct, then the solution will only come through a change in the system around which SEBs function. But before developing this *systemic thesis*, we refute the current *particularist analyses*. On this line, two streams of reasoning are called for, each party in the debate then articulating them in a specific way. The first among them is all-technical: the (public) electric sector in general, and the SEBs in particular, would lack investment capacities, which would explain the current situation. The other reason that is put forward is 'political interference', the intervention of the State

Governments not only in tariffs, but also in investment, or in day to day decisions (*clientelist* hiring and promotions, political protection in case of non-payment of bills, etc.) that is supposed to explain the whole failure of the system. In these perspectives, and emphasis being on the absence of public funds, the supporters for reforms propose the opening of the sector to the private sphere, if need be foreign, and removing the Government from the management of the sector. This is supposed to be done through so-called *structural* reforms (consisting, on a World Bank inspired line, of reforms such as corporatisation, de-integration, setting up of Regulatory Commissions etc.).

The opening up of the power sector to private investment has been gradually implemented since 1991. The practical problem – for the supporters of the financial hypothesis – is that this opening up was a non-starter. Investors did not turn up for generation – the only segment opened up initially, the SEBs remaining in charge of distribution. This reinforced the supporters of a more ambitious line – general opening up through the de-integration of the SEBs and the privatisation of distribution, also bringing around the two lines of analysis to mutually strengthen each other, contributing to blur the analysis by no longer separating *structural reforms* from *privatisation*. Indeed, the motto became 'bifurcate or trifurcate the SEBs, privatise the distribution to get the private into the generation'. The investors did not make a beeline and the few experiments undertaken or completed give reasons to believe that investors will not come – or not as much as expected. However, supporters of these lines of reform now call for an even deeper privatisation, though the play has become 'waiting for Godot'. There is now a dominant analysis, which seems to be paradoxically strengthened by the empirical failure itself of its own predictions, it is true, playing on a context where credible alternative is long to emerge.

The aim of this book is to overcome this stalemate, and to argue that it is an *analytical* stalemate. The starting point of this re-thinking of the situation is as follows. In field studies, the investigator is struck by a situation that is *a priori* paradoxical. Let us illustrate this through an example, to be generalised in the book. In certain States, the frequency of power cuts is explained by the fact that the distribution transformers often 'burn'. There are not enough of them, and the ones in the network are overloaded. Hence the need for frequent repairing.

'There is ostensibly lack of funds for buying new transformers', 'there are political orders to devote resources to other fields', are the explanations advanced. And yet... hundreds of damaged transformers are strewn on the ground. There may be tens of thousands at the scale of a State. They are not seriously damaged, at times it would suffice to change the oil, at the worst to rewind the coil. Put on the network at a low cost, they would instantly cut down most of the power cuts, smoothen the peak demand over a larger number of transformers, and thus would cut the future need to repair and ultimately save money! It is thus 'profitable' from an overall point of view. It has what economics call a social benefit, but it would as well bring a benefit to the SEBs, since the minimal 'investment' is very quickly recovered through future savings on (no longer burning) transformers.

Opportunistic Economics Do Not Explain Everything

This type of paradox has led to a series of investigations, initially devoted, with a classical bias of an economist, to the search of opportunistic behaviour, and of characteristics of the system leading to such behaviour. In other words, investigations around the classical story of inefficiently allocated property rights, bad incentives, etc. The study did focus on the hierarchic distribution of control rights and of budgetary allocation and follow up in the 'management' of the stock of transformers (which level decides what, on what basis, who records it, who carries out budgetary checks, etc.). The physical description of the hierarchical circuit of the replacement of a defective transformer being perfectly mastered by all the interlocutors, the budgetary and the accounting circuit was taken up. There, one full afternoon was needed, we had to gather together many people, obscure assistants, to go to many places, find the files thanks to the help of unskilled agents whose sole qualification is to know where which files are stored. We had to compare, for the most part, the versions of the members of the hierarchy regarding the way the costs were recorded, patient recomposition of a puzzle. Throughout this treasure hunt, our interlocutors were telling us that what mattered was what this book calls the physical circuit, not seeing the interest of this 'account circuit' which we persisted on putting to light. Finally, it became clear that the procedure of transformer repairs is as follows: the sub-divisional engineer issues an order slip for a transformer to the supply department, on the basis of a purely formal and hence fictitious cost estimate of repairing, calculated according to administrative rules whose link with the slightest reality always escaped our interlocutors. In any case, the estimated figures are without importance since many months later a new figure comes from the Headquarters, that of the average total cost, at the level of the executive engineer, direct supervisor of the sub-divisional engineer (to whom, moreover, this average centralised cost is not sent). First result: cost-wise, decisions are made in the dark. Equipped with these characteristics and knowing, moreover, that the budgets were made at the level of the division (at the level of the executive engineer) and not of the sub-division, and hence that the decision benefited the sub-division while being debited to the budget of the division, the situation became like this: 'the division pays, the sub-division profits'. In appearance, a typical text-book situation, if there ever is one, favouring this opportunism that economists affectionate so much in their models. Our interlocutors now having all this circuit in mind, the question that was at the tip of our tongue could finally come out: 'who pays?'. And here, we depart from the textbook. In an SEB, the reply is: 'no one, provided it is no one's fault'. Indeed, to answer this question, SEBs' officers forget everything—the patiently excavated process, the order slips, the budgets, and the estimates. They just speak about administrative inquiry meant to fix responsibilities for a breakdown. In the obviously quasi-general case in which there is no fault, in the mind of the officers of the SEB, *no one pays nothing*, neither any hierarchic unit in the field, nor the supply department, nor the Headquarters. One does simply execute a procedure, linked to a physical circuit; the opportunistic economist cannot explain anything.

Whither Economic Analysis?

The book develops and generalises this example. In a SEB, there are no 'costs', there are no more 'profits'. In the proposition 'there are no costs', one must not understand that the cost is nil, and therefore expect that the transformers are all repaired and fitted. But rather that the cost is neither the parameter of decision, nor a concept accessible to the officers of the SEB, thinkable by the officers of the SEB. There is no cost-benefit analysis. One has just to follow a procedure, which can by chance solve techno-economic issues, but we argue, in the long run, leads to cumulative loss that cost-benefit analysis could easily avoid. In that particular case, the procedure is to repair when and only when a transformer is defaulting. If there are repaired transformers in the stores, it can be done; if not, one has to wait. Preventive servicing, anticipated investments, are not authorised procedures despite they would have a social cum direct benefit. Inquiries have shown in a general way that the absence of cost-benefit analysis is induced by a framework of procedures, at the expense of a managerial discretion for various hierarchical levels.

What is the implication of this in the analysis of the SEBs? Simply, the techno-economic argument set out above does not stand any more: one does not 'invest' in a SEB, because one does not carry out a cost-benefit analysis. The alien notion of 'profitability' will never lead to explaining any decision and therefore to describing or analysing the functioning of any SEB. Moreover, the discourse on the profitability of the system is off the mark in a SEB. One retorts that there is need for supplementary means, that these means be 'profitable' constitutes an assertion foreign to the SEB. Above all, this gives the clue about the limits of classical analyses. The SEB lacks money? No, simply, it does not function in terms of resources it can release and *better allocate*, but in terms of physical availability in the stores. By supplementary means, any agent of SEB will necessarily understand 'additional physical means coming from the store', whatever the real impact of these, never measured, never put in balance with better maintenance, another organisation, new technical rule etc. A SEB does not reason in money, and does not make 'production *détours*', it reasons in physical goods, and makes at the most accounts *détours*. The analysis will show that in a SEB there is no money, no property right on the budget, therefore no budgetary allocation in the strict sense of the term.

The simple argument of the absence of funds hides the complexity of the procedures at work in a SEB. It does not describe reality. The preceding example on the contrary suggest other lock-ins. Likewise, 'political interference' has weak explanatory power. First, the concept of interference itself is abstract and deserves serious discussion in the infrastructure sector and especially in the power sector.

Finally, the relative failure of present reforms (derived from these two simplistic views) by itself justifies in-depth study of SEBs and the State in two directions:

(i) What are the structural factors (weight and type of procedures, forms of budgetary and hierarchical power structures, etc.) in the organisation and the decision-making process within SEBs leading to or reinforcing the problems faced by the power sector? Once these elements are identified, what is their internal consistency. In short, what is the rationality at stake in SEBs?

(ii) What could be the methods to reverse the internal rationality of SEBs, in order to implement a reform which would have some chances of success, and what is the impact of current reforms on this respect?

These are the two questions to be addressed in this book; answer to these implies a paradigmatic shift in analysis of the public sector in India.

The Analytical Method: Internal Organisation Reflects as well as Structures the Goals of the State

The existing analyses and reforms consider the SEBs as inefficient enterprises, that is to say, as (major but unfortunately wrong assumption) full-fledged enterprises that are simply 'inefficient', or departing from a norm. The SEBs are then viewed as departing from this norm in terms of (i) managerial capabilities, (ii) political interference. As the analysis stops there, it implicitly presumes that SEBs – the agents in SEBs – apart from these deviations, tend to or would otherwise tend towards a principle of efficiency. In presence of these constraints, the principle of efficiency is considered by the agents as an internal variable, that they object to and from which they react – or would react. The preceding example, which is general to the main decision-making mechanisms, shows that these assumptions are incorrect. The analytical base of the available studies is therefore afflicted with two crippling problems:

- these studies describe non-adequacy to a norm, and by doing so describe the norm itself rather than that which actually exists,
- they use concepts that are not used inside the SEBs, and thus are based on *external* explanatory mechanisms. These do not correspond to any reality of the SEBs. In particular, this kind

> of analysis neglects the study of the parameters that are actually used by the agents, and hence does not provide, truly speaking, a *description* of the SEBs. This type of analysis thus cannot serve either an understanding or a predictive purpose.

Conversely, this book favours an approach that leads to a positive reconstruction of the practices and structuring characteristics of the SEBs. It is interested in the organisation of the SEBs by going beyond the classical neo-institutional approach. The latter is indeed implicitly based on behaviourist hypothesis of opportunism oriented towards a clearly defined aim, that is to say a logic of substantive rationality. On the contrary, the book puts forward the numerous elements of procedural rationality, which structure the public administration. This behaviourist analysis therefore invalidates certain tools of neo-institutional analysis, like for example, the soft budget constraint (Kornai, 1986), for specifying the field of validity of certain others, like the analysis through property rights (Grossman and Hart, 1986).

The approach leading to these results follows the theoretical and practical approach outlined by Cyert and March (1963). It studies firstly the major characteristics of allocation of discretionary powers within the SEB-organisation — budgetary cum hierarchical power. It studies the information system. This makes it possible to define all the organisational limits in which decision-making takes place, and to study thereafter the decisions themselves, and more specifically the type of rationality to which they obey. The Marchian analysis then allows to get to the result, namely the objectives really pursued *ex-post* by the organisation. The analytical reconstruction of these objectives from the results of the stylisation of procedures makes them objectives termed by March as *a posteriori*. It presents the advantage of not being based on behaviourist hypotheses, but on *established and attested* behaviour, and specially the relevant description of the specific mechanisms gives a larger explanatory and hence predictive richness, in terms of modelling of the existing system as the foundation of reforms to be implemented.

But beyond, the methodology retained has also necessitated adopting, as descriptive concepts, the concepts that are really considered within the SEBs and therefore are operational concepts. Concepts are formed from categories internal to SEBs, thus operative, or categories used by the agents of the system being studied, and not of external categories, or categories used by the observers outside the system being studied. This made it possible to show how *the classically expected concepts are not and cannot be used within the SEBs and how the presence of other concepts reveals the very nature and the internal coherence of the system.* Proving the inadequacy of the current approaches, it also went through the analysis of what is not. It studies the 'budgetary system'...to show there is no 'budget' in the strict sense of the term... but administrative procedures. This approach was unavoidable as there are a number of concepts, which seem to be there in appearance. *The predominant analysis has either artificially imported concepts where they do not apply* (a change of status from earlier 'Departments' to current SEBs, which took place quite some time back, was thought to have put in place 'assets' where there was none before and they were there only in name), or imposed them by habit which *brings the illusion of evidence where it is not present* (for example 'costs'... and derived concepts).

Linking the characteristics arising out of the Marchian analysis, showing their reciprocally reinforcing relation within the system, allows detailing the logic of the behaviour adopted by the agents. This thus allows description of the internal consistency of organisational factors in the present situation of SEBs. This is the first question raised in this study of the structural factors at play in SEBs.

In the perspective of reform, linked to the second question (how to reverse the systemic logic brought to the fore), we have conceptually separated the analysis between structural reforms – which aim at improving the management – and privatisation – which is also designed to bridge the so-called financial needs.

SEBs as Administrations of the State: Nature and Consequences on Reform

The organisational characteristics of SEBs explain their inefficiency. Namely, a non-integrated (between physical and accounting elements) information system, the absence of internal allocation of discretionary power (budgetary and hierarchical), the pre-eminence of paper work (what is decided on paper counts more than what actually happens) prevent the operational units to come out of the framework of procedures in decision-making. This forecloses the possibility of otherwise profitable decisions, and the decisions follow *de facto* a procedural rationality (defined by Simon, 1976; March, 1978). The procedural rationality follows from the possibility, at any moment and any level, of executive instructions on the part of the State. Results may then be de-correlated from internally taken decisions. In this fluid framework, the difficulty to managerially anticipate even the predictable events makes legitimate not to consider substantive rationality. Conformation to administrative rules gives a higher stability than trying to anticipate external constraints. These interventions need not necessarily be 'systematic'; their possibility itself leads to their anticipation, which is *systematised by the agents*. An adapted system of procedures emerges from it, each decision will then find its genesis diluted in various points of this system: in that sense the procedural rationality is 'systemic'.

The recourse to administrative rules tells the real nature of the organisation. It is not an enterprise but an administration, a part of the State, subjected to its discretionary power, and which *by nature* follows many objectives, that are irreconcilable except by the direct executive instructions of the State. Therefore, the State does not *interfere* in the management of the organisation, but only acts in accordance with the administrative nature of the system. Cost or productive efficiency, meant to measure the sole productivity effects, is not a politically legitimate concept for making all trade-offs between production and redistribution, which are alien to each other. Productive efficiency is the mono-dimensional reduction of a pluri-dimensional set of parameters, that any State considers. Among these, some are given priority towards productive efficiency, and cost loses its importance as a parameter. Efficiency, an unimportant parameter for decision-making in SEBs, *ex-post* happens to be weak. *The administrative character of SEBs is the direct structural source of their cost inefficiency.*

As a result, *all the concepts and the theories derived from the concept of cost turn out to be incapable of bringing out the behavioural reality of a SEB or of its entities, to forecast, to give a base for reforms*. Thus, one does not find any trace as such neither of an investment nor of an asset in a SEB. Rigorously speaking there is no budgetary constraint, not even a soft budget constraint in a SEB, since budget is not a decision tool. Property rights are not *badly allocated*, but simply non-existent. That is, the classically raised explanation of 'transition' theories don't hold for SEBs. No hierarchical level owns residual control, given the possibility of executive instructions of the State. Not even the State Government is holding these residual rights, given the fact that the permanence of the paper work does in no way guarantee the systematic implementation of instructions.

Consequently, *reform, the way we define it, understood as the willingness to grant a central position to the concept and usage of cost in the decision-making process, necessarily goes through a change in the SEBs nature, from an administration to enterprise. We have named this process 'enterprisation'.* The study of the ongoing structural reforms, corporatisation, de-integration, setting up Regulatory Commissions, shows that they do not lead to enterprisation of SEBs in themselves. Once carried out, the SEB has changed its name but hardly its features; the major characteristics remain, only the information system has been integrated but it is not being used as there hasn't been any break in the rationality of the system as a whole. Privatisation, on its own, is a – brutal – manner to 'enterprise'. But it faces serious practical difficulties, because in the process of privatisation, investors must valuate an organisation which does not have property rights, no assets, which does not offer any hold on the forecasting mechanism based on a kind of rationality derived from a cost-benefit analysis. The investors then take important risk premiums, and the risk of selecting inefficient investors in the end very much exists (the ones that are retained are those who are less averse to taking risks initially, independently of their efficiency).

We propose in this framework a tentative outline of public enterprisation, that is to say, without recourse to privatisation (no 'selling of shares'), but with the *managerial* help of the private. The book presents an analysis of the opportunity and the risks of an attempt of public enterprisation pre-existing and preceding any privatisation. Conceptually, this outline allows overcoming the damagingly reductionist debate on 'privatisation'/'non privatisation'. In a renewed framework, the attempt of public enterprisation may ultimately lead to the absence of privatisation, as well as, to a privatisation in better conditions, depending on the success of the attempt. The issue of privatisation becomes a secondary one, both in time and conceptually. In the specific case of SEBs, and given the Indian political conditions, the practical proposals we formulate take recourse to management contracts, but this may not entail the generality of the debate.

A Posteriori Justification of the Analytical Approach

At this stage, it may be useful to justify not having considered certain questions or not having used certain classical approaches. This study addresses, in a limited manner the questions of sectoral co-ordination and competition. It does not refer to the theory of public choice, nor to the question of corruption. Let us briefly deal with them here.

- Sectoral Co-ordination: When the power sector is de-integrated to look for gain in efficiency through direct competition (in generation) or indirect competition (in distribution at the time of issuing operating licenses), there arise technical, commercial, financial and co-ordination problems. This co-ordination may continuously address issues ranging from very short-term – questions of security at millisecond levels – to very long-term – planning of a few ten years (Joskow & Schmalensee, 1983, Joskow, 1996). The new Electricity Act (2003) provides a legal framework for achieving so in the future. Setting up of adapted modes of governance and institutional mechanisms is in itself a subject of study (Glachant, 1997). In India, where we lack distance, these questions are not yet priorities as the SEBs go on functioning along administrative lines. In fact, the conditions of willingness to de-integrate are very different from those of developed countries, the ineffectiveness of this de-integration prolongs, for the middle and long-term, the recourse to *ad hoc* administrative coordination. The short-term co-ordination continues to be ensured according to technical regulations, unaffected by the organisational requirements of so-called structural reforms. Above all, the question of coordination refers to the issue of long term investments, of risks and guarantees, faced with stranded costs and specific assets. The book will briefly show that these concepts make little sense for the Central Undertakings as well, which are administrative branches of the Government of India. The book briefly mentions how to tackle these issues along with the reform of SEBs, but makes the choice to focus on the latter *in as much they exemplify the nature of the Indian State.*

- Likewise, the subtle models of emergence of competition, or the opening up to competition, concern organisations that are already sensitised and which respond to monetary constraints and incentives. Again, trading of energy, organised by the Electricity Act, 2003, has affected less than 1 per cent of the demand in 2002-03. It leaves the bulk of SEBs unaffected. In classical terms, competition concerns organisations that already have a minimum sensitivity to cost-efficiency. In this regard the words of a reformer are illustrative: "when economists come from Washington and talk to me about competition, I listen to them. I then take them to the office of Mr. X; before getting in, they realise the mess of files, in crumbling piles, on old shelves, sometimes on the floor; then they understand that the problem in India is somewhere else." To explain this, one needs to know that before this office one has to cross the 'archives', the sanctum sanctorum where all the results of the paper work of the SEB converge, heaps of files incomprehensible to the novice. More systematically, these explanations yet again recall the substantive rationality, and cannot suffice at explaining the core SEBs.
- The public choice theory is largely used to analyse the Government sector; but is however based on study of the relations between politicians and the SEBs which would tend to (i) *a priori* suppose a systematically opportunistic behaviour, (ii) leave aside certain systemic effects, and (iii) leave one to understand that politicians control the SEBs, which is systemically wrong beyond a point.
- Similarly the study of corruption alone would not bring out the systemic elements we detail. Of course, corruption matters as a constraint to reforms and is articulated to the structural framework of SEBs. For all that, it is allowed to suppose that corruption is largely permitted and rationalised by the system itself, and a large part of its bases rests on it. This is a non-tested idea but we believe that actually corruption adapts itself to the administrative nature of SEBs especially when (i) there is no integrated information to allow checks, and (ii) administrative procedures rule out substantive rationality. If true, the framework presented is self-explanatory of the entire

phenomena one come across in this large part of the Indian State that are SEBs, and is capable of ordering an answer to the questions raised. Moreover, a number of economic tools for fight against corruption are known, which are generally based on incentive outlines. The practical measures proposed here by the book, by underlining the necessary conditions for the effectiveness of these incentives, largely prepares the ground for the implementation of these 'classical' anti-corruption tools.

Finally, if we spend a certain amount of time in recalling the specificity of behaviourist hypotheses that underlie the neo-institutional approach, it is also because implicitly it was felt to be the closest to the questions studied. These tools maintain all their force once used on healthy foundations. Particularly, to define the detail mechanisms for enterprisation, taking into account the proper definition of property rights, of budgetary constraints (the risk of soft budget constraints being, more likely to occur in a private environment), and remediability (Williamson, 1994) of reforms seems the most promising approach... after SEBs will get 'enterprised'.

Plan of the Book

The book is divided in three parts. The first part analyses and characterises the functioning of a SEB. It presents a practical description of the organisational characteristics, and also of their linking to the decision-making mechanisms at work. On the theoretical aspects, it settles the debate on the validity of the analytical concept of soft budget constraint for a SEB, and specifies for the State the modalities of an analysis in terms of property rights, as well as, the pertinence of several concepts derived from that of cost. The second part focuses on the 'structural' reforms (corporatisation, de-integration, and setting up of regulatory commissions). The third part examines the role the private sector may have in enterprising SEBs, based on a model explaining the 'trade off' between public enterprisation and rapid privatisation.

The first chapter situates the SEBs in the Indian power sector, shows the limit of the analyses in terms of lack of funds or political interference. Chapter 2 conducts an organisational analysis derived from the works of James March, by characterising the systems of internal allocation of the SEBs and studying the type of rationality structuring the decision-making process. It reconstructs the practical objectives of the SEB, expresses its different internal characteristics, and brings to light the profound internal coherence of the system, its systemic rationality. Chapter 3 is more theoretical and concludes this first part by answering the question of the organisational nature itself of the SEBs – the administration – and by showing how the SEBs' own rationality follows from its nature. It rules on the choice of analytical concepts and on the conditions of application of the theories founded on the concepts of soft budget constraint and property rights.

In the second part, Chapter 4 shows that the so-called structural reforms do not alter the administrative nature of SEBs, hence do not improve their functioning. Chapter 5 draws the consequences from the administrative nature of the SEBs for their reform, by introducing the concept of enterprisation and specifies what enterprising must signify in terms of analysis by the creation – and not 're-allocation' – of property rights. Likewise, the characterisation and practical analysis of the decision-making processes serves to provide the foundation for enterprisation, in order to give the measure of the stakes.

The third part discusses the recourse to the private sector and reform of the State. Chapter 6 more specifically puts in perspective both the difficulty to reform in a public frame, as well as, the limits and political economy of privatisation. It gives a critique to the economic foundations of privatisation as a 'must be'. It studies the practical and theoretical difficulties specifically related to the 'privatisation' of an organisation not enterprised beforehand. By underlining these difficulties, it responds in the Indian case to the promoters of structural reforms necessarily completed by (rather, in their political economy: 'ordered by and subordinated to') privatisation. Chapter 7 concludes by proposing a recourse to the private experience through management contracts, signed between the State and a private partner. It provides a detailed framework for their establishment, and articulates it to larger sectoral measures.

The general conclusion winds up and recalls the outlines given to the analysis of the Indian SEBs as an integral part of the general functioning of the Indian State.

Part I

The Functioning of SEBs, their Administrative Nature and Implications

1

Beyond Simplistic Analysis

State Electricity Boards (SEBs), are the key institutions in charge of electricity in India. They enjoy a quasi monopoly on generation, transmission and distribution in their respective States. Their physical and financial distress is well known, but all the current analyses fail to explain the operational results of the SEBs in a self-consistent way. Especially, on why some available profitable measures are not taken, and what exactly is the weight of the so-called 'political intervention', compared to the SEBs' own responsibilities.

As far as the latter question is concerned, in a normative vision of the State, political choices are legitimate in the sense that they address long term social redistribution. Regarding the former question, and once redistributive choices are set, a major role of the State is to ensure the largest output through the most cost-effective option. To address these two issues, we focus on the decision-making in SEBs.

1.1. The Share of the State Electricity Boards within the Power Sector and the Indian State

This section begins by describing the organisation of the power system[1] and goes on to show that the Central Government is not, properly speaking, regulating this sector. We describe the 'historical' organisation of the sector which has produced today's inertia. Some modifications have occurred subsequent to the Regulatory Commission Act (1998). They mainly concern the creation of the Regulatory Commissions, that have taken over some of the prerogatives of the Central Electricity Authority and of the State Governments, in the States where they have been set up. Then, the Electricity Act (2003) has made Regulatory Commissions as well as some tariffing principles mandatory. It has also offered scope for future competition. These

1. For most of the statistics, the latest official figures available by April 2004, are for the fiscal year 2001-02.

modifications are extensively presented in the second part of the book. In Part II, we specially show that radical organisational alterations have not yet materialised in SEBs. The present part analyses what is referred as the 'classical system', that used to be the norm upto 1998 and continues to prevail in most of the States. Besides, and despite SEBs have been or are being 'unbundled' into various entities, it is still reasonable to go on speaking of 'the SEBs' like even the Ministry of Power (2003) or the general literature on the subject do (Godbole, 2003a & 2003b).

1.1.1. The Key Role of the State Governments

According to the Seventh Schedule of the Constitution of India, which defines the share of responsibility between the Centre and the States of the Indian federal system, the power sector is in the concurrent list. This means that the Centre sets the policies and each State is in charge of their implementation and of operationalising the system in its respective territory. The sector used to fall under the Rules framed by the Electricity Act, 1948, and its successive amendments (and, since 2003, under the Electricity Act, 2003). The Electricity Act 1948 used to specify that at the State level, the State Electricity Boards are responsible for the development and operation of generation, transmission and distribution in the "most economically efficient way". The State Electricity Boards are the entities that replaced the Electricity Departments, which were a part of the State administration. From 1956 onwards, the status of the Departments was progressively changed to Boards in all the States. The SEBs have the status of autonomous bodies. Unlike other public administrations in India, the SEBs have progressively been granted a balance sheet, when the government loans were converted into 'assets'. They have also been given the Commercially Based Accounting Rules (Act of 1985). However, they are not incorporated under the Indian Company Act (1956), a fact that contributes to granting them an intermediate status between a classical administration (which they in fact are) and a corporation (which they are not). Each SEB reports to the Power Secretary of its State Government, who is the highest civil servant under the State Minister of Power.

Attached to the Central Government, the Planning Commission determines the global level of desirable investments and, as far as electricity is concerned, ensures the co-ordination among the Ministries of Power, Finance, and Coal, and with those of Railways, Water Resources, Agriculture and other concerned Ministries. The function of the Planning Commission and the meaning of the term 'Planning' require further elaboration. The Commission reports directly to the Prime Minister. It assesses the budgetary requests and the resources of all the administrations and Ministries, at the Central and State levels. As per the Gadgil Formula, it defines the financial budgetary transfers from the Centre to the States. This formula takes into account the wealth, the income, and some developmental and social criteria of each State to allocate funds, to organise redistribution between them, and to propose a 'workable solution'. It also prepares and proposes some policies, and identifies some priority sectors[2] to be sanctioned by the Prime Minister. It then issues recommendations for the generation and the development of the electric network at both the Central and the State levels. They are quantitative recommendations expressed in terms of the number of MW to be installed, as well as, in terms of the investment ratio between transmission, distribution, and generation.

The second main institution at the Central level has long been the Central Electricity Authority (CEA), the technical adviser to the Ministry of Power, now of lesser weight[3]. Since the onset of the reforms in 1991-92, the Ministry of Power has been preparing the general policies regarding the availability of private investment and the regulation of the sector. The Ministry of Power along with the Planning Commission has an important role in the allocation of plan funds to the States. The Ministry also directly controls some Central power utilities and undertakings.

---

2. For long, a way for the Planning Commission to influence the economy over the public budgets was the obligation made to development and ensuring that both the public and the private commercial banks provide loan facilities at lower interest rates to priority sectors.

3. It sets technical norms and till 2003 gave techno-economic clearance to projects. Indeed, for every generation or transmission project that exceeds a certain amount of expenditure, the utility developing the project has to get it cleared at the Central level. This amount has been increasing over time, from 50 crore to 150 crore, and it touched 1500 crore (One Crore is equivalent to 10 million). The utility is required to submit the technical characteristics as well as the estimate of the cost of the project. Techno-Economic Clearance is granted on the basis of the conformity of the project with the standard established Rules. The standards to be used, the procedures for giving central administrative authorisation, procedures of control, are proposed by the CEA, and sanctioned by the (Central) Ministry of Power.

Regarding the development of projects and the operation of utilities, the Centre directly deals with nuclear projects through the Nuclear Power Corporation (NPC), which has a marginal generation share, and also with the inter-State projects. These are done mainly through the National Hydro-Power Corporation (NHPC) and the National Thermal Power Corporation (NTPC), both incorporated under the Company Act, 1956. They deal with hydro-electric and thermal projects respectively. Finally, the Power Grid Corporation of India dealing with the inter-State projects on transmission of power and interconnection with a view to develop, in the future, a single national interconnected grid all over India.

Another important Central institution the Power Finance Corporation (PFC), is in charge of financing both private and public power generation and transmission projects, at lower costs than the market rates in the case of public projects. It is controlled by the Government of India, and also provides for technical or managerial studies to the SEBs. Some smaller-sized private companies mainly involved in distribution and in generation also exist, such as the Bombay Sub-urban Electricity Supply (BSES) in Mumbai (Bombay), the Calcutta Electric Supply Company (CESC) in Kolkata (Calcutta), and the Tata Electric Company (TEC) in Ahmedabad[4]. Figure 1(a) presents a schematic view of the SEBs within the power sector upto 1998.

The organisation of the power sector is better understood through a historical perspective as described below. From 1948 onwards, apart from some national-scale hydro-electric projects, the key utilities of the sector have been the SEBs. It was only in the 1970's that certain major Central undertakings emerged. Indeed, after 1975, the influence of the Central Government has increased through the creation of national generation companies such as NTPC and NHPC, which are under the control of the Ministry of Power. On each plant, fixed parts of the generation capacity are allocated to each concerned State, and the energy produced is sold to the State Electricity Boards in accordance with this allocation. Until 1989, these companies also developed and operated the transmission lines necessary to connect

4. The distribution activity has recently been privatised in two States: Orissa in 1999, and Delhi in 2002, under the form of joint ventures with the Electricity Boards. TEC is a subsidiary of Tata Power Company, (TPC). BSES and TPC have taken over all but one distribution zone in these two States. TPC is also a comparatively larger player in generation since it owns 2,300 MW.

their plants to the SEBs' networks. In 1989, the networks and activities of national generating companies were transferred to a new national public company, Power Grid Corporation of India, which is also in charge of developing interconnecting lines between States. Its role is to achieve, in the long run, a single national interconnected network (the State networks remain the responsibility of the SEBs). So far, five regional networks exist, albeit poorly interconnected. Regional Electricity Boards, composed by the local SEBs, run regional despatching centres.

Figure 1(a)

The Main Institutions of the Indian Power Sector before 1998 (Without Regulatory Commissions, under Progressive Creation from 1998)

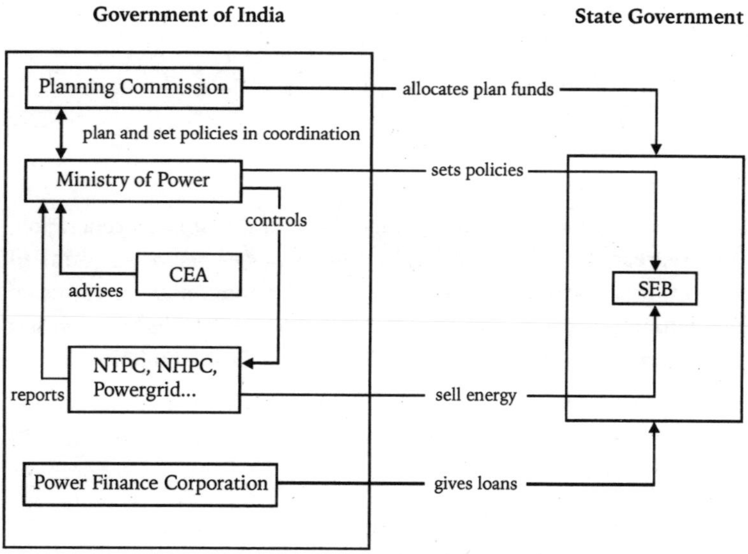

Since the 1998 Regulatory Commissions Act, (1995* for Orissa), and reinforced in the new Electricity Act (2003), the States have adjoined Regulatory Commissions, responsible for the balancing between State and consumers' interests. Figure 1(b) presents the current situation:

* Orissa Electricity Reform Act, 1995

Figure 1 (b)

The Future Functioning of the Indian Power Sector After Gradual Unbundling, according to Electricity Act, 2003

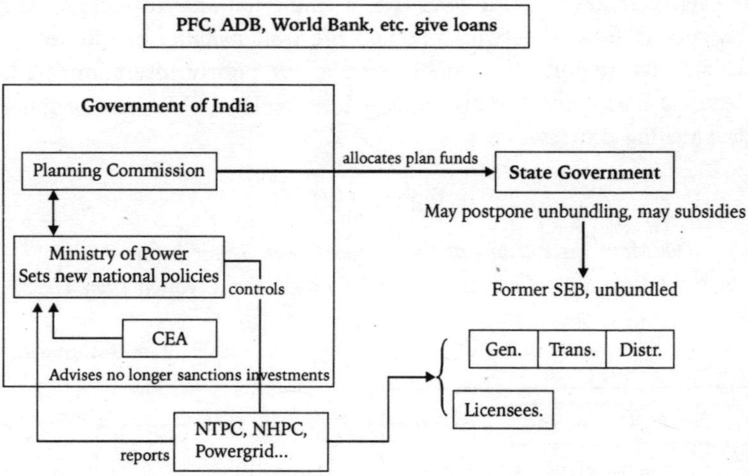

Table 1.1 shows the primary importance of the SEBs in generation. They represent a two-third of the Indian power sector in terms of generation capacity and still enjoy a quasi monopoly in terms of distribution, except in few States. As of April 2004, distribution has been privatised only in Orissa (1999) and in Delhi (2002).

Despite the provisions of the Electricity Act, 2003 to license the attribution that used to be SEBs' monopoly, the latter retain *de facto* a central position.

1.1.2. The Historical Model: Everything but Regulation from the Centre

The historical predominance of the State Governments illustrates through the fact that the Centre neither monitors nor really regulates the power sector. The concept of regulation is related not only to the process of fixing rules, but also to that of enforcing them. The Centre's role is limited to fixing rules, it has no control over their enforcement.

Table 1.1

The Generation in the Indian Power Sector on March 31, 2002

Total installed capacity	105 GW (102)
Energy consumption	515 TWh or Billion Units (500)
Technology:	
- Thermal	71% (id)
- Hydro	25% (id)
- Nuclear	3% (id)
- Renewable	1% (id)
Generation Ownership:	
- State governments (SEBs)[5]	59% (64%)
- Central Government	30% (32%)
- Private	11% (4%)
8th Plan (1992-1997)	
- needs in generation	38 GW
- actually achieved by public sector	18 GW
- achieved by private sector (93-98)	2.7 GW
9th Plan (1997-2002) : needs in generation	50 GW
10th Plan (2002-2007) : needs in generation	45 GW

Source: Planning Commission (2001), Ministry of Power (2002), and GoI (2004).
Note: Figures in brackets refer to March 31, 2001

Indeed, the role of the Planning Commission is restricted to the issuance of the plan. It does not monitor the coordination between the SEBs, the Central Undertakings and the Undertakings of other Ministries. The Planning Commission focuses only on new equipments, and not on their operation. Specifically, it is not required to look at the quality of supply or the level of losses. Even if the Planning Commission (1997) argues that "inadequate investments in the Transmission & Distribution (T&D) system is one of the major reasons for the poor quality of supply [as] the share of generation was 62 per cent in the Eighth Plan outlays whereas Transmission & Distribution had only 28 per cent share as against the recommended 1:1 ratio"[6]; however, it is not in charge of designing general schemes for power supply improvement or energy losses reduction. This example also illustrates that the design of plans has to be undertaken

5. Figure also includes the Union Territories, that are too small to have the classical State prerogatives. In their jurisdiction, the power sector is under the responsibility of the local administration, with an Electricity Department. However, their importance is very marginal.
6. After years of insistance on this issue by the Planning Commission, the situation has slightly improved, since, in 1999-00, generation had come down to 47.6 per cent of SEBs outlays, while Transmission & Distribution had increased upto 33.2 per cent.

jointly with the State Governments, and that the Planning Commission is not able to impose its views on the share in outlays. The Plans issued with the State Governments are mere guidelines rather than mandatory targets. The States have the actual discretion not only to build the new equipments, but to decide the timeframes.

Beyond these aspects, the Planning Commission has no way of checking the reports of the SEBs and the State Governments. It has to base its work on aggregate demands and on standardised administered costs. In addition, it does not even run the technical analysis itself. Most significantly, the Planning Commission long considered the average energy losses over India to be the officially reported figure of 22 per cent. This figure is completely inaccurate, as is commonly known, and is in fact rather closer to 40-50 per cent (World Bank Report, 1998). The SEBs misreport to the Planning Commission, while the Central Undertakings are monitored by the Ministry of Power. The Planning Commission again has no enforcing power.

Let us now analyse the former role the CEA used to have. It fixed technical norms and cleared projects. It ensured that, based on the technical assumptions, the formal calculation of the project costs by the utilities was correct. To clarify this point, the CEA did not run the technical studies itself, nor the economic comparisons with the income, or costs, of other alternative projects. With regard to investments, no economic evaluation such as the time of pay-back, or the internal rate of return of a project, or any other economic criteria was calculated at the CEA level, a former Member clarified in interviews. The monthly reporting on progress of works did not include recommendations for the managerial improvement of utilities once the project had begun. Such recommendations were left to the Ministry of Power in case of National Undertakings, and to the State Governments in case of the SEBs. Finally, as far as the tariff setting is concerned, the States had the discretion to fix tariffs independently of the figures sanctioned during the Techno-Economic Clearance. Tariffs for Central Undertakings plants to be paid by State Electricity Boards were based on the CEA Clearance being promulgated by the Ministry of Power. However, a former Economic Member of the CEA concurred that, due to the absence of studies of alternative projects, the tariff-setting for Central Undertakings was rather an *ex-post* clearance, based upon discussions on the manner in which the calculation was made, rather than on the level itself of the tariff.

The coordinating role of the Planning Commission is mainly theoretical. The Ministry of Power and CEA have a technical rather than an economic function. The responsibility for economically efficient investments and management in SEBs is left entirely to the States. As stated by an official during interviews, "The actual implementation is left to States, with their money". The SEBs are the heart of the system.

1.2. The Rise and Fall of State Electricity Boards

In many official reports, the work of the SEBs continues to be presented as a technical success, the focus being on achieved expenditures in new works. However, if one carefully looks at the operational results, this statement can be largely modified, and even refuted. Articulated to the politically framed low tariffs, but linked to other structural reasons as well, the financial situation of most of the SEBs is of virtual bankruptcy.

1.2.1. SEBs Presented the 'Annual Report' Way

In the annual reports of the Ministry of Power, or of each of the SEBs, the emphasis is on the amount of energy generated, and the addition of new generation and transmission capacities, or the progress of rural electrification, whatever be the mis-matching with the actual demand, or the high occurrence of power cuts or even the huge financial losses. Thus, the focus is on the quantitative levels of physical equipments added to the electric system. Using this yardstick, the level of achieved expenditures in new equipments is a direct indicator of the results achieved: greater the expenditure, greater is the success of the utility in being able to expand the system. If the SEBs are to be presented in this 'annual report' manner, then some may argue that they have been successful. Indeed, according to the Ministry of Power (2001), generation in all utilities has increased from a 4.1 in 1947 to 500 TWh* in 2000-01, the installed capacity from 1.4 GW to 102 GW (102,000 MW), the rate of achievement of State sector over the targeted capacity being 96 per cent. Moreover, the offical rate of rural electrification has gone beyond 99 per cent in 12 States out of 25, and beyond 70 per cent in 22 States. Viewed thus, the SEBs have managed to electrify the country, and to follow the demand in reasonable conditions, with the exception of a small energy gap.

* A TWh is a billion kWh, or a 'billion units'.

However, if one goes beyond the 'annual report way', the energy shortage has raised from 8.3 per cent in 1992-93 to 10.9 per cent in 1996-97, and to 11.5 per cent in 2001-02. The rhythm of new capacity addition is continuously slowing down. Still, since the report focuses primarily on physical quantities, it declares that the shortage is due to the "growth in demand outstripping the growth in generation and generating capacities" (Ministry of Power, 1997). As the report mainly focuses on expenditures in new equipments, it is hardly surprising that it attributes the energy gap mainly to the absence of additional capacities. However, if the SEBs are to be analysed with regard to their technical and financial efficiency, things appear in an entirely different light. If SEBs have been successful, this is mostly in spending money.

1.2.2. SEBs Presented Along Operational Results

Going beyond this simplistic 'annual report' view of a power sector faced with only a few investment constraints, some official documents acknowledge the problems in operation. According to the Government of India (1998a and 1998b) the issues in operational efficiency are:

- Unsatisfactory operational efficiencies, with the availability of thermal plants at less than 80 per cent, losses (including theft of power) as high as 20 to 21 per cent", and, more precisely, "high transmission and distribution losses substantially higher than normal technical standards, with a high component of non-technical losses, accounted for by poor/inadequate metering and high incidence of theft of energy.
- "Poor billing and collection, because of incorrect reporting and billing, and inadequate collection efforts, tampering with meters and misreporting in collusion with consumers".
- "Imbalance in the mix of generation sources and the undesirable proliferation of captive generating units".
- "Unmanageable size and monolithic structure, making it unwieldy, inefficient, lethargic and unresponsive to change as well as manpower related problems: poor productivity, low skills and lack of training for upgradation, low motivation levels".

Indeed, according to the Planning Commission (2002), the PLF can be as low as around 40 per cent in several States, due to the lack of transmission capacity, proper maintenance of plants and supply of coal. Also, the rate of damage of distribution transformers is very high, for instance as high as 35 per cent yearly in some circles in Haryana, leading to a life-expectancy of only a few years, as compared to 40 years in western countries. As far as the energy losses are concerned, the figure of 21 per cent that has long been reported has turned out to be notoriously fake. The Planning Commission has long considered and still does for most of the States, the official fake figures. Its annual report on SEBs, in 1997 for instance, considered a 22 per cent average level of losses for the whole of India. It is now (Planning Commission, 2001), considering to be around a 25 per cent. We have, since 1999 (see Ruet, 1999a), written that the real total figure on technical plus non-technical losses might however be around 40-50 per cent, as had also been foreseen by the World Bank (1998). These figures are now officially acknowledged (see N.K. Singh Committee Report, Government of India, 2004). Additional information had actually over time become available from the few States which have engaged in reforms and are more transparent.[7] These levels are very high in comparison to international standards (less than 10 per cent for technical and near 0 per cent for non-technical). It is difficult to separate technical from non-technical losses without reliable data, but according to the interviewed officials, a credible rough estimate with regard to the technical losses seems to be about 20 per cent, *i.e.* almost twice the international standards.[8] Such a high level of losses

---

7. For instance, Orissa, Haryana, and Andhra Pradesh used to declare roughly 24 per cent, 25 per cent and 19 per cent respectively as levels of losses. Once their reforms started they have recognised the levels of losses at 46 per cent, 34 per cent and 33 per cent respectively. This figure could probably be 35-40 per cent in Haryana. Now the Ministry of Power (2001a) reports that it was actually 51 per cent for Orissa, 45 per cent for Andhra Pradesh, 47 per cent for Haryana (and, similarly, 43 per cent for Rajasthan). Also, Punjab is reporting 18 per cent, but interviews claim that it could be at least 10 per cent more. Delhi used to declare 23 per cent, but has gradually admitted it to be 43 per cent in the first stage and is now reporting 54 per cent, while it is sometimes said to be actually over 60 per cent.

   Sources: New figures for Orissa: World Bank (1996), Gridco (1998); for Haryana, World Bank (1997), Quraishi (1998); for Andhra Pradesh, APSEB (1998); for unofficial figures for Haryana, Punjab and Delhi: interviews. Former figures: Planning Commission (1997).

8. Another evaluation is given by the CEA on what should be the norms: the UPERC (2002) recalls that "the Central Electricity Authority, after taking into account Indian conditions such as development in the transmission and distribution sector to far flung rural areas, quality of T & D equipment, meters available in the country, maintenance practices, configuration of the system, its spatial jurisdiction, nature of loads etc. has proposed that the power & energy losses should be between 8.25 per cent and 15.5 per cent". The UPERC, using mathematical methods such as Data Envelop Analysis, arrives at different results, around 30 per cent, by taking into account the actual network configuration.

shows that the network is technically under-dimensioned regarding the transits, *i.e.* in relation to generation capacity. Indeed, as the transit grows in a line, the losses increase. Investments in networks are balanced by savings in lost energy. It can therefore be concluded that the share of investments in transmission and distribution have been economically sub-optimal. Non-technical losses, on the other hand, can cover a large range of malfunctions of the SEBs, as detailed below:

- *Thefts*: they can either simply be private lines illegally connected to the wires, or shunts upstream the meter, or interruption of the meters, or lines put in upstream of unsealed meters. Such methods do not need the complicity of any SEB official to be successful, but of course, the availability of such help worsens the situation.
- *Bribing*: the amount of energy billed can be lowered by some SEB agents from the energy metered, and/or the class of consumption can be modified to allow access to better tariffs.
- *Unmetering*: a large part of the energy is unmetered and estimated, and thus often underestimated for the above reasons. A proper metering policy may either be non-existent in some SEBs, or some metering policies can face resistance or vandalism by local engineers and technicians, to maintain the income they gain from corruption.

These non-technical losses remain partially unseen due to accounting manipulations. To hide thefts and bribes, the gap between the energy produced and the energy sold has to remain unnoticed. In order to do so, the consumption of low tariff consumers is overestimated and that of high tariff consumers is underestimated, so that the official amount of supplied energy can match with a low income, the balance being pocketed. Finally, the quality of supply is poor, power cuts being as frequent as erratic. Even when the network is powered, undervoltage and low frequency (45 Hz, instead of 50, not being uncommon in North and West India) are the norm rather than the exception.

Commercially, distribution of electricity involves metering, billing and collecting; all three procedures are inefficient in the SEBs. In some SEBs, more than half of the users are unmetered, billing can face months' delays, and the dues to be collected from the users amount to crore. Table 1.2 briefly gives an illustration on GRIDCO –

an heir organisation* of the Orissa SEB – for the financial year 1997-1998. This scenario has peaked up during the nineties till date.

Table 1.2

Commercial Results of GRIDCO for Financial Year 1997-98

Area	*Total Losses (%)*	*Technical Losses (%)*	*Clients Credit (days)*	*Efficiency (kWh paid/ kWh bought) (%)*
West	39.7	17.1	181	49.6
North East	42.8	19.6	197	49.9
South	39.5	19.3	234	43.4
Centre	48.5	16.9	292	39.0

Source: GRIDCO (1998).

This problem can amount to huge figures, as shown by the results of the Andhra Pradesh SEB audit in October 1996. It reckoned that "loss of energy due to theft was getting included in the un-metered agricultural consumption; [after the audit it was] identified to be about [...] Rs. 600 crore" (APSEB 1998). If one takes the example of some other SEBs, their actual "rate of return on assets" is by far negative (figures after subsidy by the State Governments): 15 per cent for Uttar Pradesh, 72 per cent for Delhi before privatisation, and a huge 140 per cent for Andhra Pradesh (*Source*: Planning Commission, 2002).

Despite years of 'reforms', the N.K. Singh Committee still has to conclude that there is "inadequate and faulty meters", "investment being skewed towards generation resulting in non-uniform development of transmission and distribution", "monolithic and unwieldy structural framework of SEBs" (GoI, 2004). The latter point, we argue, articulates with others, and has been insufficiently studied.

1.2.3. *Tariffs and the Financial Situation: Electricity as the Lion's Share in Expenditures*

The above presentation can convey an idea of the inefficiency of

* Power sector reforms in Orissa involved the setting up of an independent Regulatory Commission as well as unbundling and corporatisation of the SEB in 1996. Generation was corporatised in the form of two generating companies, one of which was subsequently privatised. Transmission was corporatised into GRIDCO, which remained in the private sector, and is the monopoly buyer of all power from the generating companies (*Source*: Report of the Expert Group: Restructuring of SEBS; Chairman: Montek S. Ahluwalia in Reports on India's Power Sector; Academic Foundation; 2003).

the SEBs, which some State Governments dispute. But, in turn, the concerned SEBs argue on the low level of electricity tariffs.

Looking at the situation from the financial aspects, there are accumulated dues and a rise in necessary subsidies to be granted by the Governments. Though these subsidies are officially booked, they are not necessarily transferred to the SEBs, a factor that contributes to the poor supply pattern of the power system. Finally, SEBs argue, cost and tariffs are not adjusted to each other, tariffs being low for high costs. Ultimately, the debate is circular: cost with overheads and inefficiencies are too high, but low tariffs might match with cost improvement. Anyway, if one were to examine the financial trend, it is evident that the financial situation is worsening sharply. Indeed, the Government of India (1998a and 1998b) blames the poor financial health of the SEBs, referring to "irrational tariffs with heavy subsidy for agricultural consumption, excessive manpower and poor management", "skewed tariffs" involving high degrees of subsidisation, and agricultural and domestic tariffs below the cost of supply.

One of the reasons for the imbalance in tariffs is that although they should be designed in order to allow a 3 per cent rate of return on assets to the SEBs (Electricity Act, 1948), in practice the State Governments are aiming at lower tariffs for agriculture and domestic consumption. To partly balance the financial gap, commercial and industrial sectors are overcharged.

Table 1.3 gives the evolution over four years of the tariffs (national average) showing the existence of cross-subsidies, and the ensuing financial situation of the SEBs.

The evolution of the respective ratio tariff-to-cost shows that cross-subsidies decrease marginally over time. However, their level is still impressive and the industry generally pays more than the average supply cost, commercial clients pay less than industrials, domestic users paying still less (for 16.5 per cent of the sales they provide 10.5 per cent of the revenue), and agricultural users pay very little (for 32.5 per cent, they provide 4.5 per cent), if not zero in some States (like Punjab and till recently Tamil Nadu or post-2004 general elections Andhra Pradesh). The average tariff over India is lower than the average supply cost. Let us calculate it for the 1996-97 figures to show that the cross-subsidies are not a recent phenomenon. The Planning Commission (1997 & 2001) evaluates that the 'effective subsidies'[11] to the

Table 1.3

Average SEB Electricity Tariffs in India, 1996-97, 2000-01, and 2001-02.

	1996-97	*2000-01*	*2001-02*
Average supply cost	207.7 Paise/kWh	303.8 Paise/kWh	349.8 Paise/kWh
Average power tariff	158 Paise/kWh	212 Paise/kWh	239.9 Paise/kWh
Tariff / cost ratio	0.76	0.70	0.69
Category of tariff (and ratio to average tariff)			
- Railway traction	333.8 (2.11)	420.8 (1.94)	449.2 (1.87)
- Industrial	263.3 (1.66)	359.9(1.70)	378.7 (1.58)
- Commercial	260.2 (1.64)	340.4 (1.60)	426.3 (1.78)
- Domestic	103.5 (0.65)	173.4 (0.82)	195.6 (0.82)
- Agriculture	22.2 (0.14)	28.5 (0.13)	41.6 (0.17)
Commercial loss for all SEBs	9800 crore	26013 crore	33177 crore
Commercial loss after subsidy[9]	7150 crore	20220 crore	24837 crore

Source: Planning Commission (1997, 2001 & 2002)[10]

agriculture sector were 15,300 in 1997 (27,100 in 2001) and for the domestic sector, 3,900 crore (10,100 in 2000-01). From this, only around 8,000 crore (11,200 in 2000-01) is balanced by financial transfers from industrial and commercial sectors. The remainder is theoretically taken care by the State Government.

The level of deficit on the other hand increased by 165 per cent in four years from 1997 to 2001, since then it kept rising though at a slower pace. It reached 33,000 crore in 2001-02 (*Source*: GoI 2004) that is equivalent of 1.5 per cent of the GDP.

In this situation, the SEBs have to postpone their investments, borrow money and face related financial costs. Table 1.4 illustrates, through the Orissa example, the financial situation of the SEBs and their heir organisations at a time when the states were seeking for privatisation.

Given the financial burdens of the SEBs arising out of the problems discussed above, some of their suppliers can then face difficulties in

9. The figure of subsidies is a book figure. Interviews have shown that subsidies are sometimes not actually paid by some State Governments, which simply write off payable interests.
10. Most recent report available by April 2004, due to delay of publishing by the Planning Commission.
11. Defined as "average unit cost of supply minus average unit revenue realisation times the total sale of agricultural and domestic sector" (Planning Commission).

Table 1.4

The Financial Position of GRIDCO (Orissa) in March 1997

Total debts	873 crore
Expenditures	1399 crore
Recovery	1112 crore
Debts/Recovery ratio	0.79
Recovery/Expenditure ratio	0.79

getting paid for the energy or the inputs they supply to the Boards. The Planning Commission (1997 & 2001) indicates that "the outstanding dues to be paid by the SEBs to the central sector power undertakings has come to over 12,250 crore [by March 1997]", 26,400 by March 2001 and 40,000 by March 2002 (Ministry of Power, 2002). The annual losses in 2001-02 have amounted to 33,000 crore, i.e. 1.5 per cent of GDP (Ministry of Power, 2002). If one takes into account the central undertakings within all sectors, it amounts to 33,600 crore by March 2001 according to IIR (2002), and this figure is not available after 2002[12]. This situation induces budgetary imbalances. For instance, in 1995-96, 60 per cent of the bills due from the State Electricity Boards to NTPC were paid to them through centrally collected taxes, funds that would otherwise have been directed to the State Governments[13]. The payments, however, were done on a quarterly instalment basis, without any interest being charged, due to a decision of the Ministry of Power. This shows that the financial distress faced by the SEBs spreads outwards to the rest of the power sector, and ultimately to budgets of the State Governments, already in the red[14].

12. The gross subsidy, that is without cross-subsidisation by industry, was of 38,000 crore in 2000-01; Source: GoI, 2004.
13. Before financial transfers, the Central Government of India collects taxes well beyond its budgetary expenses, whereas the States are structurally in deficit. Five year budgets include financial transfers from the Government of India to the States
14. Up to the financial year 1993-94, the central current contribution (share of taxes, loans and donations) to States budgets represented 42.2 per cent (around 5.4 per cent of GNP) of the current States expenses. It decreased regularly, to dip, in 1996/97, as low as 38.7 per cent and 37 per cent for 1997/98 (4.4 per cent of GDP). Central loans remained constant over this period, but had previously decreased by 0.8 per cent of GDP in three years. Simultaneously, the States' own current receipts decreased, so current States' deficit jumped from 0.5 per cent to 1.5 per cent of GDP between 1993/94 and 1996/97. So did the total budgetary deficits (including investment expenses), from 2.6 to 3.5 per cent. The debt of Commercial banks and private sector shares in the States is growing, and so will the weight of the debt service. And last but not least, the cost of 1997's salary increase did mean an increase from 2.4 to 4 per cent of GDP to States. For the year 2002-03, the fiscal deficit of the Government of India is to be around 5.3 per cent of GDP. (All figures from www.indiastat.com).

To sum up, the State-level political decisions during the 80's have resulted in the increase of tariff subsidies to agriculture, while the promised compensation to the SEBs through financial transfers has not been made. In addition, relative neglect in the metering of the energy, and high levels of both technical and non-technical losses, have led to financial losses - even with Governmental subsidies included - in all the SEBs. Thus, the SEBs' commercial losses can be explained by a *combination* of low tariffs and of high operation costs (low efficiency).

As far as the overall impact of the SEBs financial distress on the whole economy, suffices to say that, over the Ninth Plan, the power sector has represented 14.5 per cent of the plan expenditure, and that, in 2000-01, it has represented 39.9 per cent of the total State expenditure in Andhra Pradesh, or 24.6 per cent in Delhi, for instance. Still, in addition to these capital expenditures paid by the State Governments, the commercial deficit of APSEB/AP Transco and Delhi Vidyut* Board (DVB) have amounted to the equivalent of 69 per cent and 36 per cent respectively of the total expenditures of their State Governments. Since SEBs' accounts are isolated from the Government budgets, and since few of it has been covered by subsidies (it was even nil in Delhi), the State budgets have not been directly affected by these deficits that year. However, this constitutes a short-term budgetary bomb, and a huge lack of funds for social reforms (for instance, in Andhra Pradesh, the SEB losses represent now the double of all social sector public expenditures).

Ultimately, the situation sumps up as follows: Rao (2004) states out the cost of incumbency by writing that "there is no sign of reduction in the commercial losses of SEBs. Indeed, the commercial losses from 1998 to 2000 total over Rs. 70,000 crore, which is more than the total for the period from 1990 to 1997". The question is really to know for what are these financial gaps, when the 2001 census of India shows that only 44 per cent of Indian households have an electrical connection...

1.2.4. An Outlook at the Macro Linking with Environmental Concerns

Though the book will not focus on these, long term issues on sustainable development framework have to be mentioned here. The problems at stake are recalled, for, given their size and role in the

* Electricity

energy sector in India, the SEBs will be part of the organisations whose role is to invent such a sustainable framework. Studies done for large countries, such as China, India and Indonesia, by the UN bring out unsustainable outcomes in the 'Business As Usual Scenarios'. For instance, Box 1.1 recalls the results for India in the year 2020.

The power sector as well as the SEBs are directly concerned by the level of demand for coal for electricity generation. This stands true both in terms of energy choices and energy efficiency. Alagh (2001) recalls that "the serious environmental implications of burning poor quality coal are apparent underlining the critical energy situation in the country".

Box 1.1

Unsustainable Projections for India for the Year 2020

Population	1330 million inhabitants
Urban Population	Low : 465 million; High : 590 million
Slum Population	Low : 85 million; High : 130 million
Solid Waste Disposal	100 to 110 million tonnes
Demand for Coal for Power Generation	Low : 817 million tonnes; High : 2016 million tonnes
Water Shortage	Around 10 per cent to 25 per cent between the years 2020/50
Air Pollution	Two to two and a half times the norms in trend forecast

Source: Y.K. Alagh, (2001a).

Beyond the sector-specific problems, linkages with other sectors appear. Alagh (2002) mentions the "two way relationship between transport and energy in India". Indeed, "in business as usual scenario (BAU), coal demand rises to 2 billion tonnes. Energy and transport are strongly inter-linked. Coal for power generation is a significant part of bulk transport movements. Import of oil and gas and pithead *versus* demand oriented locations of power stations determine transport need. In a BAU, Indian coal demand is 2 billion tonnes. In an efficiency scenario, it is 0.8 billion tonnes. Demand management, energy efficiency, optimal location of energy generation facilities and transport policies, lead to this outcome. Indian power grade coal is plentiful, but of poor quality and so the environmental consequences of linkage policies are high".

If BAU is to be followed, imported fuels will be around two-third of the total by 2020, which is unfeasible (see Schwank, Stokar and North, 2000). Beyond energy-conservation measures, an efficient scenario has to assume a high share of renewable sources of energy like photovoltaics and wind power. The ability of SEBs to implement them will be critical. Sustainability studies further include other hypotheses in their efficiency-based scenario. For instance, forest based non-commercial energy for the usage of households is substituted by solar, but also by nuclear and hydro-electric power. These latter forms of energy have well-known drawbacks, and the emerging analysis focuses on two aspects. At a given growth of the demand, the nature of the energy choices is of a trade-off such as 'drawbacks of some energies *versus* drawbacks of others'. The second dimension is about demand control and accompanying measures for respective drawbacks of each energy. Again, these latter aspects cannot be addressed by this book, but needed being underlined.

SEBs not only have to be made financially sound, or made delivering energy, they also have to be empowered and enabled to be reactive towards these challenges. If to be implemented the "efficient energy scenario" will strongly require the participation of present SEBs. Quite a bit of improvement sources go along good reforms. For instance, the already mentioned scope for losses reduction, or the lowering of coal-based generation plants outages, are among the (numerous) ways to explore. Indeed, too frequent shutdowns of coal-based plants lead to a high consumption of polluting oils for their too numerous start-ups. However, as this is not the focus of the present book, we will not go beyond these few examples, nor conduct any further analysis of Clean Development Mechanisms in SEBs. But it is believed that the clues the book gives for the reform of SEBs are *sine qua non* conditions for such a further environmental challenge.

1.3. From Partial Debates to a Central Question

To sum up, two sets of explanations are offered in India to explain the situation the SEBs face. Both mechanisms of 'lack of public money' and 'political interference' run short in self-consistently providing a sound analysis. This calls for a deeper examination of the kind of rationality that drives the SEBs.

1.3.1. 'India Needs Money and Hence Privatisation'

A current explanation offered to the problems of the power sector is the lack of public money. Projections on future demand, for instance in Mohan (1997) and Shukla (2000), show large upcoming equipment needs, regardless of what the considered scenario may be. Meanwhile, in the business-as-usual hypotheses, financial losses grow steeply. Even while discussing the inefficiencies in the operation of the SEBs, the Government of India (1998a and 1998b) still contends that "the most serious problem facing the power sector is the paucity of investment funds". The Government of India (1998b) argues that "need for additional resources for system upgradation would need private sector participation in distribution". Significantly, the need for reforms seems to emanate from economic concerns, though it is recognised that "to attract private capital in the industry, structural reforms in the industry would be required". This issue is hence central in the Indian debate focusing on reforms. The discussion of the debate itself is left for the second part of the book, but here let us show that the issue of resources is not the limiting factor. In other words, substantial improvement can be made within the present financial conditions. The fact that they are not made, raises some fundamental questions.

An interesting question is to understand why some politically neutral investments that are profitable under the present conditions, or that would be more profitable than others, are not undertaken. For instance, the ratio of investments in generation and network in particular proves inefficient as far as technical losses are concerned. The argument generally presented in interviews is that financial problems have prevented the SEBs from undertaking all planned projects. However, such an argument cannot be accepted as being logical. Indeed, there is no techno-economic argument to constrain the development of the network more than that of generation. Optimisation under constraints does not mean under-optimisation. Analysis shows that this situation is a techno-economic paradox. From experience derived from interview related to the World Bank loans to Haryana in the Sonepat Circle, it appears that increasing the number of transformers by less than 10 per cent, brings down the annual rate of damage, from more than 30 to 35 per cent in some sub-divisions to 20 per cent, *i.e.* an improvement of at least one-third. Such an investment is highly profitable, with a pay-back time of less than two years (calculations by the author, based on interviews). The achievement of such a result is then, in effect, techno-economically feasible. In addition, within the scale of two years, it does not imply additional means. The same applies to the availability of generation plants. The same amount of money could be more efficiently used through maintenance, rather than through the setting up of new plants.

Many profitable investments are not undertaken under the present system. These possibilities are, at the basic, improvement of plant availability (PLF), and the reduction of technical losses. Let us look at their internal profitability – investment (I), variable costs (VC), annual revenue (R) and cash flow (CF) are shown in Table 1.5. The Cash Flow is equal to the annual revenue (R) minus the variable costs (VC). The internal rate of profitability is calculated with the hypothesis of a long duration of life of assets (valid for the power sector), and at fixed figures. That is, the internal rate of return is calculated as the ratio between the cash flow and the investment.

Table 1.5

Internal Rate of Return of Strategies for Bringing Additional Power Availability

Strategies	*Investments and Cash Flow (Crore)*	*Internal Rate of Return (%)*
PLF increase up to 68.5% (equivalent to additional 4.5 GW)	I: 2,800 VC: 2,150 R : 4,150 CF : 4,150	71
Technical losses improvement (6.5%, equivalent to additional 4.5 GW)	I: 23,000 VC: 0 R : 4,150 CF : 4,150	18

Source: Ruet, 2002[15].

Although the reduction of technical losses, in itself, would mean a higher investment than that of PLF improvement, the associated variable costs are far lower. Indeed, in one case, increasing the PLF

15. The PLF has recently reached on an average 67 per cent in 2001-02, thanks to central utilities more than the SEBs. However, in terms of rate of return, the rate of 71 per cent holds in 2004, all the more that the ratio tariff-to-costs of supply as evaluated by the Planning Commission has marginally declined.

amounts to increase the running hours of the plants, and therefore saving investments in new capacities to the tune of 4.5 GW. While in the second strategy, energy already produced but previously lost in the network is made available for consumption and selling. Even under the present tariffs, PLF increase is very profitable. Classical capacity addition through new plants, on its own, has a rate of return of 4 per cent only at current tariffs (Ruet, 2002). Clearly, building new plants within the present average tariffs is not profitable, if one is looking for a 16 per cent rate of return, which is now the granted level for independent producers and central undertakings. Of course, the energy generated from new plants, according to the cost plus system, is to be paid at a higher-than-average tariff. The strict expression of this principle would lead, by definition, to a 16 per cent profitability. This, however, is not granted within the political context of tariff fixation, where only present average tariffs are granted to the SEBs.

The fact that these profitable actions are not undertaken in SEBs, is then puzzling. Beyond the partial explanations, exposed in interviews, of 'visibility' of MWs, it is interesting to note that, for similar problems in power utilities of several African countries, Girod (1993) has proposed an explanation by examining the way utilities managers were controlled and evaluated. Namely, the power ministries focused on the realisation of new works, and especially on addition of new generation and network capacities rather than on the availability and maintenance of the older parts of the infrastructure, or on its operation costs. Thus, in these African countries, there have been stronger incentives for developing new capacities than for maintenance, without any consideration for their respective economic income. The latter explanation suggests the opportunity to study the decision-making process and decision criteria in SEBs.

Though the book focuses on SEBs, the kind of cost-inefficient choices we have described similarly happens at the Centre. Indeed, some cost-efficient policies might exist, but they are not made compulsory by the Ministry of Power. This relates for instance to imposing conservation measures on the demand side or load management measures. Energy conservation methods can indeed help to a certain extent to reduce the shortages and, therefore should be accorded a high priority. In fact, the Central Electricity Authority (CEA) has estimated that by the year 2006-07 (end of the Tenth Five-

Year Plan) about 15,000 MW could be saved by energy conservation measures alone. Another 15,000 MW could be saved if demand management measures are taken up in the right earnest. Thus, there is a scope to roughly save about 30,000 MW by 2006-07 by way of energy conservation measures. On these aspects as well, the political explanation is often favoured, stating that, given the federal context, the Ministry of Power faces political difficulties in setting them. For similar lines of argument to those exposed in the case of SEBs, this simplistic explanation has to be addressed. The book will actually show, in chapter 7, that political lock-ins may be overcome, and that such a long neglect for conservation measures has also come from an administrative paradigm in decision-making.

Ultimately, our own conclusions will rather come in complement to one of the findings of the N.K. Singh Committee, that financial requirements are rather to meet the gap of a transition period (estimated to be in the tune of 72,350 crore by the Deepak Parekh Committee, see GoI 2004). However, how the 'transitory regime" should articulate to restructuring measures, and what goal it should aim at, is to be specified. This is one of the practical aims of this book to contribute to this debate.

1.3.2. The Power Sector as Driven by an Electoralist Goal: 'Bring me to Power, I'll give you Free Power'

Another current explanation given to the problems of the power sector is the influence of politicians. Again, a closer discussion of this will suggest the importance of studying decision-making in SEBs.

Politicians without a Benevolent Cause: Situating the Problem

Let us take the example of Haryana. According to a report of the World Bank (1997), "the root cause of the situation – now largely recognised and accepted by Haryana's policymakers – is the pervasive politicisation of most decisions affecting HSEB's operations and expansion, and the resulting lack of a commercial outlook in its functioning. The State has regarded HSEB as an extension of the government and has exerted influence over its tariff, operational, personnel, procurement and investment decisions to further political objectives. As a consequence, HSEB has been required to charge low tariffs to agriculture and residential consumers, and to undertake or continue unremunerative activities on behalf of the State government without proper compensation; HSEB has not been able to enforce normal remedies to collect bills, and to take bold measures to eliminate the large system non-technical losses. HSEB, impeded for many years from behaving as a commercial entity, has thus been progressively transformed into an extension of the state government, unable to meet the power requirements of the State". This position is consistent with that of the then Government of Haryana, who was a signatory to this report.

About 'Interference': Policy Directions and Executive Instructions

The statement about the SEBs quoted from the report above leaves the internal logic of the management of SEBs partly unanswered. Indeed, the SEBs managers' objective has not been inefficiency *per se*; likewise, the State Governments too have not agreed to deficits *per se*. These are only consequences of other objectives, which remain unrevealed through such analysis. The power sector vests some economic specificities. Its development has a direct impact on the agricultural production and the rural population, on the social sector, and on economic development at large. These issues cannot be addressed through market mechanisms only, and these 'externalities' of the power sector on other sectors is referred to as one of the 'market failure' situations by the economic theory. In this context, the State has to intervene, be it under the (now widely proposed) light form of a regulator. In that context, the concept of 'interference' is thus too vaguely defined and has to be questioned. Let us detail the issue of the externalities the power sector has on development through the example of rural electrification in India. As Chakravarty (1987) points out, the power sector has been used by State Governments from the mid 50's, for their agricultural development policy[16]. Special subsidies were designed for rural electrification, with precise objectives relating to the type and size of villages to be

16. We use the terms 'Government, policy, political decision' to refer to public decisions, linked with financial commitment and subject to democratic contentions. Electoralist decisions, such as low tariffs for agriculture, are still in this category. Whatever their economic implications, they are transparent, and the responsibility remains with the Government. We use 'politicians, clientelism, political influence' for hidden or non transparent decisions based on the satisfaction of particular interests.

electrified first. The State Governments made commitments regarding associated expenditures and targets were quickly achieved. The examples of Punjab or Haryana among others are significant.

In 1967, the Punjab SEB (PSEB) had achieved 1.5 million energised pumpsets, allowing Punjab to achieve the most significant agricultural production in India. In 1955, all irrigational consumption was metered and priced, but by 1967, most of the meters were not functioning and people were not willing to pay. Since proper metering necessitated a large number of employees, the Government of Punjab decided to introduce a flat rate based on the pump capacity. Subsequently, there has been political influence to not increase the tariffs though the costs have increased. From the financial year 1975-76 and subsequent years till now, the Punjab Government promised subsidies to the PSEB, which have never been fully paid because of the State Government's financial problems. After 1997, following the electoral campaign, irrigational power that used to bring 300 crore a year became free.[17] Till that stage, despite the financial amounts being high, these kinds of policies should not have prevented the SEBs from being technically efficient, provided the subsidies were clearly designed and actually granted.

Let us however specify how, beyond the financial matters, the decision-making process has actually worsened the situation. The available testimony is about Haryana, but Punjab and Haryana have the same path of evolution in issues of decision-making in the Electricity Boards, and the situation, as well as, the results are representative of many SEBs.

To undertake new infrastructure works, SEBs are dependent on their Government, who can utilise them for the purposes of achieving their political goals. For instance, according to Quraishi (1998), in Haryana, the politically given objective had been to electrify at the fastest rate. This restricted the discretion of the Haryana SEB (HSEB), that had no alternative but to electrify widespread areas simultaneously, therefore using long low voltage (LV) lines. Since doing an expenditure in LV was cheaper than in the medium voltage (MV) lines, this effectively ensured quick electrification, as more villages were covered in a short span of time. However, this low MV/

17. *Source*: Interviews.

LV ratio has quickly generated a high level of technical losses, and therefore soon added up to the financial costs of the HSEB[18]. This, in turn, has ultimately led to higher cost of supply and/or less financial resources for the process of electrification itself[19]. Ultimately, the political objective has been decided at the expense of the general SEBs' statutory role to supply at the lowest cost, according to the 1948 Act. Conversely, an ideal policy direction to implement this goal would have been to select prioritised zones within the State (based on possibility of quick returns on spent money), with the choice of the mode of electrification left to the HSEB. But still, the general scenario has further been aggravated through another form of politicisation, since, in several zones, numerous smaller political stronghold areas were prioritised with electoral considerations only.

Therefore, what is generally referred to as 'political interference' must be detailed, and bifurcated in *policy directions* and *executive instructions*. Policy directions would refer to goals fixed in a clear framework with stable rules and constraints, along with the discretion to decide on the means to reach them. This discretion is accompanied with a correlative accountability. Conversely, executive instructions refer to a series of precise and local instructions on a day to day operation. In the example of Haryana, a policy direction would have been for instance expressed like 'electrify in the most efficient way these priority areas over a ten years period of time'. The executive instruction at the same time would have have vague: 'electrify fast', and on actual day to day basis: 'electrify this village', or 'switch to this political stronghold of mine'. The above illustration on rural electrification of Haryana reflects that, even when under policy directions, SEBs can achieve a (second-best) cost-efficient management. On the contrary, executive instructions preclude to do so. In an ideal situation, if general targets are fixed but the SEBs have the discretion (and accountability) for

18. This is the case in most of the SEBs. In such a situation, reducing the technical losses really calls for a long term restructuring of the HV-LV configuration of the network. The UPERC (2002) details that, given the too high LV to HV ratio in Andhra Pradesh or Haryana, the level of losses is to remain to the tune of minus 30 per cent in these States if no restructuring of the network is undertaken. Similarly, for West Bengal and Uttar Pradesh, the UPERC reports that, though the ratio is better, it is still not adapted to the higher population densities in these States. For West Bengal, it states that the mathematical model they have used to estimate the technical losses "justifies the loss level of 29.98 per cent in the short run because (of) the consumer density". In all cases, the Low Voltage part of the network is over-dimensioned given the demand parameters.

19. This is confirmed by several technical experts, and by some officials.

relations to consumers, equipment, human resources and bill collection, to reach these targets in the most efficient way (according to given fixed criteria), then there is no major problem. Problems arise as a result of time-varying executive instructions, a factor that potentially takes place in each decision of the SEB. In this context, outcomes of SEBs' decisions are unpredictable because new executive instructions may occur at any time. Hence, the SEBs' agents cannot be held accountable for resulting inefficiencies. So, *the real problem is not that of policy directions, but of executive instructions*. This situation of being under sole policy directions has been referred by many as an unreachable ideal in the current context of SEBs, but it could be reached earlier like in other countries, France for instance, where the Power company EDF is under a 'plan contract' for five years with the State. Having made this useful analytical distinction between executive instructions and policy directions, the book will concentrate in the following chapters on the structural and organisational reasons why these executive instructions and policy directions cannot be easily operationally disentangled in SEBs' current organisation.

But, let us take this one step further. As electricity networks create externalities on development, it could be argued that the cost attached to this fastest rate of electrification has been balanced by the fastest development of agriculture, thereby helping the Green Revolution. However, the question here is of a different nature. First, whatever the macro efficiency, the point is that such a comparison, if it has been made, has been based on an objective different from the strict minimisation of the cost of supply. Years later, this structurally high cost of supply still impedes the SEBs to reach cost-efficiency, while also imposing an external discretionary power on SEBs. Electrification carried out through executive instructions instead of policy directions, has led to inefficiency and hence to lesser electrification. For the supporters of the 'interference' interpretation, the question now is to determine the various forms in which executive instructions take place.

Executive Instructions in SEBs

Both interviews and official reports testify that executive instructions are given on every equipment project. As an official has ventured to say, "the criterion is not additional revenue but the satisfaction of local needs". For instance, politicians put pressure on Electricity Boards for the location of new plants in their stronghold, ask for supply on a priority basis, even if the collection is poor, demand that these plants be allocated more credits for maintenance. For electoral reasons, consequently, investments have been dispersed in many projects simultaneously instead of on prioritisation, leading to costly delays. Just before the elections, politicians ask for immediate, visible actions. Similarly, the low *ratio* on investments in network versus generation can be explained as follows, based on corroboration by people interviewed: first, generation is more visible, as "MW speaks more than km of lines" both to populations and administrative controllers; and second, generation development implies more contracts than network, opening the door to more bribing.

As far as human resource is concerned, Rajiv Gandhi once declared, "These are not Electricity Boards, but Employment Boards". Executive instructions from the State Governments occur in recruitment, promotion, and also transfers of the agents of the SEBs. State Electricity Boards are pressurised into recruiting numerous unskilled workers in politicians' strongholds, regardless of their requirements. Hierarchical nominations (Chairman, Board of Directors, as well as officials in the intermediate hierarchy) are political. Broadly speaking, each nomination of a position in the State Electricity Boards can potentially face political pressure to support a candidate. The management of human resources in the SEB is therefore not free from politicisation. A Superintending Engineer confirmed to me that he is not free to transfer agents where they are needed without having to face pressure, either direct, or political through the SEB hierarchy. As a result of political influence, the level of (vote bank) unskilled workers is high (see Table 1.6).

Table 1.6

The Employees in GRIDCO for Financial Year 1997-98, and the Client per Agent Ratio in 1996

Total number of employees:	Transmission: 5,050
	Distribution: 25,400
Executives: 5%, Non Executives: 95%, including Unskilled Helpers: 60%	
Clients per agent *ratio*:	Orissa: 50
	(France: 440)

Source: GRIDCO (1998) and World Bank (1996).

Finally, even if the SEBs' autonomous status and regulations allow the Board to fire an agent caught red-handed in a case of corruption, interviews have confirmed that, in practical terms, the fault is very difficult to prove. Even if it is proved the unions put pressure on politicians to protect the employee, and the matter seldom reaches the Courts. Whatever the extent of the truth behind this account as narrated by interviewed officials, the evident fact is that practically no action is taken against bribing in SEBs.

Regarding the commercial function, all those interviewed insist that there is a fair amount of political protection of particular interests, and hence of corruption. The practice of political support to those users who are caught stealing power, has been confirmed in the interviews given by officials. For instance, in 1997, the Haryana SEB (HSEB) agents wanted to install some meters to farmers. A farmer beat one of them, upon which HSEB kept trying to impose the meter on him. The contention turned into riots, and some railway stations were burnt. Generally, the events do not escalate to this point, but agricultural associations have acquired a very strong influence, as have industrials. For instance, several industrials in Delhi are declared as residentials; hence they use many smaller connections, and argue against the high tariffs, with implicit political support. On what may be a more anecdotal level, the 'slumlords' problem has been expressed in some interviews. In some parts of India where large slums exist, there is an agreement between the local head of the Mafia and politicians, who then dispense with the billing of water and electricity in the slum. In exchange, 'protection fees' are paid by the inhabitants to the slumlord. A part of it is passed on to the concerned politicians. Corruption in the SEBs takes two different forms: paying more for the normal service (for connection) or helping in stealing energy (bill lowering, consumer category shifting, compliance to direct thefts, false assessment of pumps capacity). This type of corruption is directly made available by the absence of meters, flat tariffs and so on, which makes the reporting system very light and can thus be easily falsified. When information does not exist, the man in charge of the Field has the power to make people pay for his blindness. These practices are covered by the hierarchy and, in absence of checkable information, officers feel safe. Fruits of the corruption climbs up the hierarchy. On the long term, what explains the persistence of corruption is political support, interviewed people concur. However, what makes it possible is the reporting system that the book will amply analyse.

Studying the Decision-making Process and the Structural Roots of Cost-inefficiency

So, even if, as the World Bank does, the Government of India (1998b) refers to "political interference in the management and day to day affairs of the Board", this recognition does not adequately result in subsequently disentangling policy directions and executive instructions. What is required is a particularly in-depth study to disentangle on one hand the policy directions (and the way they are designed) and on the other hand, the executive instructions, that are the real roots of cost-inefficiency. Our argument is that, since neither the World Bank, nor the Government of India, analyse them separately, their analysis cannot precisely put to light the very root causes of cost-inefficiency. Their ultimate explanations on the reasons for inefficient behaviour *remain at the level of narratives at a global level, and do not address detailed facts*. Practical decision-making in SEBs must be studied in a more profound way.

Further, once the detailed path of executive instructions will be known, a second stage has to be studied. Indeed, it is hard to understand how executive instructions, necessarily limited to a certain extent, should be able to overrun a whole system, that would otherwise be dedicated to the objective of efficiency. Even in a context of endemic executive instructions, some other structural – organisational – reasons for inefficiency cannot be dismissed so easily. A minimal rationality has to be assumed for decision makers in and outside SEBs; they do not only follow executive instructions. Illustratively enough, when one focuses on the PLF improvement, this measure is not only profitable, but hardly affects any vested interest. Why are they not undertaken? What is the logic behind this? As well, better than studying the symptom of corruption, the root mechanisms that make it possible have to be detailed. Here again, the question shall become 'are there structural – organisational – causes for corruption'? All this calls for a detailed analysis of the functioning of the SEBs.

1.3.3. The Central Issue: The Rationality of the State

The previous descriptions of commonly accepted analyses of the power sector do not help in analysing why mostly inefficient decisions are taken, nor do they help in understanding the stability of the organisation. Indeed, even a deep description of executive instructions would only lead to perceiving the system as a parasite and ever-changing deviation from the (cost-efficient) norm. The core of the organisation is left undiscussed. Hence, the question of the actual mechanisms that have led to these inefficient results must be raised. 'Irrationality', which is the commonly offered implicit explanation, cannot be accepted. The Government of India deals with "irrational tariffs", while the World Bank puts stress on the SEBs own cost inefficiencies, *i.e.* irrational management. People have to be changed, this is the World Bank credo for privatisation. However, viewing people as irrational does not help to understand nor solve the issue. The very implications of the system on the behaviour of the agents, and therefore on the results of the SEBs, have to be understood prior to determining a systemic change. In this regard, *the rationality and the stability of a system that has lasted over fifty years and managed to electrify India has to be unearthed.* By focusing on the decision-making process in SEBs, the following chapter shows that SEBs have neither been asked to look for cost efficiency, nor given the means to do so. Hence, the *raison d'être* of the SEBs is neither profit nor efficiency. From this, *acting rationally in SEBs has to do with something else than focusing on costs, and the normative posture of asking the agents to behave on targeting efficiency is itself not consistent with the system* in which they evolve. The dilemma is as follows. It is considered that SEBs are irrational towards efficiency and profit criteria, in which case, one cannot ask the agents to turn rational. Indeed, the only would-be rational agent in a so-called irrational system becomes irrational himself within the system. This view leads to an *impasse* and is hence not useful in analysing and arriving at solutions. On the contrary, a positive study of the type of rationality at stake in the SEBs has to be conducted, and this is the object of the first part of this book.

This description will also help in understanding the relations between SEBs and their respective State Governments. State Governments do not have complete control on the State Electricity Boards. Both complain about each other. If State Electricity Boards have development or redistributive policies to fulfil, as well as, executive instructions to apply, this does not mean that their Governments will be later on committed to their costs. Firstly, they have their own financial problems, and secondly there are arguments on the State Electricity Boards' performance. Ironically, politicians, when sitting as Government members in front of SEB officers and arguing about inefficiencies, do not assume the populist behaviour they engage in while in their constituencies, or while giving instructions on the phone to the same SEB officers.

1.4. Conclusion

The key point in the Indian power sector is the reform of the State Electricity Boards. This is not only justified from the quantitative point of view of their size, but also because of their institutional role in distribution. Further, SEBs are, strictly speaking, not (in the economic sense) *regulated* by the Government of India. It is at the State level, that relationships between the State Governments and their respective SEB matter. As such, to understand these relations, the internal decision-making in the SEBs has to be studied, since the classical lines of explanation of the inefficiencies of the sector fail to clarify some issues. Among them, it is noticed that some profitable, as well as, politically neutral decisions are paradoxically not taken. This suffices to give relativity to the explanatory power of arguments based on lack of public funds or on political interference. One has then to question some more structural reasons for such a situation. Especially, the internal organisation matters, the decision-making processes matter, the information and the available reporting system do constrain and condition the choices to be made. At this stage, the question that emerges, is 'what impedes taking profitable decisions?' and at a larger level, how does the State take its day-to-day decisions, those that impact the larger share of the population, and also those having the highest budgetary incidence? In coming chapters, this question will open an angle of analysis for the issue of the inefficiency of SEBs. This search of structural roots conveys the general question of the rationality of choice in SEBs.

2

Procedures and Objectives: Procedural Rationality in SEBs

This chapter determines the extent and the conditions of the discretionary power left to various levels of the hierarchy in SEBs. Analysed in particular are the allocation of discretionary power through the budgetary system and the hierarchical line. In addition, the chapter characterises the way in which the reporting system enables the monitoring of the use of discretionary power. This makes clearer the stylisation of the organisational characteristics of SEBs. Within this framework, the detailed study of some decision-making processes permits us to underline the importance of the procedural rationality in SEBs. This analysis also highlights the *a posteriori* objectives of the organisation, and characterises the type of rationality at stake. Though conclusions drawn here apply to all States, this chapter is more particularly based on in-depth field investigation in Haryana, Andhra Pradesh and Orissa, that have been repeatedly conducted at different stages of reform. All levels of the hierarchy have been interviewed, from linemen and meter readers to the chairman and the power secretary. In these States, the reform process, far from precluding the analysis and definition of unreformed SEBs, sheds light on some processes which were formerly in the dark.

2.1. Theoretical Framework: Decisions, Efficiency, and Rationality in Organisations

Simon and March have re-examined some structural hypotheses generally made in the analysis of organisations. They question, in particular, the actual process of decision-making, of goal formation, as well as the kind of rationality at stake in the decision-making process. This sub-section presents the main functions that Simon & March attribute to all types of organisations. It presents the manner in which decisions arise and can be studied, as well as, the way in which goals emerge and can be discovered through analysis. This will allow us finding lines of regularity in SEBs and the State, beyond the vague 'interference'.

'Organisation' is an ubiquitous word; it not only refers to an entity, but also to the way this entity is internally structured. The first sub-section essentially refers to the latter sense, and shows the way the internal organisation constrains and structures decisions. The second sub-section, by studying the rationality of parts of the organisation – as an entity – and the rationality of the entity itself, aims at making the link between the two understandings of the term 'organisation'. The third sub-section derives the objectives of the organisation-entity from the decision-making structure and the mode of rationality. The originality of the approach lies in the fact that the objectives of the organisation will ultimately partly be a result of its internal organisation.

2.1.1. A General Panorama: Decisions as Framed in Organisation

Cyert & March (1963), have examined the "effects of organisational structure and conventional practice on the development of goals, formation of expectation, and the execution of choices". Hence, goals and expectations are not framed exogeneously to the organisational structure, but are shaped by the structure itself. The same holds true for choices. For Simon (1947), the processes at stake in organisations are decision processes: they consist in isolating some elements in the decisions taken by the members of the organisation, and setting up regular procedures to choose and determine these elements and to transmit them to the concerned members. Actually, the organisation takes away from the individual a part of his autonomy in the decision, to substitute it with a process at the organisation level. Ordinarily, the organisation:

(i) defines the functions of the members and the nature of their obligations,

(ii) gives the authority, and

(iii) sets limits to the liberty of choice.

This allocation of managerial and budgetary discretion has two consequences. First, as the organisation is allocating responsibilities to members over various fields, as well as, setting up departments, the co-ordination between the various departments has to be studied, because one's decisions affect the others' and vice-versa. According to Simon (1947), in complex organisations, decisions taken in one part of the organisation are goals and constraints for decisions taken in other spheres of the organisation. From the existence of sub-goals in such departments and the need for coordination, one important question arises. For Cyert & March, the impact of planning has to be studied, particularly the determination and monitoring of the budget, as well as the allocation and operation of managerial discretionary power. Indeed, budget is central for giving authority, setting limits to it and *has to match with given functions.*

Second, since the organisation sets limits on liberty in choice, Simon & March stress the importance of studying these sets of rules, practices, and procedures that structure the organisation. According to March, decisions in the short term are mainly to select the appropriate procedure among a set of existing ones, or if that is not possible, the procedure that requires the least modifications (Weil, 2000). This is why it is important to know the specific procedures, in order to be able to explain the organisation and predict its behaviour (we will especially analyse policy directions and executive instructions in this framework).

Before the development of the concept of procedural rationality, Gordon (1948) had identified the importance of 'short cuts'. As Cyert & March (1963) specify: "these short cuts, or guides to policy, take the form of the dicta 'Thou shalt not allow thy share of the market to go below 10 per cent', 'Honour thy dealers above all', 'Thou shalt not unionise' ". Cyert and March further specify that since "the imperative 'optimise' is less operational than the shortcuts, it is reasonable to expect that the so-called short cuts will in fact dominate the decisions, at least in the short run".

2.1.2. The Rationality of Decisions: Various Types of Rationality

Once the framework is known – that is, the allocation of discretionary power and the constraints on choice given by the internal organisation – the way decisions are made can be analysed. Methods of evaluating the efficiency of choices can be practised through the analysis of the rationality of decisions. At this point, a presentation of the main kinds of rationality the literature considers is necessary.

Simon (1947) states that, since a 'good' administration is a comportment that is realistically adapted to its goals, any theory of decisions has to cope with rational aspects in choice. According to him, in a decision process, one chooses the alternative designed to provide the adequate means to reach the desired goals. Goals themselves are often simply instrumental in the attainment of other, more fundamental, goals. Hence Simon sees a hierarchy of goals, and for him, rationality intervenes in the building of a hierarchy of links, or "means-ends". The implications of this approach, for positive and normative analysis, are two-fold.

First, rationality is local and has to be evaluated towards the local sub-goals. Simon gives an example of a commercial manager and his secretary. The commercial manager's goal is to improve the sales. For achieving his goal, among many others, he has to correspond with clients and answer their letters, which he will daily prioritise compared to other thihgs to do and actual obligations he has, like visiting stores or potential future clients. His secretary has another goal, which is to finish replying, typing and sending letters to clients and also suppliers or any other manager who has written earlier. Her sub-goal is to prevent accumulation of unreplied letters which is a rational sub-goal if one wants the structure to go on showing reactivity. At times, the manager's goal and the secretary's sub-goal may then coincide, but they may also diverge when the manager is busy developing the business and asks his secretary to write and sign new letters. In that case, the secretary wanting to follow her own procedure does not go along with ultimately fulfilling the higher goals. Any way both goals have a rationality. Hierarchical decision is necessary to priorities them, and will be based on local parameters. Similarly, it will be seen that, in SEBs, fulfilling procedures may become more rational for an agent than targeting goals that could be expected from a public structure, like looking for cost-efficiency in implementing decisions, or rapidly solving users problems.

Second, from a global viewpoint, rationality comes from the ability of the hierarchy of means-ends to reach fixed goals. Significantly, the division of the tasks and the hierarchy of goals raises the question of available information. Simon makes a distinction between the objective rationality (the rationality in facts) and subjective rationality (the rationality according to the information). For instance, to take an ineffective medicine is not objectively rational, but if the available information (which does not correspond to the facts) is that it is efficient, then it is subjectively rational to take it. The definition helps in understanding how an incorrectly designed hierarchy of means-ends can work out to be rational at every stage, while leading to unexpected results; this is how an organisation can be considered as locally but not globally rational. Indeed, distortions can occur at some levels, because of information problems, these distortions being perfectly consistent with subjective rationality. According to Simon, the access to objective rationality for individuals is impossible due to limited knowledge of the environment. This is the concept of the bounded rationality, which he places at the heart of the role and issues of an organisation. *Indeed, the role of an organisation is to allow stability in expectations under precise conditions, while giving incentives in action and fixing intermediary objectives.* The issue is therefore to achieve success in these roles. Along with the work of Gordon, a key contribution from Simon (1952) relates to his stress on the search for "satisfycing solutions" during the decision-making behaviour in organisations. In other words, on the parameters it considers, the organisation targets a level being given by the experience, and does not optimise.

Let us now examine and disentangle two interrelated but different kinds of rationality. From the works of Latsis (1972), Simon (1976), in his article 'From substantive to procedural rationality', offers a definition of procedural rationality. In keeping with his earlier work, Simon uses this term "procedural", to replace and specify the one of bounded rationality. Latsis looks at two approaches of the enterprise, namely "situational determinism" which is the classical economic vision, and "economic behaviourism", which includes a theory of the psychology of the agents. Simon uses "substantive rationality" to refer to the concept of rationality that grew up within economics, and "procedural rationality to refer to the concept that developed within psychology". He then offers definitions in more explicit terms: "Behaviour is substantively rational when it is appropriate to the achievement of given goals within the limits imposed by given conditions and constraints. Notice that, by this definition, the rationality of behaviour depends upon the actor in only a single respect – his goals. Given the goals, the rational behaviour is determined entirely by the characteristics of the environment in which the behaviour takes place". Conversely, "behaviour is procedurally rational when it is the outcome of appropriate deliberation. Its procedural rationality depends on the process that generated it".

This is consistent with the approach of March (1978), who analyses the details of the decision process, and for whom the procedural rationality explains the impact of these details on choice behaviour (as exposed in Weil, 2000). An example given by Simon (1976) makes the meaning of the concept very precise. In the case of the Cournot duopoly[1], "the choice that would be substantively rational for each actor depends on the choices made by the other actor, since it will affect the market; none can choose without making assumptions about how other will choose". *Hence no single substantive solution exists independently from the subjective specification of forecasting procedures. In that context, agents deliberately, and in a 'rational' manner, adopt a 'myopic' but workable strategy.* The issue is not at all a problem of missing information. Keeping this point in view, Simon invokes Cournot as having proposed "a particular solution for the problem, which amount[s] to an assumption about the *procedure*[2] each actor would follow [...]. All [challenges of the solution proposed] rest on postulates about the decision process". Here again, the situation is not a question only of bounded rationality. There is no 'missing information' on what would be 'existing facts', simply because these facts – or how each one anticipates them – are not fixed and do not exist apart from practical experience. The result, with both parties being rational, will entirely depend on the procedures – or, to use March's term, the details of procedure – of the expectations they have and how they assess one another.

As the concept will be a focal point in analysis, let us clarify the position that will be adopted regarding the understanding of the procedural rationality. Simon pre-supposes objectives as exogeneously given for the whole organisation, and hence can derive a normative analysis on the adaptation of the sub-goals, or hierarchy of means-end, to the general objective. In this context, procedural rationality can refer to the rationality of the procedure towards the aim. March

1. In which two companies only produce the same product for a single market, and have to yearly optimise their production capacity. For each company, the optimum depends on the decision the other company will take. However, there is no information on this competitor's decision (but the previous decisions he took), and each company has to evolve very assumptions on its competitor's behaviour.

2. Italics by Simon.

however aims at showing how the internal organisation has an effect on the specification itself of the objectives. They are not specified in themselves, but are an *a posteriori* product of the organisation. *A posteriori* in the sense that they emerge after the decisions, but also since their very identification can happen to be not so clear for the managers themselves, and appear in light of the results of decisions. March maintains the distinction between bounded and procedural rationality, contrarily to Simon. The coming sections implement on SEB's analysis a combined approach. That is, the theoretical construction made by March will be retained, and objectives will be *a posteriori* derived from the study of decisions, since they will be considered to be influenced by them. Hence the radical impossibility of a normative analysis will remain. But, however, even if the rationality of the procedures cannot be causally rooted in and devised in consideration of the objectives, a further step shall remain available. Procedures can still be examined through the lens of their consistency with the organisational structure and constraints. The analysis and the demonstration of the presence of procedural rationality will then be decomposed in two steps:

(i) to show that agents mainly follow procedures, that shape and design the characteristics of choices, and

(ii) to show how these procedures can be causally derived from the structural organisation.

According to Cyert & March, some general findings in decision-making emerge, which can be summed up by the general statements (the 'short cuts'): 'avoid uncertainty', 'maintain the rules', 'use simple rules'. This issue will turn to be of absolute importance in SEBs: when political orders can happen anytime, following bureaucratic rules makes safer than trying to optimise on the ground of an unpredictable future.

2.1.3. *Objectives of an Organisation as* a Posteriori *Constructed*

Let us now deal with the 'organisation's goal'. Cyert & March (1963) question this concept by assuming that "people (*i.e.* individuals) have goals; collectivities of people do not". Therefore, they propose to 'search something analogous' and propose a method of *a posteriori* deduction of the goal that applies to each level of the hierarchy of goals dealt with by Simon. Cyert and March question the argument that the goals of an organisation are the goals of the entrepreneur or the hierarchy, since the actual goal will be the resulting effect of the local sub-goals (that may be not be objectively consistent with the targeted entrepreneurial goal). This classical interpretation of the entrepreneurial goal is considered to be a myth by Cyert and March. The key point for March (1962) is that the attribution of a superior objective to the organisation is an *a posteriori* interpretation of its behaviour. A description of the elementary process seems therefore useful to him, even if it leads to the same observable characteristics, since, in this way, one can better question the properties of the model built, and hence evaluate more efficiently the effects of a modification of some processes. Consistently with this framework, Cyert and March (1963) argue that the way objectives are formed depends on:

(i) bargaining process within the agents, which fixes the coalitions,

(ii) the internal organisational process of control, through which objectives are stabilised and elaborated, and

(iii) the process of adjustment to experience.

Thanks to organisational process, the objectives of an organisation are in reality more stable than a simple model of coalition would suggest. This comes from the existence of "mutual control-systems" for enforcing agreements. For instance, "one such mutual control-system in many organisations is the budget. A budget is an explicit elaboration of previous commitments [...]. As there are usually severe costs to the department in exceeding the budget, so also are there severe costs to other members of the coalition if the budget is not paid in full. As a result, budgets in every organisation tend to be self-confirming". Also "a second major mutual control-system is the allocation of functions [...] when we define the limits of discretion, we constrain the individual or sub-group from acting outside those limits; but at the same time, we constrain any other members from the coalition from prohibiting action within those limits [...]. The allocation of discretion in an organisation chart is [also] largely self-confirming". An example of this in the case of SEBs is: SEBs underplay the importance of maintenance, to stress on infrastructure expansion instead. The classical explanation is that they are given such a mandate to expand the system. However, we have already mentioned that in the long run, this under-optimisation leads to (otherwise avoidable) costs, then constrains the resources and thus constrains the ability to expand. Looking carefully at the decision-making process, following section will show that, due to improper coordination between stores and field units, this maintenance is hampered by procedures favouring new works. Thus, SEBs are structurally bad at maintenance. They in turn have an incentive to over-stress their heavy engineering construction role and overstate this objective and the narratives attached to it. This shows in the annual reports (so many MW, km, have been developed), but this role is *a posteriori* constructed out of a failure to also maintain the existing equipment.

Let us now articulate this methodologically and proceed to the decision-making in SEBs, and proceed to:

- study of general patterns of allocation of power (financial, hierarchical),
- study of some decision-making processes as embedded in these patterns,
- identification of the type of rationality at stake in the decision-making,
- building of *a posteriori* objectives of the organisation.

2.2. Organisation as a Frame: Paper Budget, Absence of Allocation of Power, Non-Integrated Reporting System

The study of budget, hierarchy and reporting in SEBs will show that their internal organisation leads to the absence of an allocation of a formal discretionary power within the structure. This in turn gives space to the predominance of some procedures, as the next sub-section will show. For clarity of exposition, the hierarchy in SEBs is described in Figure 2.1.

The Chairman of the SEB reports to the Power Secretary of the State Government, who reports to the Ministry of Power. Under the Chairman, there are several 'Members of the Board'. Each of them is in charge of a Wing. The more important wings are the Technical wings (dealing with new works, stores and workshops, where the material is repaired), the Operation wing, with a geographical organisation of work, the Finance wing, the Accounts wing. In each wing the hierarchy is the same: under the Member of the Board who heads the

Figure 2.1

The Hierarchical Organisation in SEBs

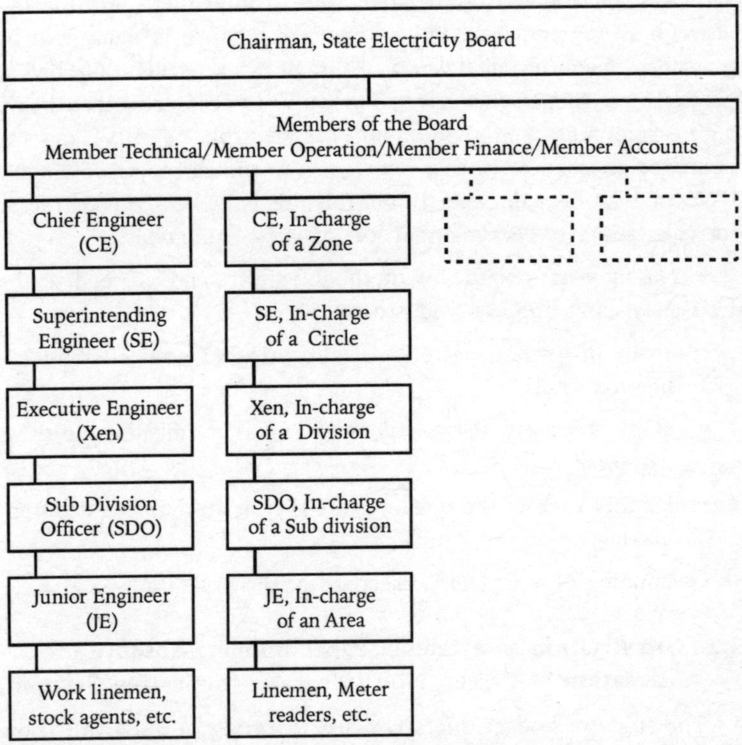

wing, there are Chief Engineers (CE). Under the CE come the grades of Superintending Engineer (SE), Executive Engineer (Xen), Sub Division Officer (SDO), Junior Engineer[3] (JE), and finally the simple agents. Members and CEs sit mainly in the Headquarters, or occasionally in the secondary Headquarters. Headquarters will in the following Chapters refer to the upper part of the hierarchy, and includes the Chief Engineers, as well as, the functional staff directly reporting to them. The part of the hierarchy from the SE to the JE, including the simple agents will be referred to as the Field. Since a

3. This term only refers to a grade, and is in no way indicating the age of the concerned person. One can retire as a JE.

special focus will be on the operation wing, let us present its geographical organisation. The Board is divided into a few Zones, headed by a CE. These Zones are divided in Circles, each of them headed by an SE, they are further divided in Divisions with an Xen. Then one finds Sub-divisions, with an SDO, and last, Areas under the duty of a JE. The JE conducts the technical operations on site. The SDO sets or transmits the priorities between areas and passes the collected revenues to the Xen. The Xen is the operational relay between the Headquarters and the Field. He gathers the day-to-day reporting and his division is the key accounting unit. The SE is the strategic relay between the Headquarters and the Field. He supervises the works of Xens and sets or transmits priorities at an aggregated level. He works in consultation with the CE and other SEs belonging to the same zone. CEs represent the Members of the Board and are responsible for ensuring homogeneity of action across the Circles and Zones. All the objectives to be followed are on paper set up by the Board, including the way they should locally be dis-agregated and implemented by the Field. The system is hence centralised. Following sub-sections will show that, from this description of responsibilities, actual decision-making always involves several hierarchical levels, and that the power to decide is never fully granted but rests in procedures of technical and administrative sanctioning.

2.2.1. A Budgetary System Without Allocation of Money

Let us analyse the budget as a tool for allocating discretionary power. Especially, let us compare the public budget with the three dimensions economic analysis vests to money: a means of exchange, a general equivalent, and an intertemporal reserve. The budgetary system of SEBs is based on public accountancy. The expenditure involves three categories, (i) the 'capital' section, related to new constructions, (ii) the 'establishment' section, related to staff expenses and administration, and (iii) the 'revenue' section, related to maintenance. The budget has to be sanctioned by the State Government. Actual revenues from the sales are not budgeted; only the expenses are, as is customary in a public accountancy system. The making of the annual budget is based on the actual expenses of the previous year (plus an annual increase, officially less than an additional 10 per cent), and is defined Division-wise. More precisely, the SE files a budgetary demand for each Division in his Circle. Then a budget is defined by the Headquarters to each of the concerned Divisions. Lines of credits are specified and strictly attached to precisely identified activities. This is the general scheme valid for every SEB in India, as defined by the Central Ministry of Power, through amended versions of the Electricity Act (1948). After six months of operation, a re-evaluation takes place, based on actual expenditure. The budget has no role of reserve at the Field level, as it is yearly-based; in other words, unspent allocations will not be transferred to the next year.

The important point is that this budget is operated according to public accountancy rules. There is neither the possibility of re-allocating funds from one of the budgets to another (capital, revenue or establishment), nor to re-allocate funds, within one budgetary line or from one activity to another. This means that, the budget in SEBs has only partially the classical properties of money in economics, or of an autonomised account for a unit of an enterprise. Budget is not even a partial equivalent between goods and resources, as inter-line and inter-type transfers are not available. Hence, once the budget is sanctioned, the power of arbitrating between maintenance and new works is not in the hands of the Field. Neither the Division nor the Circle have property rights over this budget. They cannot use it the way they consider to be the best. If not used, it is lost.

There is no direct allocation of actual cash to Field. Once the budget is decided, physical inputs of Divisions and Circles are physically provided directly from the Board, and accounted on paper. This is granted on duly argued requests by the Field, along a process starting only at the moment the needs occur. More precisely, for each expense in the 'establishment' section of the budget (fuel, papers, office material, etc.), as well as, in the 'revenue' section of the budget (expenses on maintenance, repairs, and whatever is related to the technical operation of the network), authorisation is formally requested through or by the Xen. Broadly speaking, the process is as follows. To begin with, the concerned Field Officer has to fulfil the procedure of acquiring technical then administrative sanction of the validity of the purchase. According to the various kinds of expenses, powers are formally attributed to each level of the hierarchy. In practical terms, however, several levels of administrative sanction are required for any expense. Next, the requirement is transmitted to the

Headquarters, which grant the expense. No cash is given. Instead, the inputs might be directly – physically – provided by the Board or a different unit. So-called expenditures are in fact cleared at the level of the Headquarters in accounting books. Even where that is not the case, or where the market supplies the inputs, the Board still does not directly allocate cash to the Field. In this case, a procedure is followed in which the supplier is selected during the phase of clearing the administrative sanction, and the Board notifies the local branch of the State Bank of India to give the money directly to the supplier. The only difference in the two types of supplying is the interlocutor who is dealt with – with some implications regarding the type of the procedure – since a supply from the market requires a tender notice. Practically speaking, Circles ask for monthly credits, and allocation of funds to their bank account remains at the discretion of the Headquarters. In fact, only the wage portion of the establishment budget is provided automatically. The operation of the 'capital' budget (new works) is even simpler. Material is transferred to the stores, then to the work department that is building the new equipment, and subsequently asking the Field for a certificate of acceptance. The store neither 'buys' nor 'purchases' the materials, as the Board only notifies the bank to pay the supplier. In addition, no store – attached to a specific area – is the 'owner' of its stock, as any store from any other area might require some of its materials. As far as collections are concerned, they are directly transferred to the Headquarters.

To sum up, whatever be the action undertaken by the Field, no actual money (that is, no power to arbitrate) comes into the hands of the Field officers.[4] Indeed, the so-called budget allocation does not even allow the Field the use of discretionary power to arbitrate within two similar actions in slightly different places or at slightly different times. A decision is separate from any other one, and each follows a separate path. This means that, beyond its general characteristic of public accountancy, in no way does the budget play the role of a general or even partial equivalent in exchanges.

Conversely, in enterprises, the budget is classically designed to be a managerial tool for the Headquarters, allowing a monitoring of the totality of expenses, while decentralising the budgetary constraint and

4. Only small items can be actually purchased by issuing a cheque.

responsibility to locally arbitrate to the Field. This decentralisation can be possible only if the credits in the budget serve the purpose of being – at least partially – a monetary equivalent between the actions one needs to arbitrate. SEBs function with an administrative-type budget, a so-called 'allocation'. Conversely, in a real enterprise, as opposed to SEBs, decision-making cum accounting units are defined. Once granted a budget, it is actually transferred, at fixed times, to their local accounts. Then these units have the rights and responsibilities over decisions and afferent expenses upto a fixed level of delegated financial power. They later on report on these expenses. This allows fast and decentralised decisions, and puts the burden of responsibility (hence acts as an incentive) on local managers. For instance, a public enterprise like the French power company, EDF, has since long applied this system. This does not exist in SEBs. Even operational day-to-day action cannot be taken efficiently and rapidly at the local level. In the constrained framework of public accountancy, the goal of managerial freedom is not met. This is a book-currency budget, or a paper budget; it is not actually allocated. The paper budget at stake in SEBs simply precludes this kind of decentralisation.

A Digression: Why Public Accountancy is Adapted for Some Sectors and not for Others

Due to the role of the budgetary system as illustrated above, one also needs to look at the notion of public accountancy. The point is not to argue that public accountancy is unsuitable for every sector. As far as regalian functions of public health, education, or defence, etc. are concerned, the outputs can hardly be valued, since being non-commercial. Public accountancy is then useful for purposes of monitoring the level of expenses. In addition, where an activity involving investments (such as roads) is concerned, public accountancy is useful, as long as the commercial side of the activity is nil (road use is free). An extra load on a road leads, in the short term, only to traffic jams, and not to additional costs to the road authority. On the contrary, power overloading affects the state of the technical system itself. So, power system planning, if addressed with an economic approach, implies the computation of avoided costs. In this sense, there is no economic calculation that can be compared with investments and avoided costs in roads. The public accountancy system is useful for roads, where this question is not stringent, but in the case of the power sector, it leads to major cost inefficiencies. Finally, some infrastructure investments rely on a standard technology, whatever the capacity of the traffic, which is not the case in the power sector. In fact, when the traffic increases on roads, the short-cut 'increase capacity' materialises, either in the form of new roads or in new lanes on existing ones. Whatever the level of use, the technology remains the same. As far as an electric network is concerned, however, 'increase the capacity' raises additional questions: apart from new lines or new wires, does the voltage level have to be changed, does the network have to be reconfigured, do new transformers have to be added, do some lines or areas need to be bifurcated? What about the trade-offs between the location of plants and the development of the network? All these techno-economic questions are the focus in the electric system, as stressed by Joskow & Schmalensee (1983). It has been seen that, even in the simple case of rural electrification, technical choices always have to be made; taking into account all these elements requires a decentralisation of decision-making. The absence of the latter, *de facto* denies the very techno-economic nature of an electric system.[5] The latter cannot be a mono-technique.

2.2.2. *A Hierarchy Without Allocation of Power*

Let us focus on the hierarchy in Operation, and Technical (Works and Stores) wings. In Haryana SEB (HSEB), for instance, this is defined by the HSEB Notification No. 130, dated 18th December 1991, on revised financial powers. Let us look at some examples of the SE and the SDO, (an SE may have a 200,000 customers in his Circle, and an SDO 20,000 in his Sub-division). As a first step in each decision, a 'preparation of estimates for work' is done and 'technically sanctioned'. Second, it is 'administratively approved'. The allocation of power for technical sanction and administrative approval is detailed in Box 2.1.

Box 2.1 shows that the amount of delegation of power is very low regarding administrative sanction of new works. Everything is virtually decided at the level of the Board itself. On technical sanction,

5. Actually, if one fully examines the road example, public accountancy efficiency can be questioned as soon as the technology is to be radically questioned: new large highways or urban elevated highways. However, in the electricity sector, the limits of public accountancy occur immediately, as soon as one deals with something else than mere planning.

Box 2.1

The Allocation of Power for Technical Sanction and Administrative Approval in Haryana

- Administrative approval of Works (either under capital or revenue head of accounts): On capital expenses, the SE and the SDO have respective power of Rs. one lakh[6] and Rs. 25,000 only, subject to the condition that "the work is directly remunerative" and "subject to technical justification". In any case, these conditions have to be cleared from the hierarchy, by the financial member in the case of the SE. As no budget is actually allocated, the requirement for availability has to be given by the Headquarters. On repairs, SE has a Rs. 50,000 power, and SDO Rs. 10,000. This has to take place on projects "already sanctioned by the Board". The power of buying new cars is with the CE only.
- Technical sanction, *i.e.* preparation of estimates for works (different attribution whether on capital or revenue). The SE has a power of Rs. 5 lakh in capital expenditure, and the SDO only has Rs. 50,000.[7]
- Power of purchase: Purchase of material for approved projects or civil works is available up to a limit of Rs. 1 lakh for the SE, subject that (i) there is a tender organised, and (ii) there is "approval of the next higher authority". The SDO is limited to Rs. 2000, under the same conditions. In the case of emergency, the SE has a Rs. 20,000 power and the SDO Rs. 2500. In both cases, "a certificate should be given that the material has been purchased on competitive rates, after ascertaining the rates orally", and "emergency has to be defined in details". On the other hand, in the same category is classified the power of the SDO to "draw the materials from the stores (...), for which due provision has been made in a sanctioned estimate". For this matter, he is given "full powers". This actually happens, however, only through the paper budget system, once the administrative sanction is procedurally given. This corresponds only to the right to ask for what should be actually granted through a classical budgetary system. Indeed, it is specified that these so-called full powers are "subject to the limit of provision for respective items in the estimate or budget allotment".
- Acceptance of tenders: Roughly the same limits, the same provisions and the same need of higher authorities apply.
- Exceeding estimates: SEs are allowed up to 5 per cent or Rs. 2500 whichever is more, and the Xen 5 per cent or Rs. 500 whichever is more.

Beyond this, SE and SDO are allowed to sanction dismantling, in case of thefts, up to an amount of Rs. 2500 and Rs. 1000 per case respectively. On Field, only Xens and SEs are authorised to write off irrecoverable arrears (Rs. 500 for the SE).

Source: Delegation of financial powers, SEBS.

6. It can amount up to Rs. 6 lakh, when the point is to follow a procedure of setting new connections, and in this case only.
7. In the case of new connections.

the matter is not directly linked with actual financial power, as the technical sanction does not constitute the actual decision. Even in this case, however, the delegation is very limited. To sum up, in the framework of the book currency budget, the power of decisions left to the Field is very low. Further, the power of decisions implying direct purchase from the market – and not through the internal store system – is even more limited, next to non-existent. It can be concluded from this that:

(i) the actual discretion of external purchase is very limited,[8]

(ii) internal allocation of inputs is subject to stringent conditions, and

(iii) in both cases, the number of clearances at various levels is high; prior to a decision, at least three levels are involved to prepare a technical plus administrative sanction. Following that, it still has to be cleared by Headquarters under the budgetary process or the authorisation of expenditure through the bank.

This leads to the fact that, at every level of the hierarchy, officers spend a substantial part of their time clearing formal requests. This need for multiple sanction implies that every officer has tall piles of documents to sign, in which a clerk shows the officer where to sign. Both direct observation in offices and the fact that basic errors remain, show that these reports are not read when signed. The day is finally rhythmed by tides of the helpers moving piles of files. In addition, the time taken to have a decision cleared can be very long. On close examination, it is clear that the separation of the two levels of sanction and the framing of the decision process within a book currency system leads to the *de facto* absence of formal discretionary power left with the Field. This latter point, as well as the delay in action, is illustrated in Box 2.2.

To sum up, virtually every decision in the SEB has to be taken collegially, between at least three levels of the hierarchy, often with the involvement of the Headquarters. The manner in which the procedures lead – with more or less stringency – to the orientation of the decision-making is detailed in a further sub-section.

8. Other minor examples could be given, like the fact that toner ink can only be purchased by a CE, or the purchase of uniforms by the SE, if authorised by his CE.

Box 2.2

A Practical Example of the Absence of Discretionary Power: The Upgrading of Computers

The following example is taken from the HSEB, and more precisely from UHBVN[9]. In October 1999, it was felt in a Circle that upgrading two computers would allow the Circle to operate the newly computerised information system in a more synthesised way . The officer responsible for the Circle computer cell applied for the upgrading. The Managing Director[10] (MD) agreed – a new name was given to the former function of a member of the Board for the distribution activity – and transmitted the request to the concerned CE. Unfortunately, the CE retired, and the MD was transferred. So the procedure was started again (a fact that demonstrates how far requests are attached to occupants of a post and not to the function of the post itself). The new MD gave his approval on principle. Under the SE, the estimate was prepared, then sanctioned by the SE in the Operation wing. A tender was requested and conducted. After issuing a report on the results of the tender, the original applicant in the computer cell submitted it for administrative clearance to the SE. Since the amount was under Rs. 10,000 it was felt that the Xen from the Works wing should issue it. By now, the whole process, starting from the second agreement at the MD's level, had taken two months. Two additional months have been necessary to finally obtain the money from the Board and upgrade the two computers at a cost of Rs. 8700. The interviewed officer has detailed that, in other Circles where the agents were less dedicated to this result, the process was still under administrative clearance, six months later.

At the borders of the SEB, it is interesting to consider the nature of the separation between the SEB and the Government. As recalled in Chapter 1, interviews show that politicians give executive instructions. Frequently, there is motivation to start projects before the elections. It shall be detailed here that this happens through direct notification of the concerned Members of the Board or CEs by the Minister or the Chief Minister. Beyond these unwritten facts, it also appears that the separation between the SEB and the State Government is *de jure* unclear. Decisions regarding main new works are taken by the Standing Committee, which comprises the Chairman, the Members of the Board and the Power Secretary of the State

9. Uttar Haryana Bijli Vitran Nigam (UHBVN) has been created further to reform the HSEB, to deal with the distribution in the northern part of Haryana. Although reform had supposedly taken place, this example is taken to illustrate the classical SEB system, where the reform hasn't changed much. The name only has changed, not the practices.

10. Further to reform, officially new posts have been created, not previously existing in the classical SEB system, to make them closer to the corporate entities. The MD, in his Zone vests some of the prerogatives of the Technical and Operation Members, and directs to the CEs.

Government. The respective roles of the Chairman and the Power Secretary are also unclear. The Power Secretary is required to ensure the link between the SEB and the Government regarding financial aspects and the policies to be followed. By way of example, the case of Haryana, discussed in Box 2.3 is illustrative.

Box 2.3

The Posting of the Power Secretary and of the Chairman in Haryana, from July 1998 to March 1999

In Haryana from July 1998 to March 1999, two Chairmen and three Power Secretaries have successively occupied the same post. Starting from a situation with one integrated SEB, headed by a Chairman and under the supervision of a distinct Power Secretary, the SEB has been de-integrated. Since then, the Power Secretary has cumulated the function of Chairman of the generation activity, while the Chairman of the SEB remains the head of transmission and distribution. Then both have been transferred and charge of the new Power Secretary has been assumed by the Finance Secretary, while simultaneously being Chairman of generation, whereas a new Chairman was posted on transmission-cum-distribution. When transmission and distribution have later been separated, posts of Managing Directors have been created. Soon after, Managing Directors have been transferred, and the former Chairman became the MD of transmission. At that time the Finance + Power Secretariat has been bifurcated again and the new Power Secretary headed the Generation + Transmission as a Chairman, the two MDs of the two newly created distribution zones formally reporting to her.

Hence, Box 2.3 shows that the formal separation between SEB and State Government is not compulsory on judicial status. The analysis of the procedure of subsidies fixation will show that it corresponds in many respects to a *de facto* integration of each SEB as a department of its respective State Ministry of Power.

2.2.3. *A Reporting Without Integrated Information*

Let us demonstrate that the reporting system does not allow hierarchical monitoring or external control on the SEB's efficiency.

A Dual Technical Reporting

Detailing the technical configuration of the network can be useful (Figure 2.2). In transforming stations, from the 132 kV[11] lines of the

11. 1 kV = 1 kilo Volt, i.e. 1000 Volts.

transmission network, 132 to 33 kV transformers feed the distribution network (33 kV and below, down to low voltage). In sub-stations, from 33 to 11 kV transformers, depart the 'feeders', that are 11 kV lines. On these lines, all over cities and rural areas, distribution transformers ensure the conversion to low voltage.

Figure 2.2

The Technical Configuration of the Network

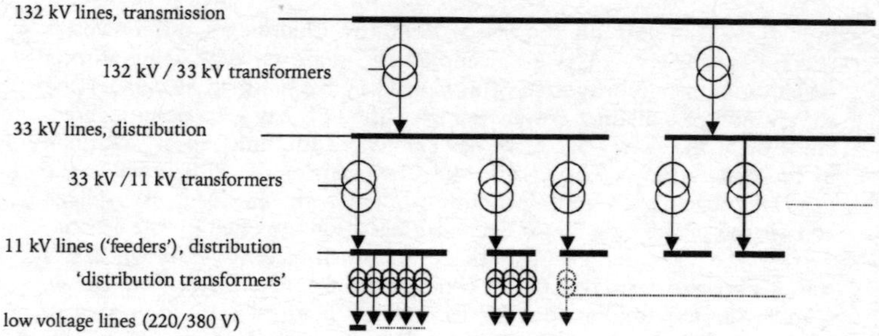

One major element of the supply activity is the measurement of the supplied energy. This requires meters at the substations (132 kV/ 33 kV), at the departure of each individual feeder (33 kV/11 kV), on each LV line, as well as, with each client. The metering of the clients allows the billing, while the metering at other levels enables detection of non-technical losses and knowledge of the total level of losses at every level of the system. A proper metering therefore would allow a yardstick competition between the different hierarchical units, and a monitoring from the Headquarters. However, it happens that there is no metering at the Division level, and hence their actual consumption is unknown. For instance, by April 1999, roughly 50 per cent of the feeders were unmetered in HSEB, according to its Chairman. Also, an interviewed consultant argued that by December 1998, the Andhra Pradesh SEB had all the information on revenue and collecting but was unable to provide information (on a Division-wise basis) on the revenue efficiency, the losses, or the costs, because of the absence of meters at the level of the sub-station and the feeders. After four years of reforms, this was still the case in some places in Orissa by April 2000, recently confirmed in official reports in February 2004 (GoI,

2004). Benchmarking is then often not available in SEBs. Each distribution unit can therefore claim innocence about losses or relative innocence due to its backwardness.

Another kind of problem arises from the absence of proper metering in each low voltage line, and likewise at the users level. This makes the proportion of technical and non-technical losses unknown. If we look at official figures by February 2004, that is after a decade of so-called reforms, figures are striking: 100 per cent metering at 11kV level took place in 11 States only ; 6 States have a performance between 26 to 99 per cent, while 11 others (including the 'privatised' Orissa) are below 24 per cent. Worse, at the consumer level, only Himachal Pradesh and Kerala report a 100 per cent metering, majority of other States being balancedly distributed from 50 to 99 per cent, the State of Delhi along with Jammu & Kashmir and North Eastern States have the pathetic record of a less than 50 per cent metering (GoI, 2004). Box 2.3(a) details both the grey areas and misreporting they allow.

Box 2.3(a)

Grey Areas in the Reporting System

The reporting system does not even attempt to estimate energy volumes in respect to collection. Two types of reports are made in this case, one dealing with collected bills - in rupees - and the other with energy losses - in kWh units. Reports are issued by the Field to the Headquarters, without any comparison of the two kinds of information at the Field level. On one hand, energy reports implicitly suppose (this is implicit in the reports, but explicit in the interviews) that the agricultural consumption has been underestimated, and some 'corrections' occur. In some cases, the SDOs - who issue these reports - put on paper their corrective assumptions, but in other cases, they do not. These practices have been acknowledged by the APSEB, after an audit in October 1996. The audit reckoned that, in APSEB in 1998, the "loss of energy due to theft was getting included in the unmetered agricultural consumption; [after the audit it was] identified to be about [...] Rs. 600 crore". It explained that technical calculations were made first instead of trying to use commercial information. It elaborates that "as has been the practice in all the SEBs in the country, the APSEB was showing the difference between the generation and the sales as the agricultural consumption plus technical losses. Technical losses have been computed to be in the region of 18 per cent to 19 per cent, and hence the remaining energy was attributed to agriculture". After being issued at the SDO level, the figures are compiled at the Circle office, where the assumptions on duration of supply generally disappear from the reports, and are then sent to Headquarters. On the other hand, regarding reports on money collection, when collections are

Contd...

Contd...

made they are directly transferred to the bank. The Division office directly issues reports to Headquarters. In the case of billing, the collection efficiency is sometimes not completely accurate, as it is measured by comparing for one month the energy billed during this month and the money collected during the same time, without distinction between current and older bills. The collecting efficiency can therefore be higher than 100 per cent for several months. This indicator is therefore not helpful for management. It remains the same even if completed by the amount of outstanding dues, since the manner in which penalties for delay are integrated is far from clear, and as there is no precise monitoring of the clients who are late in paying. Another factor relates to the fact that billing is partly computerised, sometimes by outside 'computer companies'. In this case, the dues to be recovered are booked with a delay, and that is only when the computer company gives back the results. As far as liabilities on pending dues are concerned, the restructuring of HSEB accounts showed that, before its 'corporatisation' in 1999, up to a thousand crore of liabilities, HSEB had no idea of the identity of the defaulting payer for roughly 120 crore. At the Board level, the billing indicator combines several zones with different practices and different delays in their procedures and is simply of no use for direct management. It only makes some sense after several months, when all Divisions have provided definitive results. Hence, there are two types of reports, the engineers being more concerned with the technical reports. Since the hypothesis on consumption duration is made under discretionary assumptions at the SDO level, the comparison at the Headquarters office is not feasible. In any case, even at the level of Headquarters, reporting does not constitute an integrated system, since the technical reports are sent to the technical wing, and the reports on amounts collected to the financial wing. No comparison takes place between the two kinds of reports, since technical reports are originally designed to be integrated in planning studies, and financial reports are mainly intended to provide an administrative justification of the origin of the transferred collections.

Broadly speaking, the reporting system can be characterised as plethoric but inaccurate and incapable of efficient monitoring. In Haryana, for instance, according to a consultant, interviewed in 2000, roughly 90 per cent of the reporting was manual, which is quite significant for an organisation dealing with a 3.5 million users. This figure used to be 100 per cent in Orissa. On examination, one can also see that many errors occur.[12] In Haryana, a consulting company found 177 different types of reports – some of them not standardised

12. For instance, I noticed several very obvious errors in already officially sanctioned reports, and it is widely acknowledged that different reports might give different figures. As these errors are caused by copying figures from other reports, it can be difficult to discover which report is the accurate one. Numerous manual copies of the reports are either made – which takes time and multiplies the risk of errors, or if there is only one copy, it is regularly sent for sanction and returned with delays.

– where finally, 70 turned out to be enough and the number of recipients has been substantially reduced.

In such a system, where information is not integrated, the reports cannot be used as centralised managerial tools. For instance, after the reduction in the number of reports in Haryana over the first semester of 1999, a synthesised report at the Circle level, showing in one page the main indicators, was only made available by February 2000. This happened in one Circle, after an independent initiative by an agent. This has been neither generalised, nor even actually used in this Circle. Conversely, in an enterprise like the French Public Power Company EDF, at each operational level, expenditures are compiled simultaneously with and compared to quantity of electricity supplied and the amount collected. This allows for quick decisions and efficient control by the Headquarters.

Accounting System

In 1985, SEBs were provided with a 'commercial accounting system', through the Electricity Supply Annual Accounts Rules (1985). Basically, it introduced the double entry accountability. Specifically, "the cash basis of accounting, *i.e.* the practice of booking [...] when money is received or paid and not when accrued shall not be adopted", "reserves [shall] not absorb charge against revenue", "payables to one party shall [...] not be set off against receivables from the same party", "losses shall not be capitalised". The aim of the reform was to trace out the respective impacts of various decisions and activities.

The actual system, however, departs from this framework in many ways. Interviews have confirmed that State Governments do not actually give the subsidies; instead, a part of them is cleared through a partial erasure of debts. The remaining part is left unpaid. In this case, what should be done in book accounts regarding the paid part is to write subsidies in the revenue accounts, and then make a second entry regarding the erasure of debts. This is not done; on the contrary, the two steps are combined and only the final results are shown. Moreover, the unpaid part should be shown as receivable dues; this, too, is not done. Ultimately, the so-called 'subsidies', in their entirety, are booked in the revenue account, although this does not correspond to reality. It is therefore virtually impossible to know, from a SEB book of accounts, whether subsidies have been actually given or not. This is the reason why the CEA (1998), in its review of the financial performance of SEBs, considers two extreme cases, which are the subsidies fully paid *versus* the subsidies not paid at all. Reality may be anywhere in-between and Box 2.3(b) exemplifies some distortions.

Box 2.3(b)

Accounting Discrepancies in SEBs

Several problems also arise concerning the assets. Normally, the fixed assets register should specify the acquisition value. Consultants confirm that "no SEB has known this value for the last 10 years, the more that could be found is 4 or 5 years". Moreover, the land acquisition value shown in some SEBs is not consistent with evaluations for comparable lands. It is interesting to trace the process of asset building and booking. The Headquarters issues orders to take material from the stores, after which the works wing builds the assets. The construction unit then has to issue a completion certificate to increase the fixed assets; and the operational unit has to issue a certificate to accept it. If one of these two is missing, the assets may be booked in 'inter-units transfers'. This category should be very low but happens to be quite high in the SEBs of Haryana, Tamil Nadu and Uttar Pradesh, according to CEA (1998). In other situations, it can also transpire that fixed assets are booked as such prior to the acceptation certificate, or even prior to the completion one. In this case, fixed assets might exist on paper but not on the Field. In addition, capitalisation of interests is seldom undertaken.

The explanation usually given by consultants is that the number of chartered accountants is very low (roughly 10 out of 50,000 employees in HSEB), the accounting work being left to clerks who have received a very basic training.

A more argued approach, based on IMI (1999), states that from the Division level upwards, the accounting is a unified commercial accounting, but that, from the Sub-division level downwards, the system is filled with "statements and statistical information only, instead of accounting entries". An examination of accounting in SEBs thus involves issues of completeness as well as that of consistency. A former Power Secretary of the Government of India once declared that the book accounts of SEBs are "a terrible mess, with no link with reality".

More generally, the whole reporting system is not designed to provide information to be used in decisions, but to offer an administrative reporting, allowing administrative inquiries. It can be qualified as non-integrated, since technical (repairs), physical (energy) and commercial (billing, revenue) figures are neither put in front of each other in any report, nor in front of their respective accounting.

2.2.4. *Summing Up: Stylising the Organisational Characteristics*

From the above analysis it is evident that the whole structure of a SEB is characterised by the absence of formal discretionary power. *The budget does not allow any actual power on decisions, which are to take place through procedures of administrative sanction.* Regarding the positioning of officers in the hierarchy, there is no discretionary attribution of tasks, since every decision must go through formal agreement at several levels. Managerial pressure is not available, as there is no strict allocation of power over human resources. Reports deal with technical matters, and their number is plethoric, but their information is useless in decision-making, since there is neither integration of information nor control. Finally, there is no reliable accounting system; accounting rules are transgressed in many ways. The reporting system basically comprises *ex-post* records of results and decisions for administrative reporting, *i.e.* for providing a basis to check the implementation of centrally defined procedures. In this case, using the term 'information system' is not valid, as the term refers to a utilisation of the information generated as an input in decisions. It should also be noted here that the system does not serve its purpose, since inaccurate – and even fake – reporting occurs. All these are contrary to what exists in an enterprise.

Finally, SEBs are characterised by a paper-budget, an absence of formal discretionary power, a non-integrated reporting system. A deeper analysis of the procedures that operate within the SEBs will allow us to better understand which kind of rationality is in place in SEBs, what is its inertia, and how this hampers reforms.

Rao (2004), from other sources, confirms that "Accounts are not finalised for many years by (SEBs). Asset registers are either not kept or are out of date and so it is impossible to know what to take as the asset base for purposes of calculating return. In Uttar Pradesh, the restructured distribution companies – KESCO (Kanpur Electricity Supply Company) and the Uttar Pradesh Power Corporation Ltd) and the Uttar Pradesh Power Corporation Limited – do not maintain the asset registers. During the Kanpur privatisation process, the consultants realized that there was no record of the number of transformers, feeders, etc. with the board. A similar situation arose during the privatisation of the Delhi Vidyut Board. In Himachal Pradesh, the HPSEB has not finalised its accounts and does not maintain an asset register. The regulator (the HPERC) in its tariff order for 2001-02 has directed the board to prepare and maintain a fixed asset register. Unfortunately, there has been no improvement".

2.3. Procedural Rationality in SEBs: "We are Doing Paper Work"

Having studied the organisation of SEBs, let us look at their functioning. From the top to the bottom, ensuring the physical continuity of supply is the most time consuming activity. This ranges from ensuring that generation plants will deliver energy down to reacting in case of power cuts in distribution. Within organisational characteristics of SEBs, the stress on the continuity of supply justifies (i) executive instruction from the governmental level, (ii) a relative disinterest for other activities on the part of Headquarters, (iii) quasi-exclusive priority on this for the Field, at least on paper, and (iv) even misreporting in some circumstances. Four decision-making processes that turn out to be important in a power organisation are studied in a more detailed manner. Two of them concern the Field: (i) repair of distribution transformers, and (ii) attention to revenue aspects. Two others concern the Headquarters: (iii) subsidies fixation, and (iv) planning. For each of them, the procedures on which they depend will be described in order to show that the decision-making is ultimately shaped by the procedure, which corresponds to the descriptive definition of procedural rationality given by March. A second step aims at showing that the following of these procedures is rational given the SEBs' main organisational characteristics.

2.3.1. The Field: 'the Technocrats'

Field officers spend a considerable amount of time in making the system technically work, and trying to coordinate with each other. Box 2.4 illustrates that the main variables of concerns of Junior Engineers, Sub Division Officers and Executive Engineers are related to maintaining the continuity of supply, checking the availability of materials, recording the complaints on metering and billing, as well as fulfilling political decisions on connection. They are only marginally

Box 2.4

The Usual Day of an SDO or of a JE

The day of an SDO is filled with the common solving of technical problems with JEs. Of course, in the process, the Xen is consulted by phone, and his agreement on solutions has to be acquired. But, beyond, that he has to address user complaints, which may be linked with excess billing, wrong reading of meters, demand for replacement of defective meters etc. By early morning, the SDO has about 15 people in his office, whose declarations he has to read, have discussions with them, add some comments and instructions for the attention of the concerned JE. Subsequently, the JE is meant to check the cases and report to the SDO, who will issue some notifications for metering replacements – if available in the store – or start a procedure of bill regularisation, which has to be administratively sanctioned according to HSEB (1991). The flow of complainants does not stop before 11 a.m. An SDO declared that "everyday, up to 11 a.m. no rest is possible, this is the procedure". Indeed, the complaint centres are designed only to record technical problems, not to deal with billing concerns. The agents from the collection office, the 'revenue section', could deal with billing, but it is felt by the SDO that they would be reluctant on that and display some passive resistance, and that the users would be satisfied only by meeting the SDO. An SDO argued that "[the agents from the collection office] say they don't convince the people". A collecting agent confirmed that "the people are happy only if they meet the SDO, and, due to political interference, we have to receive them". In fact, the Board has transmitted Government instructions to receive people. In between, JEs come to the SDO to deal with technical problems, and have to wait until some users' requests are cleared, and until the Xen can be reached on the telephone. Meanwhile, the SDO signs orders for petty purchase, prepares a report on assessed and realised revenues, (which is a large paper, hand written and full of figures struck off and amended by hand), then the report on assessed and realised revenues, but category-wise this time, which is a different report.

able to provide new connections, not so much when and where it is required and accepted, but when and where the material turns to be in the stores. The stress on technical issues can be asserted by pointing out that the interviewed SDOs define their duty as being to "maintain the continuity of supply, replace meters, attend to breakdowns, maintain the existing transformers". There is no mention of collection of payments, which is separate and recorded by untrained clerks.

To sum up, Field Officers focus on technical matters, considering the problems of the consumers as either secondary (revenue side) or a constraint precluding them from doing their job (the complaints). However, when actual decisions to solve technical matters are not available, due to shortage in stores for instance, fulfilling the procedure is ultimately the most important task; decision-making and problem-solving come later. And actually, even when 'decisions' are made, these do not necessarily lead to actions, or if they do, they do so with delays that are mainly due to parameters being out of control. One could go as far as to say that the activity of the Field can be analysed as that of pushing paper work ahead, and going back to actual implementation only once clearances have progressed in other wings of the Board. In this context, it is more important to follow the demand procedures or the inquiry procedures. Hence the importance of analysing some procedures at stake in the decision-making process. The following sub-sections demonstrate that what is important in SEBs is to move the 'paper work' ahead. That is, to follow procedures, to file requests for technical sanction, administrative clearance, and formal request to stores. Fulfilling the paper work shall be defined and understood as filing these demands and filing justifications on the realised outcomes. The paper work uses and feeds the paper budget and the non-integrated reporting system.

Procedural Rationality in Operation: The Example of Distribution Transformers

Here is what happens when a transformer is damaged in a Sub-division.[13] The SDO, with the clearance of the Xen, issues a store requisition. The store replaces it with a new (or repaired) transformer; following this, the damaged one is repaired in the workshop, before being returned to the store if it can be repaired, and then being ultimately being returned to whatever Sub-division that faces a damage. Every manager in the Field knows this theoretical physical circuit. Needless to say, from this theoretical scheme, several delays can occur.

Due to the absence of reliable information, the Headquarters have no way of controlling the operation of transformers through techno-economic calculation. To monitor this activity, therefore, there is an administrative circuit, based on inquiries starting with the placement of responsibility for the burning, and checked by the hierarchy on a sampling basis. The SDO is required to inspect 100 per cent of all the damaged transformers; the Xen to inspect 25 per cent of the damaged

13. Beyond the analytical interest, this issue is a very practical one in some States facing a high level of transformer damage.

transformers ranging 200 kVA and above; and the SE 50 per cent of the damaged 500 kVA and above.

The Headquarters monitor the situation through an annual constraint on the rate of damage, not to be exceeded.[14] If exceeded, an administrative inquiry is implemented. The concerned officers have to explain why it has happened, and to prove that this is independent of their actions. This type of monitoring leads to an attitude of 'mutual protection' among Field officers. It is common practice to declare, in damaged transformer reports, that all the necessary protections were installed and that the operating conditions were normal. Hence the damage is attributed to an 'internal fault', that is a defective or a used component of the transformer itself, not detectable by external checking. The reports, stating that the necessary controls have been made by the SDO, the Xen, and the SE, are further written up and sent, without any correlation with actual checking – they are either not done, or are delegated to very junior officers. The logic is not to foresee events, but to justify *ex-post* that they had occurred despite appropriate measures taken by Field officers, and that proper procedures had been followed. To sum up, the notion of cost never appears while arriving at a decision. The transformers must be made to run as long as possible. When and only when they are burnt, are they to be repaired. Finally, there is neither actual budgetary monitoring – based on costs – nor actual administrative efficient monitoring tools for the Headquarters.

How is this 'Rational' in a SEB Context?

Let us now discuss the consistency of these practices with the general characteristics of the organisation. The annual rate of damaged distribution transformers is abnormally high in some SEBs (more than 30 to 35 per cent in some sub-divisions such as Haryana), due to over-load for the limited number of transformers. This situation is a techno-economic paradox in the Indian context. Actually increasing the number of transformers by purchasing new ones to a tune of 10 per cent[15] would imply only limited expenses while being highly

---

14. The target is of 18 per cent in Haryana, although 30 per cent is a common 'achievement'. By way of comparison, it is not even 1 per cent in France.

15. Or even by simply repairing those numerous transformers laying on the ground, that are a common landscape in SEBs.

profitable through removing all the burnings. This would result in savings in repair, which would soon pay back the initial expenditure. Let us go beyond the usual explanations of political interference or lack of money. On the contrary, it is possible to establish that, at the Field level, the paper budget system itself precludes the generation of the additional savings in transformer repairs. This is a result of a paper work system. If one looks at budgetary procedures, possible Field's actions on transformers does not include building new ones nor repairing in advance. Whatever advantages there may be, the Field does not have the power to take this decision. As far as the Headquarters are concerned, the absence of a feedback on the decision through a proper information system renders the decision of building new transformers only a budgetary headache. In an enterprise (as opposed to SEBs) with delegation of powers, proper accountancy and an information system, the local manager (i) has access to techno-economic calculations, (ii) has the power to do whatever is in turn profitable. This in return ensures that (iii) the Headquarters can check and control his activity, but (iv) the manager himself can use this system in order to prove the quality of his decisions. In other words, in an enterprise-type organisation, decisions can be made in an efficient decentralised manner. This further spares time to Headquarters, and leaves them focusing on strategic concerns, which they have no time for in a SEB.

Again, all this is not available in a SEB. Therefore, in a SEB, only decisions that can occur are those concerning the repairing of transformers because of the procedures in place. Such a decision is directly linked with the procedures at stake in attributing the inputs, and not with the absence of money at the Board level. Similarly, the fact that no preventive maintenance is done, and that only *ex-post* repairs occur, can also be understood as arising from the same logic; the Headquarters are even more lacking an evaluation of the benefits of preventive maintenance. *It is in this kind of situation that the decentralising role of an actual budget is missing*. In the study of this decision-making, it can be seen that the outcome of the decision depends mainly on the procedure that is followed to make it. Within this context, the behaviour of the Field officers is rational, as they have no discretionary or budgetary power to look for technically superior solutions. Within the organisational context of the SEBs, which is a paper based budget, implementing such procedures is rational from the point of view of the Headquarters. In the absence of the decentralising tools that would allow monitoring based on controllable parameters, the solution of checking that some identified procedures have been respected becomes rational. Keeping in mind this analysis of the behaviour of Field officers, as well as, the analysis of the reasons for the Headquarters to maintain these procedures, one can conclude that decision-making on the operation of distribution transformers is based on procedural rationality.

From that standpoint, the behaviour of Field agents is fully explained though it leads to lower efficiency compared to more substantive rationality, available in an enterprise but not in a SEB. In fact, due to the absence of discretionary power, the only way to lower the rate of damage would be to make new equipment from the capital budget. However, as budgets cannot be diverted, the Field has to wait for transformers to burn before they will take action. So, transformers burnings can not be avoided and thus virtually vests a 'fatality aspect' in this system. As far as *ex-post* control is concerned, the absence of integrated information calls for technical norms only, based on rates of damage, along with respect of procedures. Once the damage has occurred, the cost of repair is of no importance, since in no way can it become a monitoring tool.[16] Reforms will then be all the more difficult to implement, that the system has a strong consistency.

Procedural Rationality with Relation to Revenue

Generally, the information on losses is not available. However, even when figures are estimated, no action is taken. For instance, in Andhra Pradesh, although there was no metering at the feeder level in Hyderabad, there was a meter at the sub-station level. It has been roughly known for many years that losses in Old Hyderabad were far higher than in the new areas of the State capital. In spite of such knowledge, no action was taken till April 1999. Bills are not always sent. Anecdotally, a former Power Secretary of the Government of India, living in Delhi, in order to confound the officials of the Delhi

16. If one were to look at dynamic analysis, and at the manner in which the rules for decision-making are made, it is conceivable to imagine some attempts at decentralisation, either at budgetary levels or in relation to discretionary power. However, this kind of transformation is in nobody's power in the hierarchy, except the Chairman or the Power Secretary. But they also have continuity of supply priorities to address, and huge amounts of clearances to give, being at the Centre of the paper work system. The system thus can hardly be changed from within.

Board – claiming a proper note of billing over the capital – had once asked them why in that case he had not been receiving any bills for the last six months. Regarding the level of Transmission and Distribution losses, targets are not fixed in each SEB. In HSEB, there is a target, which is to be within 30 per cent, regardless of the initial level of the Division. In order to do so, JEs are required to check meter readings, and to check some connections. They report having done so, but the number of checks is inflated. Only the number of detected thefts and the amounts charged are accurate. However, even in Haryana, the existence of a target is recent; according to interviewed officers, only once earlier, in the financial year 1980-81, was there a Chairman who happened to be tough on losses. Then "the officers began giving wrong figures". Box 2.5 illustrates the non-application of procedures issued by the Board and the hypocrisy of the paper work.

If one looks at the number of circulars issued by the HSEB over 1997-99, one notes that actual implementation is not carried out, as deadlines are regularly moved ahead. It is also interesting to see the pattern of circulars. They are not based on numerical targets that the Field officer would enforce with the powers they possesses. Instead, procedures have to be followed and the formal discretion left to the agents is nil. This absence of formal discretionary power left in their implementation can again be explained by the lack of a proper information system. The circulars require many personal actions by the JEs and more by the SDOs, who are obviously unable to conduct all the requirements, because of the time they end up wasting during the day due to the general disorganisation of the work. The position of the SDO is particularly uncomfortable in this system, as circulars are inflexible in content and threatening in tone. This is so, not only if he does not comply with some checking, but also in case of users' discontent. It is for these reasons that misreporting becomes a common practice. Officers at the Headquarters know it, thus the numerous circulars can be understood as actions taken to show that they have done their job of monitoring the Field, even if the absence of effect is anticipated; in other words, hypocrisy. An important procedure of the Headquarters is to issue these circulars. They do their paper work. The SE behaves similarly while issuing Memos that only repeat instructions already issued by the Headquarters. He passes them up and down; paper work in progress. So, the whole activity on

Box 2.5

Some Circulars and Notifications Issued by the Headquarters, Relative to Revenue Realisation in Haryana, over 1997-1999

Unauthorised Connections and Arrears of Payment

In Haryana, the circular 8/97 states that "there are reports that some unscrupulous persons are still indulging in the act of stealing electricity by directly tapping the lines unauthorisedly [...]. JE/Assistant Foremen in charge of the area shall be given one month time to get all such unauthorised connections removed [...]. On the expiry of the one month period, surprise checks shall be conducted by the respective SDO, Xen & SE [...]. Strict administrative action against the JE/Assistant foreman [shall] be initiated for his lapse in detecting the unauthorised connections". The circular 19/97 requires the JE to make a 100 per cent check on tubewell connections. The circular 3/98 requires a checking that there is no industrial use on domestic connections, the one on 5/98 asks to check the accuracy of meters, the 6/98 to disconnect users where there is an outstanding amount, the 7/98 to check the users defaulting for more than Rs. 5000. The circulars 14/98, 15/98, 24/98 order the recovery of a first quarterly instalment for outstanding bills by the end of June 1998. Circulars 28/98 and 29/98 provide an easier time limit to achieve this. Also, numerous faxes and memos occur to recall attention to these circulars or to extend them, right up to a fax by the CE/Commercial dated 14/5/1999, and a Memo issued by him, dated 13/8/1999. The circular 13/99 deplores the "accumulation of outstanding dues as a result of timely actions not being taken for disconnecting the supply of defaulting consumers". It recommends "surprise checks between 5.30 & 8 p.m." (in spite of the fact that this last point is not enforceable without union agreement). At some periods, over a few days, memos and faxes from the Director operation, CE/commercial succeed themselves on a daily basis. The SE generally formally confirms these messages already transmitted to all the Field officers, by asking the Xens to "please direct all SDOs and JEs under your control to adhere the instructions strictly and should be implemented meticulously". A memo dated 14/6/99 complains against "checking reports not (being) on the prescribed PROFORMA". After two years of paper work, nothing has changed, except for the height of the pile of accumulated paper.

Source: HSEB

the revenue side is focused on following procedures, or positioning oneself in relation to them. Focus on revenue as such does not occur, far less on 'profit'.

How is it Rational within the SEBs' System?

It may be recalled that increasing the revenue is a secondary objective in many SEBs, if it is an objective at all. When it is, it has been seen that procedures are numerous, unrealistic (since other obligations do not allow time needed by officers), and even ambiguous (in the sense that some of them recommend toughness and some others are designed to prevent it). In the context of a poor information system, the Field officers know that monitoring will be low on this issue. Moreover, it is widely accepted that political protection may arise at any time and Field officers have an incentive not to act.[17]

It is in this context that the Headquarters issue several circulars and memos. As State Governments have their own financial problems, they complain about the SEBs performance. When this happens, all the levels of the hierarchy can claim that they have done their paper work, and explain that the results are unmet because of scarcity of means or time. Indeed, an argument given by a Field officer is that "they want the outputs without giving the inputs". Therefore, as long as the paper work is done, SEB officials can argue *vis-à-vis* the Government.

In this context, the absence of discretionary power (regarding the budget, but more stringently on managerial power) leads to a process of bargaining (between the Field and the Headquarters) over the respect of procedures, and over the issuing of procedures (between the State and the SEB).

2.3.2. *The Headquarters: 'The Bureaucrats'*

Procedural rationality also occurs in the fixing of subsidies and in planning.

Procedural Rationality in Fixation of Subsidies:
"If they take money from me, they take orders from me"

The role of the State Power Secretary is to negotiate the subsidies with the other Ministries (Finance mainly) of the State Government, and to co-ordinate the actual supply of power from the Central Government Undertakings, like NTPC, NHPC, sometimes not independently from political deals. As far as the Chairman is concerned, his main aim is to ensure security in the supply of energy, from the same Central generators and to the customers. His objective is also to look for financial assistance, but in this case financial consideration is not important on its own, but is rather a by-product of the continuity of supply, as the following analysis shows.

---

17. A SEB official declared in interviews that even "if able to prove that this user stole energy", then the politician might answer "I know, he's sharing with me". "Politicians are so shameless", he added.

Viewed from the point of the State Government, two contrast approaches on a continuum of methods are theoretically feasible for fixing of subsidies. These tell a lot about the parameters on which they are based. Subsidies can either be discussed as an economic category in itself which aims at adjusting the gaps between tariffs and costs. In this case, it is independent from expenses in capital and establishment sections, and also from dues to the suppliers and the actual level of collections in the revenue section. In other words, it is independent from the daily financial position, whose monitoring would be left to the Board, for only focusing on creating long run equilibrium conditions with clear and fixed rules (this is what some Regulatory Commission now try to implement). Alternatively, the global situation might be considered, with a look at all these issues, and hence ultimately as treasury in itself. But then, subsidies become an adjusting variable. In this case, *ad hoc* subsidies are fixed with this focus on the treasury, and adjusted to provide the amount necessary for the clearing of book accounts. It is then more subject to the discretion of the Governments. The former system would allow transparency of rules, by fixing the method of calculation, while leaving the other activities to the responsibility of the SEB. The latter actually opens up the space for *ex-ante* uncertainty in the level of subsidies, while considering the global situation. In this case, whether the Government were to be benevolent to the SEB or not, the allocation itself could materialise in many sub-cases, according to the manner in which the money is given. For instance, financial transfers give liquidity on short run. This is not so for debt re-scheduling or the writing-off of interests, which have effects in the long run, but do not help liquidity in the short run. The actual system is the second one. Indeed, no *ex-ante* provision is put in place. Meetings on subsidies occur on the demand of the Board, on a "crisis basis", as a Power Secretary acknowledged. There are no set rules for calculation, and the amount that is negotiated has to occur. The Board's demands are based on the tariffs of subsidised categories of consumers. Generally, the State Governments do not commit *ex-ante* to these tariffs. Some of them consider that they only have to deal with the agricultural subsidies, and with some concessional tariffs that are designed for poor consumers.[18] For instance, a Power Secretary stated

18. When the first 50 kWh are sold at cheap tariff, for instance.

that, except from these categories, domestic tariffs shall be relevant in the context of cross subsidisation, which he considered "the matter of the SEB", despite tariffs are fixed by the Government. Apart from the category, Governments can also argue about the level of agricultural subsidies. It is true that, given the lack of information, SEBs can overestimate the unmetered agricultural consumption. An official stated that "SEBs provide calculations by exaggerating". Once an agreement on the level of subsidies is reached, the method by which the subsidies are paid still depends upon the contextual situation of the finances of the Government. Financial transfers are fixed so as to provide the minimal support needed by the Board to continue to supply power. The transfers can also come from the diversion of capital funds, if so decided by the Government. This can easily be done on non-plan funds. After financial transfers, the balance is cleared through rescheduling of debts. This does not actually provide liquidity in the short term, as would be the case if some debts were converted into assets. In such a case, the newly categorised assets will give future claims for recovery to the Board, but that will still be considered under State Government's discretion only. The Board cannot anticipate the amount of given subsidies, firstly because the total amount in itself will depend on the current finances of the Government, and secondly because a part of the subsidies will be 'given' under a book-currency budget only, that is at least delayed. In other words, in theory the Boards are given a right in the future but the right is not guaranteed. For this reason, the Board cannot be sure that its liquidity situation will be fully taken into account. In this context, the term 'subsidies' is itself an improper one, as the amount given is not based on a consideration of 'subsidised' tariffs to be recovered, but on external considerations.

Let us now analyse the criteria taken into account in the fixation of subsidies in particular, and the financial relations with government in general. The (very short-term) continuity of supply is clearly more important for SEB, as well as, for State Governments than investment, maintenance, or clearing of dues, that is, than the long-term continuity of supply. The clearing of dues is not considered as important in itself, but as a 'by-product' of ensuring the continuity of supply, a Power Secretary acknowledged. To elaborate, crisis situations often arise when the suppliers, for instance NTPC, or similarly, some equipment suppliers, threaten to stop delivering the inputs to the

Board. Then, a part of the dues has to be cleared in order to maintain further supply. If not possible, the crisis arrives and the Board calls for a meeting, discussing the issue of subsidies, and also that of the funds available. Ultimately, the outcome is designed to take care of the crisis in the short term, the Government using it to technically clear the general matter of the financial relations with the Board.

To complete the present discussion on the subject of financial links, let us specify that, contrary to the autonomous status of SEBs, their dealings with the Central Government Undertakings are not conducted face to face. Instead, this is channelled through the State Government. The Power Secretary, the Finance Secretary, the State Ministry of Power or even the Chief Minister of the State might intervene in some debt re-schedulement with NTPC or NHPC, or on some agreement to write off interests on arrears of dues. As an official declared, "we give guarantees, but we also have to put pressure, moral and political". Another official recognised that, even if supposedly autonomous, SEBs depend, due to their financial conditions, on State Governments. The same official stated that "if they take money from me, they take orders from me". Speaking on this issue, a Board official acknowledged that, being "a part of the administration of the Government", the State Electricity Boards cannot argue. The financial boundaries of SEBs are hence malleable depending on the discretion of the State Government. In this regard, it can be asserted that the relationships between a Chairman and his Power Secretary might not be unequal. Indeed, in some political contexts, the Chairman "might be influential enough to bring the Chief Minister in the negotiations". An interviewed official said that, depending upon the personalities of their holders, the two posts can be exchanged in terms of precedence. But the fact remains that the Board is in the Government sphere, in which financial aspects are only a by-variable in the issue of ensuring the continuation of the physical supply. There is no link between payments and energy to be supplied. Rather, these factors reflect the respective bargaining position of government bodies. The actual variable that is considered is the availability of administrative bargaining capacity through a political process. This is done in real time, without any forward-looking scheme.

To sum up, the procedure is not written here, but it nevertheless exists, based on physical crises in the continuity of supply. The whole procedure is directed by this physical issue, and financial aspects are actually a by-product of it. So, the negotiation on subsidies is hardly done for its own sake, in the sense that it is not actually separated from constraints related to continuity of supply.

The Logic of this System

Erratic monitoring of this issue, based on irregular meetings and decisions taken under contextual rationality (March, 1978) might seem puzzling, since the relationships between Boards and States are based on both connivance and the stick. Indeed, State control of State Electricity Boards is somehow forgiving: as they fix the tariffs and impose policies without paying subsidies, they, in turn, "extend loans and give help by way of capital subsidy", an official said. He agreed that, in spite of the fact that "there are five- or one-year plans, the budgets were not used for the purpose originally meant in consultation with the Planning Commission". "Theoretically, everything is under Government control, but State Electricity Boards were in the red and the priority of the Government was agriculture, so State Electricity Boards were not strictly monitored", he added. Another confirmed that, in this situation, operational efficiency was not an objective for State Electricity Boards, whose tendency was to ask the Government for support through credits or simply to accumulate losses. A consultant agreed that "as it was a priority sector, the Government funds came and were less of a worry for State Electricity Boards".

However, this process, based on problems in supply, has some advantages to both sides if the content is taken into account. First, as the Government clearly will not commit to subsidies and will not allow a fixed frame in absence of reliable information, it is beneficial for the Board to await crisis situations. Indeed, the issue being one of liquidity, in order not to stop the supply (in reality most of the energy is supplied anyway, be it for political reasons, from Central Undertakings; financial transfers just allow not blocking the system), short term cash is preferable to future unreliable promises. This cash is more likely to come if supply, which is a concern for the Government, is at stake. Second, the Government, also under treasury shortage, might prefer waiting for the crisis to come, in order to delay the payments, so as not to 'waste' subsidies that might not be well-spent and lead to a crisis anyway. Last but not least, the State Government has an interest in waiting for crisis situations simply because such a strategy makes it easier to press for, and get accepted, some re-schedulements and minor diversions of plan funds. Finally, under the structuring hypothesis of unavailability of information, and hence of unclear allocation rules, the process itself is consistent with procedural rationality.

Procedural Rationality in Planning

The planning is done by the planning wing of the Headquarters, based on the peak consumption at each sub-station, with a one year advance. Obviously, as the metering at the sub-stations level is hardly widespread, estimates have to be made. Proper estimates based on inquiries by the users, or close coordination with some other administrations, do not exist as confirmed in interviews of the Haryana Electricity Regulatory Commission (HERC). According to HERC, the load forecast is based on gross figures, and not on aggregation of micro estimations. Planning should integrate various costs, like the costs of works and equipment, but also the cost of technical losses. These calculations are limited to rough rule of thumb estimates. As the actual configuration of the Field is not known, the calculation of cost is based on administered costs (average costs given by the previous accounts of the Board). In the selection of projects, generally no alternative projects are considered, which means that only the more 'obvious' project is considered in the first step. For example, extension of existing lines, and the addition of transformers. The configuration of the network is not questioned. From the project decided upon at this first step, the cost is calculated by using the administered costs. If the project is found to be under the limit, it is sanctioned. Only if the cost happens to be higher, is an alternative project studied, and a second step taken in the process of planning. From interviews, it is clear that no complete master-plan study is done, and that there is no study focusing on long term development of the network, including re-organisation and re-structuring of the meshing of lines and of the levels of tension. Because of the lack of information, planning is even conducted on the basis of problems actually faced during the operation, hence involving a delay in solving them. There is no integrated approach between the costs of new works and the costs of operation to be expected in the future which depend on technical choices. Neither is the financial return of the projects evaluated, nor is the time of implementation optimised.

So, costs are hardly checked. When they are, such checking appears only at an *ex-post* stage, making sure that theoretically devised costs remain within administrative limits. Unfortunately, the true organisation of the planning process does not integrate them, since the basic tools, which are minimal comparisons and integration of basic operation costs, are not used. The development of the network is rather seen as a process of solving present issues *per se*, that is, without taking into account the future, without considering the cost variable, and, in terms of the technical plan itself, without clearly seeing the externalities between the generation and the network, *i.e.* without having a systemic vision of the power sector. Implementation of the sanctioned works depends on the availability of material and ultimately on the priority given to some politically decided projects. In any case, even among the sanctioned projects issued from the planning wing, the actual priority will be set up through interaction with the political level.

Planning under Politics *versus* Cost Rationality

The planning activity is obviously done under bounded rationality, as it only focuses on solutions close to the symptom (Cyert & March, 1963), with a satisfycing criteria (Simon, 1951). The procedure at stake could however be considered as being too rough, since some important elements are not integrated into it, as pointed out before. Indeed, beyond technical issues, a cost return based planning system allows a decentralisation of the investment choices. When the criteria of profitability is fixed and set up according to refinancing capabilities, the result is that decisions on new works are based on sound objectives. In addition, the level where the decision is taken is lowered. Subsequently, the accuracy of data increases, and the decisions are arrived at sooner. However, in SEBs, the fact that, some costs are not taken into account, financial return is not evaluated, the time of implementation is not optimised, and that no systemic approach is developed, is consistent with the low level of available information, and the absence of discretionary power. Prioritisation between projects relies on comparisons between politically driven projects and planning wing projects. The criteria are (i) what additional load the project carries and (ii) where it is carried. From this prioritisation, the actual building is limited by the level of available inputs, in terms of materials and workforce. The financial considerations occur as in the context described in the negotiation of subsidies, that is, based on felt political priorities. Hence, due to the process of selection, it is rational for the planners not to consider costs, and the basic kind of bounded rationality that is at stake is procedurally rational.

2.3.3. *Procedural Rationality and Paper Work*

To sum up this sub-section, the analysis of the four decision-making processes has shown how far procedures influence, constrain and shape the final form of the decision. Beyond this point, the behaviour of focusing primarily on procedures, and not on costs is consistent with the given general characteristics of the SEB organisation, a paper budget, a non-integrated reporting system, and the absence of allocation of discretionary power. This particular mode of behaviour has then rationally emerged, instead of some others types of behaviour one could think of. The rationality at stake in SEBs is procedural rationality. More precisely, this focus on procedures is not so much attached to achieving some technical goals through the following of these procedures. It is rather attachment to procedures *per se*, as a goal and as an end in themselves. In this regard, doing the paper work attached to procedures is the most important issue; the paper work matters, and the presence of paper work in lieu of cost analysis emerges as an additional characteristic of the organisation.

2.4. The Rationality of the System and its *a posteriori* Objectives

The question of the inner rationality of SEBs, raised in Chapter 1, can now be answered. In addition, the *a posteriori* objectives of the Field and the Headquarters can be deduced. Let us recall that rationality would also mean the way the system has developed its own sustaining logic. These are all elements that hamper reforms, and that will need a radical change, as developed later on in the book.

2.4.1. *The Rationality of the System: Consistency and Self-enforcement*

In SEBs, decision-making does not involve analyses of relative efficiency. The classically referred explanation is that the trade-off between different solutions have already been sanctioned at the political levels. However, the previous analysis shows that, beyond political intervention, the SEBs' organisational structure itself precludes doing this. There is no focus on cost and benefits because there is no formal discretionary power, either on budgetary or on human resources. Moreover, the absence of an integrated information system leads to the same result. Ultimately, decision-making in SEBs is based either on Government's direct executive instructions or, on positioning towards procedures, either by showing a paper compliance with them or by arguing on the reasons of non compliance, by invoking other procedures with a higher priority.

Let us see how these elements not only sustain, but reinforce each other (and will constitute a strong, systemic, resistance to reforms).

Consistency Between the Characteristic Elements

One can now discuss in detail the internal consistency of the system, as well as, some mutual enforcing mechanisms, by analysing the inter relations among the following four elements: executive instructions, absence of formal discretionary power, absence of integrated information, and importance of procedures. This can be visualised in Figure 2.3.

Figure 2.3 distinguishes between necessary consequences (double arrows) and strengthening mechanisms (dot arrows). It has been seen that the absence of formal discretionary power and of an integrated information system prevent focusing on cost (not available) but legitimate recourse to paper work (arrows 1 & 2). The resulting inefficiency is systemic. That is, the structure of the organisation, in terms of delegation of power and of available information, leads to the procedural rationality of focusing on paper work as *in-built in the system*. This structure is rooted in the fact that the State gives executive instructions. A necessary condition to that is indeed the absence of formal discretionary power, that would otherwise allow SEB officers (whether they are from the Headquarters or the Field) to partially oppose these instructions. Indeed, officers' opposition declines if the decision relates to collegial responsibility and if their personal action cannot be found (arrow 3). The relation is therefore also causal, since the absence of formal discretionary power is indeed a *sine qua non* condition for substituting executive instructions for policy directions. Additionally, if the politicians want the cost of the executive instructions not to be seen, in order to prevent arguments from the SEB officers or from other political parties, the fact that there is no information system helps hiding the consequences (arrow 4). The presence of executive instructions contributes hence to framing what is more a reporting system for *ex-post* control than an information system for *ex-ante* monitoring. Ultimately, as there are executive instructions that can always arise on any action taken by the officers, no effect of the decision can be devised with certainty. Following the modelling made by Heiner (1983) on procedural rationality, the emergence of paper work can be explained through the need to cope against uncertainty (arrow 5).[19] *The four elements are therefore not here by chance but derive from a single and unified logic, that is all the more difficult to tackle. Modifying any of these elements while leaving the others untouched would place decision-making in a crisis situation.* Let us take an example. What happens if decision power is officially delegated to identified hierarchical levels (formal discretionary power)? Then, arrow 3 leads to open crisis with politicians' instructions, since the officer can now be identified as the one whose responsibility was to take the decision. Similarly, impossibility in the present system to focus on costs has been exemplified in all the four procedures studied.

Figure 2.3

The Inner Rationality of the SEB System

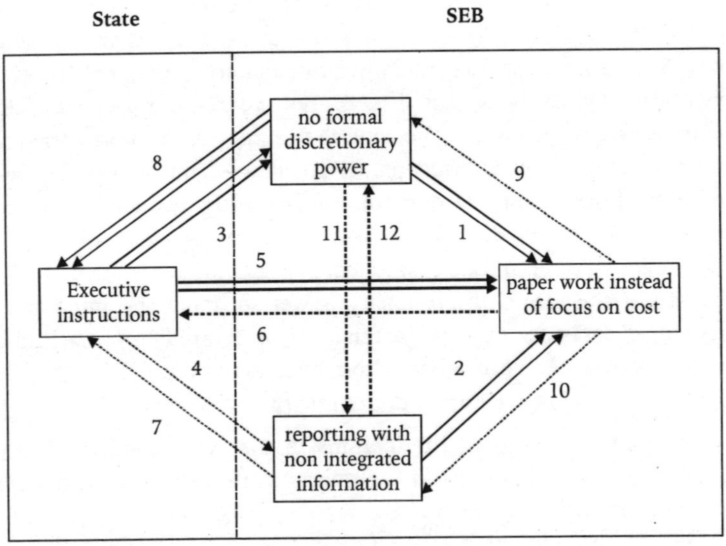

19. The possibility to analyse this last point through a property rights approach is discussed in next Chapter.

Mutual Enforcement between the Characteristic Elements

There are also some feedback effects that lead the system to self-enforce. Since costs can hardly be checked *ex-post* on a detailed enough way to allow monitoring by the State, it becomes all the more necessary and consistent for the Government to rely on executive instructions, whose effects can be checked on a specific basis. (arrows 6 & 7). These relations are of a self-enforcing nature rather than being a strict necessity. Indeed, the moment the third characteristic of SEBs – that is, the absence of formal discretionary power – is no longer present, then the two others do not lead to executive instructions. Under this hypothesis, even if there is no focus on costs in SEBs, some systems of incentives can be imagined for *ex-post* monitoring by the State, in a compatible manner with policy directions. However, as the State maintains absence of discretionary power for the SEB to retain its own power, this leads to the inability of the SEB officers to take some actions, like major new works, restructuring decisions, or even proper allocation of material and human resources in operation. The State has in return no choice but to intervene, be it for the sole purpose of running the organisation. They finally have to be dealt with directly by the State, either the Power Secretary or other Secretaries, or politicians themselves (arrow 8). This relation is also causal and systemic. Finally, since SEB officers can face administrative inquiries, they may protect themselves by justifying that they are not granted the power to take some decisions (arrow 9). They are also somewhat comforted by the non-integration of the information, which allows them to avoid detailed and argued questioning (arrow 10). Subsequently, two additional dot arrows need to be discussed. They link the absence of formal discretionary power and the non-integrated information system. In the absence of the formal discretionary power to frame and implement structural decisions, the importance of integrated information is reduced (arrow 11). Also, where information is missing, one can hardly implement an effective formal discretionary power (arrow 12).

The above analysis of the lock-ins in the system will form the basis for practical proposals for its reform in the second part. It shall be noted from the Figure that the separation between the State and the SEB has been left permeable. Indeed, it has been previously shown how, beyond the possibility of executive instructions, the SEB does not have the control over its main financial parameters and decisions.

In this regard, it is subject to the decisions of the State and does not control its 'border'.

Let us compare SEBs' characteristics with those of an enterprise, and how the difference alters decision-making or the reaction to external 'shocks'. First of all, to be given this label, an enterprise, even a public one, has to be separate from the Government, in the specific sense that the Government may not intervene beyond mere policy directions (as defined earlier, which equates to policy directions that shareholders give in a private case). Then the enterprise implements these constraints keeping in mind alternative operational ways and cost-efficiency. It does not mean, that the enterprise will neither be 'fully' efficient, nor choices affected by its own inertia (past decision, past records, internal organisation). However, it will explicitly integrate costs, in an independent and decentralised manner. For that, a proper cost-oriented information system is developed, and responsibilities are made clear. The schematic way to represent it is just the reverse as it is in SEBs, as figure 2.4 shows.

Figure 2.4

The Inner Rationality of an Enterprise-type Utility

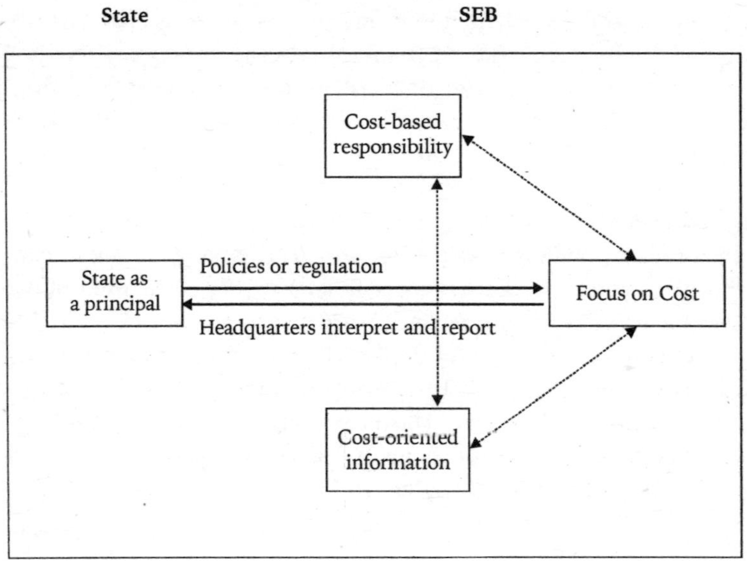

From this, let us look at how a SEB (respectively a public enterprise) would differently react to an external shock. Such as an unexpected increase in the consumption, or a major problem in a generation plant. In both cases, a sustainable solution for getting extra energy has to be found. An enterprise can act and its action is besides predictable. It will ask a generation company to provide an extra amount of energy, compare the costs of supply and try to optimise its own available plants given the cost differentials and peak level. Answer would be quick and cost computed. It can even be asserted that, most probably, in an evolved competitive environment, the enterprise would have secured in advance some of this amount through notional contracts. For an SEB, political agreement would be required, and sanction on unplanned, unbudgeted costs would be required, in a situation where no procedure exists to calculate it. Then the implementation of new generation operational timings would require lots of paper work. Ultimately, in the long run, the share between new owned sources for generation or external sources will not be clear (not predictable). It will all depend upon political negotiations and arbitrage: is the State Government able to get some extra power from the Centre, NTPC for instance? If so, is it willing to give a guarantee, which more or less depends on its relationships with the Government of India. Depending on the answer to these questions, and later depending on its capacity to renegotiate its financial situation, the SEB might alternate (this is further unpredictable) good or bad financial position for the same action. Ultimately, the financial position, and thus the outcome of the shock for the SEB will even be de-linked from its decision to increase or not the supply. Besides, the 'reaction' could similarly be an absence of reaction, which in a sense is what has happened during the whole 90s, when capacity addition has been so low. This example is not a mere 'thought experiment'; discussions with a former Power Minister of the Government of India have revealed that this absence of action and this de-linking between technical decisions, costs, and financial impacts has sadly been the rule till 1995 as far as inter-state energy transfers were concerned for instance. This dichotomy between SEBs and what would be an efficient autonomous public enterprise will be rendered more systematic in next Chapter.

2.4.2. *Construction of a posteriori Objectives: What Does the State Really do Through SEBs?*

For March, the objectives of an organisation are actually *ex-post* narratives and justification of what has actually (and sometimes unexpectedly) emerged. In this sense, they are to be qualified to be *a posteriori* objectives.

Let us compare the *a posteriori* objectives of the agents with their declared ones. The declared long term objectives of the Headquarters are to increase the capacity, the number of kilometres of lines and the generated energy. In other words, they are to increase the *size* of the Board on technical parameters. This technical and quantitative objective is constantly recalled in interviews, and its pregnancy in minds can be seen among others through the technical bias in the way annual reports are presented. A secondary declared objective is the dedication to increase the revenue, claimed by the Headquarters of the Board. The declared objectives of the Field are to increase the number of connections, as well as, to increase the quality of the voltage. This has to be realised through technical means. Acknowledged – if not publicly claimed – objectives of the State are to increase the access of the irrigated agriculture to the consumption, as well as, the number of employees and the satisfaction of some political clients within local constituencies.

Chapter 1 has already shown that these declared objectives either have not been fully obtained, or could have been obtained faster and in a more sustainable manner, or at a much lesser cost. The previous analysis of the characteristics of the organisation, procedures of decision-making, and type of rationality at stake, helps us in understanding why objectives are not being met adequately. Because of the system, and in fact, in full consistence with it, the Field officers only focus on short term supply, under an *ex-post* approach. What is more, they only focus on meeting their minimum responsibilities. On the non-technical aspects, they concentrate on clearing themselves by showing commitment to users complaints and Headquarters complaints. Both technical and non-technical aspects are dealt with through the attention paid to the paper work, and at the end of the process only they materialise into some action. As a consequence, the *a posteriori* objective, that is the objective actually targeted in consideration of the actual decisions, is to handle short term situations on paper. The latter can be characterised as emergency. Indeed, Field officers only consider disequilibriums on technical and non-technical matters. Disequilibrium is the norm. Headquarters are also in a comparable situation. The *a posteriori* objective is to deal with short term, and even day to day scarcity of physical resources. Numerous officers complain about the perpetual emergency situation, saying that "day to day activity prevents us to foresee". The focus is also on fulfilling political executive instructions. As there might be, in some cases, a claim from the States on the inefficiency of SEBs, the Headquarters have in this case an additional *a posteriori* objective, which is to show commitment to the refutation of this claim, but not to actually look for efficiency. Paradoxically, despite the open reciprocal recriminations between the Field and the Headquarters, the convergence in their *a posteriori* objectives should not be surprising. Indeed, March (1962) points out the existence of "mutual control-systems" for enforcing agreements, which are the budget and the allocation of functions. The mechanism is one by which, "[by defining] the limits of discretion, we constrain the individual or sub-group from acting outside those limits; but at the same time, we constrain any other members from the coalition from prohibiting action within those limits". This is then manifested, in the context of SEBs, into *de facto* collective decisions between Field and Headquarters. It can hence be said that, on many issues, the objectives are those of the Board as a whole.

The issue of *a posteriori* objectives of the State shall be left for the next Chapter, as the subject requires more insights into the characterisation of administrations. At this stage, however, it can be said that the objectives do not include efficiency, as its elected members continuously ask for political protection. Thus, whereas the State could have the declared objective to increase efficiency, the unavailability of monitoring leads to the system itself becoming inefficient. In this sense, these objectives can be considered as being *a posteriori* ones. It can therefore be said that the *a posteriori* objective of SEBs as a whole has never been efficiency, and that it rationally cannot be such as long as the main characteristics of the system remain.

If one is to consider the fulfilling of these *a posteriori* objectives, the operation of SEBs can be considered as successful. The supply has lasted over fifty years, and electrification has taken place. Since, within the rationality of the system, the question of relative efficiency is not relevant due to the impossibility of alternative scenarios, the goals have to be declared as achieved. When not possible, official figures and misreporting do the rest. They could ultimately be analysed as a self reproducing and protecting procedure that has emerged over the years.

2.5. Conclusion

The analysis of the characteristics of the organisation and the type of rationality at stake permits us to understand that the objectives given by the State to SEBs are not at all based on cost-efficiency, nor even on long run supply efficiency, but rather on short term technical concerns. This analysis, conducted by using the concepts of March *et al.*, shows that the system is rooted in something deeper than the so-called 'political interference'. In particular, it sheds light on structuring organisational characteristics: absence of formal discretionary power, reporting with non-integrated information, procedural focus on paper work and not on costs. These elements are interdependent and strengthen each other in a way to render every isolated reform difficult to implement. The key aspect is that, given systemic unavailability of discretionary power or information, relying on paper work instead of costs becomes rational. The point here shall not be misunderstood. If paper work leads to cost inefficiency, as compared to a situation where costs would be targeted, this does not mean that inefficiency is targeted *per se*, but that strong inertia to reform is in-built in SEBs' internal organisation. Let us now similarly examine the role of the State beyond the simple existence of executive instructions, and let us look for some elements of causal analysis at this level. Particularly, since the costs are not used in decision-making in SEBs, the theoretical, as well as, practical pertinence of cost as a concept will be questioned.

3

A Decision-making Theory of the State: Administrations and Irrelevance of Cost-related Concepts

This Chapter places the previously stylised facts in a consistent and causally derived framework. It essentially shows how the organisational characteristics are derived from the administrative nature of SEBs. It also shows how some usual economic concepts and theories cease to be valid in the analysis of the running of SEBs. Especially the concept of cost is alien to SEBs, since it is neither used in them, nor does it explain or clarify the decision-making within them. These latter theoretical results, demonstrated from stylised organisational characteristics, hold for many administration-like organisations of the Indian public sector, we argue.

3.1. An 'Administered' System

Let us go beyond the judicial status of SEBs, and deal with their very nature as an organisation. To serve that purpose, a survey on the nature of enterprises and of administrations is conducted. Let us show, from the analysis provided in the previous Chapter, that SEBs are administrations, not enterprises, and that the procedural rationality and the paper work system are ultimately derived from this administrative nature. Finally, the administrative coordination between SEBs and other electric organisations within the State apparatus is discussed.

3.1.1. SEBs are not Enterprises, but Administrations

Definition: Enterprises *versus* Administration

According to E.C. Banfield (1976), compared to an administration, an enterprise has only one objective. Its parameters are easy to measure and can be expressed in monetary terms. This can be the maximisation of profit for a classical private enterprise, or in the case of a public enterprise in natural monopoly, this objective may become the minimisation of the long run cost of supply. This involves a highly integrated measurement and control system, with rules to solve the conflicts in decision-making, based on economic criteria (evaluation of return, cost comparisons, etc.). Milgrom & Roberts (1990) state that "a firm is a business organisation with a central office that has substantial discretionary power" and has "substantial independence from other discretionary powers as Courts, Governments, Agencies". These independence and discretionary power express themselves in the ways the enterprise organises its internal functions. Cyert & March (1963) recall that this discretionary power materialises, among others, into an autonomy in financial and budgetary concerns, as well as, into independence in the human resource management and in the allocation of managerial power.

Conversely, in administrations, according to Banfield, there are several objectives of different, heterogeneous natures which are at best unprioritised, or may even be contradictory to each other. By the term 'heterogeneous' it is meant that they may be productive, allocative, social, legal, military, and so on. Conflicts are not subject to resolution through a robust decision criterion. Decision-making ultimately depends upon the use of discretionary power on the part of the Government, be it on financial, budgetary, human resource, or managerial concerns. Here lies the legitimacy of the State, and the question becomes of its appropriate disentangling/articulation with the production and economic sphere. As far as infrastructure is concerned, the contemporary answer lies in the articulation between the State & policies, the regulatory power, and the regulated utilities.

Definition

Ultimately, there are two necessary conditions for an organisation to be an enterprise: (i) the existence of a main monetarily expressed objective – its derivative being the use of an adapted information system – and (ii) the absence of an external discretionary power. Should one of these conditions remain unfulfilled, this would imply that the organisation is not an enterprise, whatever its official designation may be. For instance, Hirschhausen (1995) analyses the socialist system in Eastern Europe, through a study of 'combinats', the name of eastern European production plants. Combinats have been mainly analysed (by Kornai 1992) as public enterprises, or public firms. However Hirschhausen shows that Combinats used to be given, at the same time, productive, social and population control objectives. The relative importance of these objectives used to vary according to the changing political equilibrium. Consequently, Combinats were not enterprises, but administrations. This delineation between an enterprise and an administration can appear to be too clear-cut. However, it is consistent with the works of Cyert & March, or Simon and offers an operative base for such a delineation. In the final sections of their book, Cyert & March (1963) focus on goals such as profit, sales, inventory, production, on information linked with these goals, and on prices and outputs. Through these categories, they refer more explicitly to enterprises. They add that these are "if not unique to firms, at least more characteristic of firms than of other organisations". In a different way, Simon (1947) had already laid stress on this concern for the enterprise. Of course, Simon's objective is not to essentialise the enterprise, nor to evolve a 'pure' model. He of course differentiates between the global goals (in their diversity) and the sub-goals, and this definition is compatible with the fact that the hierarchy of means-ends within the enterprise may not be purely profit-oriented[1].

This definition does not imply any superiority of one form over the other, and only reflects a difference in nature. The issue, and the main concern of the book, is to know which organisational form is more adapted than the other to the social and economic decisions to be taken currently in the power sector in India. Enterprises deal with productive matters and can subject their production to a single monetarily expressed objective, since the effects of decisions are subject to financial evaluation. Politics, and hence administrations, have by nature to deal with competing interests, such as those described earlier. As Giraud (1998) points out, it is the duty of

1. Even though he agrees that profit might not directly account for the decision-making of most of the members of an enterprise, he points out that the possibly countering argument that enterprises are in practice not fully and substantively acting on profit motives, is actually misleading. According to him, it is fruitful to view enterprises as units primarily motivated by the search for profit – and exposed to several secondary constraints -, acting through a network of decision processes that introduces multiple approximations in the search for profitable solutions. But then this reference explicitly remains the profit.

politics to clinch the debate. Conversely, economics is only capable of detailing allocative consequences of decisions, but has no legitimacy to clinch the related trade-off and their respective domains have to be defined. Every decision has its pros and cons. By nature, in administrative matters, there is no formal and lasting rule for trade-offs in decision-making, which is ultimately made through Governments' discretionary power. This has two consequences:

- First, administrations are best adapted to complex, multi-faceted decisions whereas the enterprises are more suitable to tackle cost-based and lasting decisions in productive matters. *In our concern, the question becomes to know if the best arrangement could not be a mostly cost-based management of the power sector for the bulk of the consumer, while targeting subsidies for some section through explicit and separate channels and regulation.*
- Second, trying to evaluate the efficiency of an administration through a single criterion makes no sense, from an internal point of view. Indeed, this would mean evaluating the achievements of an organisation on the grounds of criteria it might not consider itself, or consider only incidentally. This may give a normative goal, but does not allow to understand why this external goal is not reached and how the decision-making process needs being modified in order to do so. *This opens the question of the right concepts to choose to analyse SEBs, which the next sub-section will thoroughly deal with.*

To fully explore the consequences of Banfield's definition, the question of the *public electricity enterprise* has to be addressed. We argue that public power enterprises can exist, provided (i) minimal provision of services of common interest[2] is clearly defined, and (ii) the principal's objective is monetarily expressed (being, for instance the minimisation of the long run cost of supply). The objective is then clear, monetarily expressed, non-contradictory, and a developed information system allows checking the results and elaborating incentives. The examples include the 'plan contract' between the French public power company EDF and the French Government.

2. This also refers to the French concept of 'public service', now acknowledged by the EU 'economic directives', which delineates the 'public good' part of infrastructure services. This concept has allowed to disentangle what can be provided by the private and what has to be either provided by the State or strictly regulated by the State

SEBs as Administrations

The analysis of decision-making in SEBs has clearly shown the absence of allocation of formal discretionary power within SEBs, and, in *lieu* of that, the existence of an external one, under the form of executive instructions.

Also, the objectives at stake within a SEB are not based on monetary criteria. The same applies to the *a posteriori* objectives of a SEB as a whole. Indeed, even on the social objective of electrification, the result has not been obtained in the most efficient way, in terms of long term rates of electrification.

For these reasons, and according to the definition given earlier, SEBs are not enterprises but administrations. They are a part of the State, as the analysis of financial links between the State and the SEB has clearly demonstrated. Then, what are the multiple, confronting objectives of State Governments?

Multiple Objectives of the State Governments

Objectives that State Governments assign to the SEBs have been wrongly coined as 'political interference' in current analysis of SEBs when they actually are consubstantial to the SEBs as administrations. Namely, they are redistributive goals, electrification and employment. They all arise under the form of executive instructions. The prior definition helps in understanding that this is not 'interference', but the true logic of the administrative nature of the SEBs. Of course, any State Government has a minimal concern for financial parameters through its budget, since at least some situations of treasury shortage might happen. And, even if they are in a position to obtain some facilities through bargaining from the Government of India, they ultimately have to face financial constraints. But this is addressed by them as a by-parameter and neither as a single nor as a forefront parameter.

The State Governments only consider financial aspects as an adjusting parameter, occupying at best a second level position. First-level parameters are related to comparisons over political advantages between different sectors. To illustrate this, let us explain why the State Governments largely do not react to financial parameters. First, the financial results of SEBs are technically not shown in the budget of the State, what allows higher political margins. For instance, if subsidies are booked as *payables* by the State but not actually paid to

SEBs, the loss does not affect the next budget of the State.[3] Then, both the book accounts of the SEB and the state budget look fine, though there is a discrepancy between them. Similarly, the responsibility for retirement schemes rests with the SEBs, and, since public accountancy does not show this kind of future liabilities, these funds are not provisioned. Second, decisions are taken locally and effects on SEBs' efficiency are only seen later on, at an aggregated level, while political benefits are instantaneous, and efficiency costs are delayed. So, in the process of giving executive instructions, politicians do not need to bother with cost variables. Of course, in the long run, the arrears accumulate and the situation worsens. The issue is not so much that SEBs do 'political production'; it is that, even from the point of view of the State, the financial constraint is not considered under an integrated (costs *versus* benefits) approach. That way, SEBs do not even select the cheapest techniques of political production, as already underlined with the example of rural electrification.

The Organisation of the System as Derived from its Administrative Nature

Since, by nature, political objectives can not be reduced to a single criterion, they call for political arbitration. As long as these objectives are included in the system, recourse to executive instructions is therefore a necessity. Executive instructions constitute the top level of the means-ends hierarchy and frame the whole structure of the SEBs. They are structurally linked with the administrative nature of SEBs, and are the practical manifestation of the external discretionary power of the State. This allows the State Government to change the weight it gives to various objectives. Executive instructions are not only consistent, but also consubstantial to the whole system. The organisation of the SEB-system as a whole is derived from its administrative nature.

Let us detail how executive instructions articulate with decision-making in SEBs. As underlined by Cyert & March (1963), this administrative nature does not mean that all decisions are taken only arbitrarily by the State. Executive instructions are even not the norm. According to the huge number of issues that need to be solved daily, and the fact that the system 'works', that is, supplies electricity, one

3. Because payable are not shown in public accountancy. As an example, the Maharashtra Government budget looks fine despite his State is virtually bankrupt given the numerous, guarantees it has extended.

cannot imagine that it relies only on executive instructions. The previous Chapter has been dedicated to finding out what the lines of permanence and of stability within SEBs are, and has aimed to show the rationale of the procedures. Illustrative of the actual number of instructions, when the issue of posting appears in interviews, all officials declare that instructions come on transfers and postings. However, when asked practically when such instructions appeared last, and under what conditions, answers are elusive. This cannot be attributed to the shyness of interviewed agents, many of whom give crude information on other aspects. A similar scenario takes place when discussing the so-called political protections for users who do not pay the bills. Uniqueness of the decision is hence not the point in SEBs. Politicians directly deal with the top levels which transmit to the Field. The key aspect is that *executive instructions ultimately acquire a structuring status through an anticipation effect*. They are not systematic in the sense they do not occur for every decision, far from it. However, they may potentially occur for any decision, or after any decision. Which means that, during a decision-making cycle, agents are faced with the potential 'expropriation' of the outcomes of their current decision, since any further executive instruction can occur.

Consequently, facing this potential instability, the rational answer for ensuring higher stability is to respect procedures, since benefits are not granted. These procedures provide the missing stability. Hence, not knowing on which issue executive instructions will arise, every outcome is considered to be potentially affected. Financial parameters finally stop being considered by themselves. As a result, the system, through strict procedures, leads to *a posteriori* objectives that are always in disfavour of cost efficiency. More important than the actual instructions, then, the perception of their importance is the key of the system. Executive instructions are not *systematic*, but become *systemic*, since the agents *ex-ante* (and very rationally) integrate them in their behaviour. The existence of executive instruction justifies the procedural rationality in SEBs.

Analysis of decisions shows the absence of comparisons between alternate strategies, be it in planning or in operation. Moreover, the reporting system focuses on initiation of new works, regardless of their completion or their quality. The power sector is ultimately organised around a *mono-technique*, that is where the importance of technical choices is marginal and where the technique is standard. It is based on new works and maintenance limited to *ex-post* repair. This mono-technique vision would actually be valid for an infrastructure sector to be quantitatively developed from scratch, as an input for the rest of the production sector. It would then be rational that the reporting focuses on quantities, and on 'expenditures' rather than on 'investments'. Under these assumptions, an integrated and developed information system becomes unnecessary. A public-accountancy type budget also becomes sufficient. In turn, the whole organisation of the decision-making is a consequence of the administrative nature of SEBs. This is summarised in Figure 3.1.

Figure 3.1

The Inter-relations between the Nature and the Organisation of SEBs

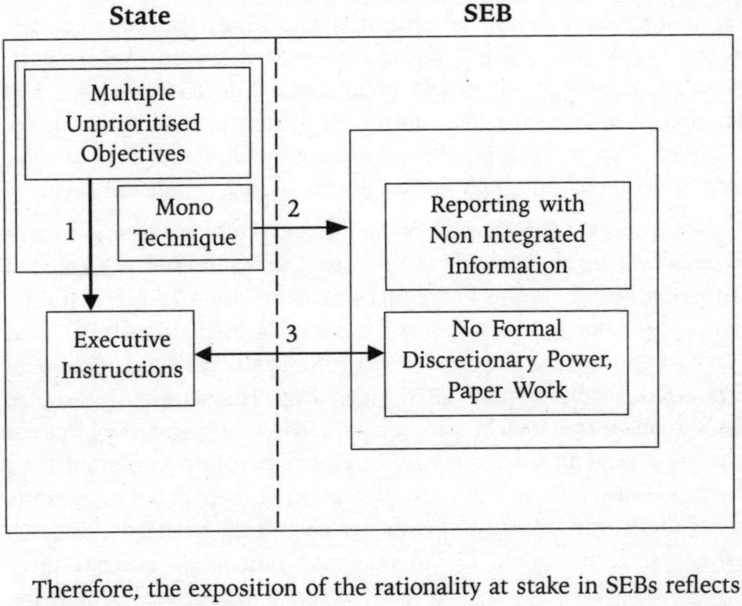

Therefore, the exposition of the rationality at stake in SEBs reflects an organisation where the issue of efficiency is not at all internally relevant. This comes ultimately from its administrative nature, oriented towards the pursuit of irreconcilable objectives required from an electric sector seen as a mono-technique. We shall say that it is operated through an administered monitoring. This model, suited to a non-electrified country and where human capital existed but was limited, such as newly decolonised India in 1947, is by and large unsuitable to a mature power industry of a country such as contemporary India. The derived absence of practical focus on costs results in the relative cost-inefficiency of SEBs. Hence, under a paradigm of cost-efficiency, SEBs are not organisational forms. Even if inefficient – which could mean that lots of efficiency improvement opportunities may be available – the internal organisation does not bring enough power to its agents to catch these. At that stage, one can notice that *the fact that SEBs produce electrical power is not topical in the analysis. The fact that they produce political power, jobs, redistribution, and revolve around administrative procedural rationality matters much more.* In that way, and without entering into the details, the demonstration that it potentially applies to many other sectors in the public sphere is quasi-immediate. Ruet, Saravanan & Zérah (2002) or Ruet (2004a) exemplify this for water and sanitation, but also public mining or handicraft departments at the State Government level in India. The delineation between the State (with its administrations) and its public enterprises, beyond official status of organisation, would require a further research, but the scope of the method exemplified here on SEBs looks promising. Let us explore it for the whole power sector.

3.1.2. Administered Links between NTPC, NHPC and SEBs

Co-ordination between the SEBs and some of the Power Central Undertakings like NTPC, NHPC, and Powergrid, is similarly done through political executive instructions. Co-ordination among Central Undertakings is also based on an administered system, under the Central Ministry of Power. The aim here is not so much to fully characterise some Central Undertakings, but rather to replace SEBs in the institutional environment they interact with; we will therefore deal with planning and new works only.

NHPC, strictly speaking, faces development problems due to political choices, since the construction of new hydro-plants always implies the relocation of people. Ultimately, the concerned levels of Government monitor each step of development. The initiation of projects, as well as, the final decision, rests in an agreement between the Government of India and the State Government, and does not belong to NHPC. The manner in which populations are relocated is the responsibility of the concerned State Government. As far as the implementation process is concerned, NHPC also, mostly follows Government intimation. As far as NTPC is concerned, plants are developed on the basis of demands issued by State Governments, and transmitted by the Ministry of Power, Government of India, after a preliminary agreement between the two levels of Government. The Central Ministry of Power selects the sites; by focussing on coal supply and water availability. Financial sustainability of the concerned SEBs does not enter the picture. Therefore, NTPC does not control the financial risks. The planning process is mainly based on engineers' rules; and the investment decision process is largely external to NTPC, depending on the discretionary power of the Government of India, in spite of its corporate status (under the Company Act, 1956).

Similarly, relations between NTPC and Powergrid, for instance, are dealt with in an administrative manner. Joskow & Schmalensee (1983), among others, point out that, in the planning and building of plants and a network, each one is a specific asset to the other. That is, it has to be used in coordination with the other organisation. A network is designed to evacuate a given amount of power and is less useful if the generation is modified; at the same time, the plant has to rely on the evacuating capacity of the network, and each can suffer from the delay in building the other. If the two builders are not integrated within the same structure, a contract has to deal with the financial and institutional procedures to solve the potential conflicts.

On this important issue, it is interesting to note that no contract is signed between NTPC and Powergrid, even for guarantees against delays, though it may imply severe financial consequences. It has been argued in interviews that such contracts are not needed, as "NTPC and Powergrid depend on the same administration". It is the Ministry of Power and not the courts, which will address any problem. Whatever be the efficiency of such an institutional arrangement, it thus clearly makes more sense to analyse NTPC and Powergrid not as two independent corporatised companies, but as two distinct parts of the same administration. The Central Ministry of Power provides a hierarchical form of co-ordination between them. Box 3.1 details the administrative functioning of Inter-State Transmission. It identifies in central public undertakings the key features of an administration: absence of a genuine cost-benefit computation, focus on procedures and political arbitration. Interestingly, this example shows a situation where the arbitration has been in favour of cost-efficiency; but, this is also true that this had happened at a time when the Minister was an economist...

Box 3.1

Administrative Nature of the Inter-State Power Transmission Monitoring

From the nineties onwards, the Southern grid has become structurally deficitary in terms of available capacity to match the demand. Conversely, the Northern grid has become reiatively excedentary at least at some point of time in the year, or under some conditions of hydraulic reserves. In 1996-97, electricity growth in India, was only 3.7 per cent. This growth was minus 8 per cent in April 97 and 2.85 per cent in May 97. With special efforts it went up from 7 to 8 per cent from June to October 97. In November 97, demand in the Northern, Eastern and Western region started slackening. In spite of full reservoirs a number of States backed down hydro-electric generation. Energy deficits, as high as 12 to 14 per cent, went down to 6 to 8 per cent. Large generating units like Rihand, Badarpur, Kahalgaon, Talcher, thermal units of Damodar Valley Corporation and in the State sector, plants like Bhatinda, Ropar, Kota, Kolaghat and Titagarh had to back down. But the Southern Grid was still having large deficits. In these circumstances, not only political good sense, but also a techno-economic analysis of this situation reveals that this makes sense to transmit power across grids in India. Indeed, would the fixed costs of all these plants be allocated to a larger volume, generation, the cost per unit would decrease in the same tune. Indeed, if the PLF is low, overhead costs per unit would be high. The central Government decided to ask the CEA to work out back-to-back arrangements between public generators (either Central or State) and SEBs. Alagh mentioned that "interestingly, once the technical feasibility was worked out, the economics became a bottleneck; the Eastern Region SEBs as also the Central parastatals with excess capacity, wanted full cost reimbursements". He detailed that some units wanted Rs. 6/kWh of electricity.

Actually, how to analyse this? The public generators, in this scenario, would actually make profit by supplying at a lower tariff, while they make losses by refusing, and effectively loose money. This comes from the fact the fixed costs have to be paid already anyhow, and that supplying the Southern grid would amount to variable costs only to be paid. Then, if paid to them at any tariff superior to the sole variable costs, the generators earn cash-flow that ultimately help them repaying their variable costs, even if the tariff is not at the level of the full-cost.[4]

Alagh stated that "Inefficient rules never make sense. Here were units willing to shut down but would not supply at marginal cost, the first rule for profit making". The lessons from this example are three-fold. First, these (Central included) public undertakings do not focus on costs *versus* benefits. Indeed, the right cost to consider would be the short run

Contd...

4. In effect, the full-cost computes all the expenses, including the cost of depreciation of capital. The economic theory shows that, for provision of goods to be sustainable in the long run, they should be paid at the full-cost (also-called the long run marginal cost). However, it also shows another prescription in a situation of excess production capacity in the short run. In that case, if an extra part of the production can be sold at any tariff superior to the variable production costs (also-called the short run marginal cost, or simply the 'marginal cost'), this is beneficial to the producer.

...*Contd...*

marginal cost, what Alagh and the whole of economic theory calls "the first rule to profit making". Second, they do so because they actually follow procedures. The whole system of CEA administrative techno-economic clearance for tariffs is based on computation of long run expenditures as earlier mentioned. Though in this particular case it would make high economic sense to these public undertakings to get rid of these procedures, they simply cannot. Third, the political discretion has settled the issue, since the Minister, has forced through an "availability" tariff, based on opportunity cost efficiency principles and over 600 MW power was shipped to the South. In this matter the political arbitration has favoured the supply and economic (efficiency) principle, but the important point for us is that these three aspects of this decision-making show the administrative nature of the Central public undertakings.

Source: Interview

As far as the Central Government is concerned, another example, the Programme for Accelerated Generation, Evacuation and Refurbishment (see Box 3.2) shows the structural weakness of an administered system in the long run, whatever the success of well designed measures in the short run. This drawback resides in the fact that *an administered measure has no in-built economic mechanisms that allow good decisions to sustain and survive political changes*.

Box 3.2

The Programme for Accelerated Generation, Evaluation and Refurbishment

The growth of energy production in 1995-96 was only 3.7 per cent. In April 97 it was minus 8 per cent and 2.8 per cent in May, with energy deficits crossing 12 per cent and peaking deficits 18 per cent. The Government of India decided to introduce a programme of administrative monitoring and support to turn around the crises. This consisted of plant level monitoring and support in terms of cash flows, physical input availability and other organisational support like sorting out workers problems. Over a 100 units were monitored and supported from the Ministry of Power. This programme was called PAGER—Programme for Accelerated Generation, Evacuation and Refurbishment. From negative growth the electricity sector, particularly thermal plants, turned around in a dramatic way from June 97 to February 98, but was further given up.

Source: Interview

This programme, based on a "dual arrangement, namely support to incentive based systems and also administrative arrangements", as Alagh names it, may be required in transitional policy periods.

However, they have to integrate in-built economic mechanisms with enough decentralisation of power to be credible and lasting.

These few examples suffice to show that the Central Undertakings, both in their relations with SEBs and with other Central Undertakings (this is true of other public suppliers as well), are parts of a *single administered system*. They are in fact subsumed in a larger political game, where they are used by the Central Government as arguments in negotiations with States. Several former top officials of the Central Ministry of Power confirmed in interviews that the decision to allocate new capacities to States, through NTPC and Powergrid for instance, was highly linked with considerations of political coalitions linked with various other subjects.

3.2. The Proper Use of Analytical Concepts: Cost, Soft Budget Constraint and Property Rights

SEBs are administrations, and not enterprises. This is not neutral as far as their analysis is concerned. Thus, one should be careful in the choice of descriptive and analytical concepts used to describe them. Concepts have their range of validity and are misleading if used beyond this domain. Especially, and in spite of their apparent generality, the concepts of costs and soft budget constraints do not fit to SEBs as we show now. Their use is even particularly misleading. As far as the theory of property rights is concerned, it may be quite useful and operative, but at the express condition to be used only in a precise manner that we will also describe.

3.2.1. Budget and Cost as Non-operative Concepts

Cost and Cost-related Concepts as Non-cognitive Structures and as Irrelevant for Analysis of Public Administration

Let us demonstrate that classical enterprise-related concepts, ultimately based on costs, are not pertinent in analysing the functioning of SEBs in particular, nor public administration in general. Since a description always refers to choices made by the observer, we feel that, properly speaking, a 'description' deserves this name only if it allows an identification of mechanisms at stake, in order to predict, even with limitations, simple issues. The uselessness of cost-related concepts in the SEBs context will be demonstrated in two steps. First, they are not internally used in SEBs and thus do not correspond to a decision mechanism existing in SEBs. Second, even if they can always be reconstructed by an external observer, they have no explanatory effect, no *impact* on the SEB behaviour.

Definition

Related to this, let us specify that we will consider an economic concept as simultaneously referring to:

(i) a set of stylised facts, (in a diversity of reproducible situations, similar events, regularities, can be identified and stylised without loss of quality) and

(ii) a cognitive structure on other stylised facts, that is, a set of relations with other sets of stylised facts (or concepts).

The cognitive structure integrates explanatory and predictive mechanisms, as it specifies how the 'other facts' are integrated into the evolution or the building of the studied fact.

In dynamic, or once the concept is applied to a case, the concept in its generality aims at attributing the whole stylisation and its sets of stylised relations to the identified set of (particular) facts. What makes it relevant, is, through its stylised regularities, its ability to particularly relate (establish relations) with other facts particular to that case. This relation, to be solid, needs being testable.

This definition deserves an illustration. For instance, as far as the concept of cost is considered, on the first level, it encompasses the fact that a set of inputs is used for a the production of an output. That implies that this set (i) is used instead of others (from this comes the notion of higher and lower cost), and (ii) is used for this particular purpose instead of another productive use (linked with the idea of opportunity cost). But on a second level, it also relates to other concepts, such as decision or investment for instance (or assets, tariffs, etc.), in short, a set of actions. That is, the cost is a parameter for an investment, the latter being a set of actions (works, organisation of them, timetable, operation of the results of the works and collection of monetary returns). When the cost explains decisions on investments, tariffs and so on, then only does it become a cognitive structure of decisions.

To be a full economic concept, the cost must absolutely include the manifestation of the links between the costs as facts on the one hand,

and the decisions on the other hand. How does it materialise? First, the cost is an *ex-ante* parameter for decisions and that way links the decision to other facts (sensitivity to costs in decision, whether qualitative or quantitative). Second, it is an *ex-post* information on how the decisions have been taken, through the knowledge of the influence of decisions on costs. Ultimately, the concept of cost relates to and explains decisions only if costs are internally taken into account in decisions, and what is more, taken into account in an explicitly specified way. Otherwise, the cost is not a cognitive structure, and hence not an explanatory concept.

In SEBs, decision-making is based on procedures and paper work, which does not integrate costs, but rather, technical and administrative standards. For example, let us recall the field investigation on transformer repair procedure. When questioning SEB agents about the precise budgetary circuit (who issues orders, paper bonds, whether cash memos exist, who computes the costs, who clears them etc.), neither the question nor its relevance was understood by Field officers, whether they were SDOs, Xens, either from the operation wing, or from the stores. The physical circuit was recalled again in answers. When the meaning of the question was ultimately understood, only accountants without any managerial responsibility were able to answer. This means that the Field officers simply do not focus on these issues, and what is supposed to be a so-called budgetary monitoring by the officers, is only an *ex-post* reporting made by accountants.[5]

Decisions within the SEB do not depend on costs, and simple relations between costs and decisions cannot be derived, even at a global level. For instance, whatever the purchase cost of an item, or whatever the cost of losses in the lines, or whatever the operation costs, the decision will follow a proper path of administrative procedures. Indeed, a reduction in the cost of purchase of transformers will not necessarily lead to initiating more replacement procedures at the Field level. On the contrary, the Field will instead still go on filing demands based on occurrence of burning transformers. At the Headquarters level, in negotiation with the State, the filling up of the Stores will not be based on costs. Conversely, once the *ex-post* external reconstruction of cost is observed, it is impossible to relate it to a single decision, or even to a simple set of well-identified decisions, for

5. And no actual stress is laid on that, as reports are issued late and with a low reliability.

decisions have occurred over several pluri-hierarchical administrative stages, with additional changes. As these changes can concern a different set of technical matters than the one considered at the first step of the decision analysis, the panel is moving, and they cannot be used as a yardstick. Hence the costs cannot serve as a cognitive structure for the decision-making in SEBs. Cost is therefore not a suitable concept for the analysis of SEBs and has no reality in them.

At this juncture, one could argue that, since they can be calculated (by consultants, economists...), therefore they exist. We shall demonstrate that this is not the case. Hirschhausen (1996), Giraud (2000), point out that measuring of a cost is feasible under the condition that a system of prices is available. The cost of supply, for instance, can be computed, in cases where SEBs produce outputs to be paid or at least delivered to a system where a general monetary equivalent exists, or where they use inputs that ultimately have to be paid or at least to be taken from this system. In that case, the cost is an opportunity cost, compared to a different usage of the same inputs.

The results of such a computation have already been discussed in Chapter 1. But the key aspect is to find out, after these calculations are technically made as successions of mathematical operations, if the result can be put in relation with other costs or decisions in the rest of the system. Here it depends on the system one takes into account. If one looks, for instance, at the way the tariffs – more or less reflecting the costs – influence the industrials, then the cost will be related to the investment decisions of some of them, or also to the budgetary constraint of consumers, or even the decision to turn to captive generation. These decisions will depend on the cost of supply, they will be a cognitive structure of some investments of the private sphere in the Indian economy. Through the costs themselves (as a measure of the general equivalent of goods that are consumed), it will also directly affect the available consumption in the remaining areas of the productive activity and have ousting effects. Hence it is a valid internal concept for the Indian economy as a whole. That is, if the system considered is the 'outside' of the SEB. But if one takes a look within SEBs, then every cost calculation is an *a posteriori* reconstruction, and it remains an external criterion for the SEBs themselves, that is, a criterion considered only by observers external to SEBs. In this sense, it does not relate to any opportunity cost within the SEB, because costs are not related to decisions. It loses its predictive power, and even its descriptive power.

For instance, suppose there is a relative increase of prices of the transformers in the Indian market, while labour remains cheap. As extensively discussed already, nobody either in the Field or at the Headquarters, will decide to foster the preventive maintenance in the short run. In the long run, policies depend on anything but this cost (political consideration, availability of plan funds, World Bank support, or proximity between stores and Circle office, etc. but not this cost). In other terms, the assertion "we (the external observers) *think* the costs, therefore they *are* (as effectively in use and as having a predictive power in analysis)" is wrong. *We may think costs, but they do not exist. We are wrong in thinking then, as far as the 'inside' of an SEB is concerned, and these thoughts will tell us nothing workable about the functioning of any particular SEB.*

We shall now demonstrate how none of the cost-related concepts either explain or relate to choices, sales, new works, or to monitoring of the working force.

No proper allocation of budget exists in SEBs. At the same time, budgets are actually not considered in decision-making. Hence, there is a double impossibility of speaking about financial or budgetary constraints. Constraints are rather on physical availability in stores. So, financial aspects are substituted with physical ones and 'budgets' are mere books where one more or less keeps records. The most important criterion for the Headquarters is the administrative constraint relative to the Government's agreement to furnish the necessary equipments to make the system function, that is, to make the SEBs' suppliers continue supplying the inputs (be it under an administered mode). Instead of costs, the main criterion is based on the ability to show that procedures have been respected. The concept of budgetary constraint is thus rendered void in SEBs.

Properly speaking, neither does commercial activity exist in SEBs, nor does the concept of sales relate to something existing in SEBs. Instead, SEBs at most supply a good, but do not sell it, in the sense that they are not really eager to have it paid, nor do they take decisions based on volumes of sales. The activity consists of showing on paper that procedures to supply the good have been followed.

Quite illustratively, as a Power Secretary declared: "Tariff is seen as a taxation by the Government". Again an administrative process.

Likewise, neither investment nor assets exist in SEBs. The concept of 'investment' relates to the concept of benefits. An investment is made in order to get benefits. These benefits are devised so as to be in excess of occurring costs and to allow further budgetary choices. Since these concepts of cost and budgetary choices are ineffective in SEBs, 'new works' occur, but 'investments' are not made. This implies that new works are not made in order to improve the revenue or with regard to other budgetary choices, but are technically made when cleared by an administrative process. The concept of investment has no sense in SEBs, as the expenditures relates to nothing. Illustratively, during interviews, an officer asked, "What do you mean by 'investment'?" In this matter, it is interesting to note that SEBs have been initially set up without assets, only developing and operating technical devices built on State expenditures. So-called 'assets' have in fact been booked in accounts *ex-post*, along with an evolution in the status of SEBs, in 1985. At that time, the Central Ministry of Power took this policy to make them theoretically financially autonomous. As stated by an official, "equity came for external reasons". Equity came on paper externally but did not materialise internally. So, SEBs have no assets, but equipment, and this latter concept is used in the whole book instead of 'asset' which has no relevance to SEBs. Similarly, 'new works' is a descriptive concept where 'investment' is not. The planning process has been sufficiently dealt with for us to be able to conclude straightaway that the concept of planning, in its cost-related implication, is ineffective in SEBs.

To sum up, if one wants to make predictive analysis, or if the target is to change the system or advise on this change, cost-related concepts are inoperative. Then, only two solutions exist. The easiest of the two is to develop an internal comprehension of the system (the analysis), the second is to incorporate into the agents' understanding and behaviour some concepts that have either been unconsidered by the system or external to it (the reform).

Administration *versus* Enterprise: A Reduction in the 'Thinkability' of the Environment

Not only SEBs' agents do not use costs, they are also unable to conceive or to 'think' them. Indeed, the ultimate stage of the organisational structure of SEBs is the very 'unthinkability' of the concept of cost within the system. An analysis of transformer repair again illustrates this.

Let us elaborate further on the concept of cost. In a choice situation, a decision is not taken out of a context, but in comparison with an implicit or explicit reference scenario. Even if the reference is not further specified, the implicit reference scenario can be 'nothing is done' or 'we follow the procedure', or 'business-as-usual'. Then when an action departing from this is considered as a decision, it implies a whole set of consequences (facts) and it compares to a second reference set of facts, which are respectively the consequences of the 'inaction' scenario or the 'follow the procedures' scenario. In that respect, the cost of a decision implies a difference of monetary outcomes resulting from a confrontation of two scenarios. In the case of the operation of transformers, the stringency of the procedures on budget allocation makes only one scenario available. That is, transformers are repaired when damaged and only when damaged. Since no diversion from other budgets is allowed, it is simply impossible to imagine a scenario of *ex-ante* maintenance, or more radically to think of putting new transformers 'in excess' in the short run compared to the reference scenario, in order to avoid overloading, and to limit in the long run the number of defaults. Only the reference scenario is available, due to the absence of internal discretionary power. In interviews, when proposing any change in the decision-making process which would lead to a more efficient situation, the only answer was that additional means were needed, *i.e.* physical ones. This is the only solution available and thinkable if one takes into account internal parameters.

This example shows the very impossibility of thinking from outside the system, that is, the very inconceivability of the concept of costs, even as a set of facts. Let us take a precise example. During the field inquiries, once the accountancy circuit was reconstituted, one of the results was that transformers were ordered at the subdivision level, while accounted from the divisional level budget, raising the question of who (meaning which level) was ultimately 'paying' for the damaged transformer. This question has obviously no sense in the SEB context the way we have deconstructed it, but allows to identify the distance agents have from this system (since, after all, they work in a system where costs do not exist but they live in a world where they do exist). The answer was quite illuminating. Officers dealt with administrative control procedures on legal responsibility and could not at all concentrate on the accountancy. The answer was: "Provided no one is responsible, no one is paying". Neither the Field, nor the Board. This has 'no cost'! Out of this, the techno-economic calculations made in Chapter 1, showing that SEBs may improve their financial situation through profitable actions, only attract internal reactions of incredulity such as: "Additional means are needed". Indeed, the assumptions made are only possible outside the SEB system, the prevailing techno-economic logic is only externally available. The internal one is a *techno-procedural* one. Thus, these profitable measures can be implemented only in a radically altered system.

The question has no internal relevance but can be imagined (thought) by an external observer. It however can no longer be thought by an internal actor. *There comes the hiatus between the organisation on the one hand and both consultants and reformers on the other.* What we shall call *reduction in the thinkability* comes directly from the organisation. Money has, among other properties, the function to be a general equivalent as well as an inter-temporal reserve. In enterprises, the allocation of money enjoys these conditions. Since the concept has no relevance in SEBs, the most profound consequences on these two properties have to be studied. The action no longer relies on costs or monetarily expressed measures, but on physical availability. This shift is two-fold.

First, from a multi-product choice, made available by the fact that money is a general equivalent, the system goes in the reduction of the choice to a single physical product, whose physical availability in stores becomes the limiting factor. If not present, the availability of other physical factors will not help, as the property of substitutability has been lost. Second, the reduction in thinkability is also temporal. The item has to be available in stores at the moment it is required, and one cannot rely on its forthcoming availability nor 'pay' for it if unavailable. It is under this context of double reduction of the spectrum for action, that the action itself stops taking the form of a decision to become a matter of administrative authorisation or sanction. This implies that there is a formal shift from a choice arising between several possibilities, made on a quick time due to the temporal flexibility, to a procedure on a mono-technique which has to be followed on a lasting path, due to the absence of temporal latitude.

The link can be explained by using the theory developed by March (1987), who states that "decisions are not so much made in organisations as they develop within a context of meaning. Organisational information processing seems to be driven less by uncertainty about the consequences of specific decision alternatives than by a lack of clarity about how to talk about the world – what alternatives there are and how they related to stories we think we understand, how we describe history and how we interpret it". SEB agents *describe history and interpret it through procedures and technique, not through costs and technique.*

The result of irrelevance of cost is that the leading concept of normative economics – efficiency – is structurally alien to SEBs. Indeed, since efficiency is the outcome of cost-based comparisons, the concept of decision between alternate uses of existing assets under budgetary constraints, is missing in SEBs. Cost-based efficiency is unthinkable in the system, simply because no related criterion exists.

3.2.2. *The Footprint of 'Indian Socialism'? Soft Budget Constraint and Analysis of the State*

The running of public organisations is widely discussed in the economic literature and even more in the 'transition' and 'reform' literature. In the case of productive organisations especially, models based on soft budget constraint (SBC) and property rights (PR) theories have turned out to be natural candidates for the framework of such exercises, as they aim to explain why and how efficiency standards are not met in public organisations. They also underlie reforms in former so-called 'command economies', and they inspire the reforms in India. However, SBC theory does not apply to, and leads to severe misunderstandings on what an SEB is and does. The core of our argument will be that, since costs are not a valid concept in analysing SEBs, such a description based on opportunism toward cost-based parameters has no relevance for SEBs. PR are then discussed separately.

The Soft Budget Constraint: A Behavioural Concern

The concept of SBC has been mainly developed in order to deal with public productive organisations in socialist countries, and ultimately extended to enterprises – public and private – in mixed economies. Basically, while making their decisions, enterprises and managers know that, *ex-post*, they will have financial facilities accessible through negotiations, generally with the State. Opportunistic enterprises thus integrate this element *ex-ante* in the decision-making, and take inefficient decisions.

Kornai (1986) re-specifies the definition of SBC he gave in his earlier works (Kornai 1979, 1980), to correct misleading interpretations. The term 'budget constraint' (implicitly: 'hard constraint') "refers to a behavioural characteristic of the decision-maker: He is used to covering his expenses from the income generated by selling his output, or by earning returns on his assets". Kornai elaborates that "this is not a book-keeping identity nor a technical relation, but a rational planning postulate". This issue of planning postulate is central: Decisions are made in view of the incomes, by knowing that only the sales or the assets will generate them. Then Kornai is able to define, in contrast, the 'soft budget constraint': "Softening of the budget constraint appears when the strict relationship between expenditure and earnings has been relaxed, because excess expenditure over earnings will be paid by some other institutions, typically by the State". Kornai brings to light four mechanisms of softening of the budget constraint:

(i) 'soft subsidies' appear as soon as they are "negotiable, subject to bargain, lobbying";

(ii) 'soft taxation' as soon as "rules are negotiable, subject to bargaining, political pressure", or if "fulfilment is not strictly enforced";

(iii) 'soft credit' covers situations where "credit contracts are not enforced" or when "postponement, rescheduling" appear; and

(iv) 'soft administrative prices' apply to any "permissive cost plus principle that almost automatically adjusts the price to costs".

When these processes are at play, the results of the organisation no longer depend from its sole decisions. Kornai argues that "the reported and final profitability depends at least as much on the generosity or tight-fistedness of different subsidy-granting or tax-levying authorities, as it depend on success or failure in operation".

However, these processes, even if noticeable in an organisation, are not enough to become explanatory and predictive mechanisms.

Indeed, Kornai specifies that "a further condition of 'softening' is that the decision-maker expects such external financial assistance with high probability and this probability is finally built into his behaviour". But the behaviour matters. In other words, one can find situations where bargain or lobbying exists at some point in the managerial process (as a set of facts), but without relating to the set of decisions. That is, there can exist some cases where the most important part of the decision does not focus on subsidies, and *subsidies are a by-product of administrative decision-making,* as in SEBs to keeps the books clear. Hence, the concept of SBC will not relate to other sets of facts, and may not be operational if not *objectified in behaviour*. Further, Kornai conceptually distinguishes between the goals and the hardness of the budget constraint. He argues that "hardness of the budget constraint is not a synonym for profit maximisation [but the] budget constraint is hard if persistent loss is a matter of life and death [...]. What is really important is the psychological effect of the constraint [...]. Profit maximisation refers to the internal goal-setting of the decision-maker in the firm; the softness-hardness of the budget constraint refers to the external tolerance limit to losses". In other words, SBC does not have implications on goal setting.

Having made the above clarification, it should also be understood that SBC is not equivalent to an absence of focus on benefits and costs. On the contrary, the notion of limit is still pregnant, and there is a focus on it within the organisation. Indeed, "even if it might be softened, the budget constraint has at least some influence on the behaviour of the firm or on other micro-units". More precisely, "the firm can start a project even though it may have the subconscious suspicion that the cost will be more than planned and the revenue less". In his statements, Kornai addresses the fact that some attention is still paid to costs and benefits.

Since the study of managerial behaviour is to be the cornerstone of the present chapter, let us detail here the implications of Kornai's definition. SBC has several behavioural assumptions: First, the decision-maker focuses on expenses and incomes. He might be focusing on other aspects, as he can have different kinds of goals, but the issue of a limit ultimately remains. Indeed, Kornai notes that the external assistance is not automatic, but rather requires active lobbying and reciprocal favours. Second, the important point is that the decision-maker is able to have this focus, *i.e.* he has the discretionary power to integrate these monetary variables into his decisions. Formally, SBC can hence be viewed as an extension of the concept of budgetary constraint. This extension arises by integrating additional sources of income from surrounding institutions, designing new mechanisms, but with remaining opportunistic behavioural assumptions. Formally, the decision-maker under SBC has the same behaviour as the one under 'hard' budget constraint, based on substantive rationality.

How is SBC Theory Generally Used to Analyse SEBs?

An analysis of SEBs as public enterprises under SBC (especially under soft subsidy and soft credit) underlies current reforms. For instance, Regulatory Commissions are partly being set-up to 'harden the budget constraint'. Indeed, advocates of SBC theory interpret the facts differently from this book. They underline that the Field has the discretionary power over the budget, since it can make its costs and expenses accepted. If needs are above the initial budget, additional funds will be provided, driven by operational constraints. Moreover, advocates of SBC theory assume that, in an actual system of scarcity, agents have incentives to use the budget as long as equipments are available. The budget constraint would be considered as soft in this sense.

The analysis of SEBs as under SBC takes place within a whole corpus of economic literature applying this concept to public sectors over the world. For instance, Sun (1999), dealing with 'State-Owned Enterprises' (SOEs) in China, thinks that: "Soft budget constraints are a result of centralised ownership of key economic resources, incomplete information and agency opportunism". On practical implementation he offers however a slightly different view: "unconditional government support (allows) enterprise management to pursue multiple objectives from which (it) derives utility". He details that, in a context of "negotiated targets", a minimal required level of profits as well as a maximisation of workers welfare would be two plausible goals in 'SOEs' in China.

Soft Budget Constraint as Inappropriate in Describing SEBs

We however maintain that reasoning on SBC is not appropriate. This concept does not apply in describing the running of SEBs. It does not serve this purpose by offering either explanatory or predictive mechanisms through a cognitive structure on various decisions. Indeed, as far as *internal* relations between the Headquarters and Field are concerned, it has been clearly demonstrated that the concepts of costs or benefits are not part of the action of the Field officers. Rather than expecting help, they even face a lack and sometimes a quasi-absence of material support from the Headquarters. But beyond this feeling, *no initiation of any paper work, and hence no result of it, is driven by considerations of expected financial help*. They are rather driven by technical constraints that are identified in a rigid framework led by techno-administrative procedures. Internally, SEBs does not follow the behavioural assumptions rooted in the concept of soft budget constraint. Beyond this aspect, the categories on which soft budget constraint relates are not present in SEBs. The phenomenon of financial help might be at stake, but rather as a by-product of procedures. It does not constitute a cognitive structure to any characteristic of the system.

The question of soft budget constraint *between a State Government and a SEB* is more subtle. Indeed, a SEB presents, at least formally, separate accounts, and some meetings occur on loan plus subsidy matters[6]. But, as the subsidy fixation procedure has been studied, it appears at this stage that the frontier between SEBs and States is at least permeable, as SEBs *de facto* do not have the granted financial autonomy on borrowing, payments or incomes. How then are they dealing with the subject?

One shall first notice that the models of SBC developed since Kornai presuppose a substantive rationality towards profit which, even though it is slightly relaxed as compared to the strict hypothesis, still implies an assumption of discretionary power allowing to look for profit or at least for cost-related concepts. Such a discretionary power of the Headquarters on the running of the SEBs is missing due to executive instructions and the paper work system. So, the Headquarters are not able to design strategies behaviourally based on anticipation of subsidies. The functioning of SEBs cannot be described by that. First, operations and maintenance are technically driven. They are initiated when field problems arise. Then, actual action occurs

6. As loans and subsidies are not formally separated in these meetings, they will be treated as a whole, and the discussion of concepts of soft subsidies and soft credit gathered in one of soft budget constraint.

subject to availability of material. It can even be said that the operation appears as a 'natural phenomenon', mainly independent of any active will in the SEB.

As far as new works are concerned, they result from negotiations between the State and the SEB. However, they are initiated on some repetitive planning procedures, with final arbitrage mainly left to the political level. In this sense, they are quite external to SEBs, and hence not subject to any behavioural opportunism of the Board. Lastly, as seen in Chapter 2, the procedure of subsidy fixation is only a by-product of the supply activity, and does not relate to other categories in the SEBs. The concept of SBC does not apply to SEBs-State relationships. Booked subsidies are only a way to (sometimes partly) record an assistance that is ultimately physical, simply because it is physically driven. Like other cost-related concepts, subsidies have no analytical substance in SEBs.

To sum up, soft budget constraint theory cannot be used to analyse SEBs since (i) there is no substantive control over these aspects and (ii) the consideration is not on the level of subsidies (supposed to be negotiable), or the level of the constraint, but simply of a total irrelevance of the concept, both in internal relation between the Field and the Headquarters and between the Headquarters and the State.

3.2.3. A Clearer Explanation: Theory of Property Rights and Analysis of the State

An Introduction: Property Rights Matter

Demsetz (1967) underlined the predominant economic role of the allocation of property rights, that is, the question of who is the bearer of property rights. His article deals with situations where several users have access to a common resource, and the financial consequences are either faced by all of them or by some specific persons. In such cases, overuse of the common good might arise. In the case of imperfect contracts or of inability to perfectly contract out, Coase-style[7] re-negotiations are unreachable. Demsetz provides the example of

7. Based on the first Coase theorem, which specifies that, in absence of cost to transact (transaction costs), the socially optimal use of a resource can be realised whatever the ownership on the resource, through appropriate financial transfers. When contracting is costly, the optimum is no longer reachable (this is the second Coase theorem) and the outcome is sub-optimal, hence ownership matters as far as social utility is concerned, see Coase (1960).

preventing the building of a dam, in the absence of defined property rights for the local residents.

Negotiations with an engineer/enterprise carrying out the project may succeed in stopping it. However, another engineer/enterprise may follow, and negotiation has to occur again. Likewise, many can successively come and the negotiations turn out to be costly. In this situation, Demsetz argues that, over time, property rights tend to emerge (either for the local residents, for the public, or for a private party). For Demsetz (1967), property rights are the rights to exclude others from the use of the resource, as "an owner expects the community to prevent others from interfering with his actions". In Demsetz's paper, property rights go along with the specification of the financial impacts of actions, as "property rights specify how persons may be benefited and harmed, and, therefore, who must pay whom to modify the actions taken by the persons". Furthering this line of analysis, property rights theories and models have developed, which focus carefully on the impact of the allocation of rights on efficiency. In his paper he does not further analytically develop the concept.

More Complex than the Naïve 'privatisation': Cash Flow Rights and Various Types of Control Rights

Analytical improvement of the concept of property rights has led to the clarification of the distinction between control rights, which are the rights to take decisions, and cash flow rights, which are the rights to appropriate the financial results linked to the decisions (as well as the obligation to face the financial losses), which Demsetz does not disentangle in his paper. From this conceptual improvement, the property rights theory focuses on the respective incentives of several parties involved in decision-making. It derives the respective incentives from various allocations to the parties of the rights to appropriate cash flows and the rights of control over decision-making.

The idea is simple: if the agent who takes the decision (the holder of the control rights) is not the owner of the cash flow rights, he has less incentives to perform. But here the results again depend on the possibility to *ex-ante* contract out on the outcomes of the use of the resource. If feasible, as in the first Coase theorem, allocation of property rights does not matter: incentive mechanisms can be put in place and, in any case, *ex-post*, a more efficient share in the outcomes can be reached through (non-costly) transactions.

Property rights theory really finds its substance from a (real) world of 'incompleteness of contracts'. That is, in situations when it is impossible to imagine and anticipate all the possible outcomes of a decision. In that case, no *ex-ante* contract or agreement between the parties can possibly take everything into account. In these situations, unexpected outcomes may be *ex-post* expropriated by one party at the expense of the other. Rational agents of course anticipate this *ex-ante* which leads to a distortion in the decision-making, for instance in investment, compared with the first-best outcome, and hence to inefficiencies (Grossman & Hart, 1986). The normative prescription of property rights theory becomes to vest both rights with the same agents as much as possible. This is an incentive-based mechanism. Of course, the notion of contract has to be understood in a broad sense: within an organisation, many rules which set powers and their limits actually define control rights.

For this will turn out to be central in analysis, let us specify the mechanisms at stake, and show that the recent developments of property rights theory have actually set the focus on control rights. Grossman & Hart (1986) and Hart & Moore (1990) further separate control rights into 'specific' and 'residual' rights of control. The former are the rights in decision-making that are specified in the contracts. The latter are all the remaining rights on decision-making that have not been specifically written in the contract, because of incompleteness of contracts, or *ex-ante* uncontractibility.

Evolving on this, Grossman & Hart actually define ownership as the purchase of residual rights of control. They give the example of a power-generating plant using the coal produced by an adjacent mine. *Ex-ante*, all the states of nature cannot be known. That is, in this case, many variables that might turn out to be important in the future relationship, cannot be anticipated or listed. For example, the rate of ashes in the coal supplied by the mine to the plant may happen *ex-post* to be a key issue in the relation (or may not, this is unknown *ex-ante*), e.g. because it is high in some parts of the mine, for instance. Grossman & Hart show that the allocation of residual control rights (that is, who will be able to impose technological adaptation to the other) matters on the *ex-post* outcome. Indeed, in case residual control rights were attributed to the plant, the latter would be tempted to impose on the mine to select the parts it exploits. In the other type of allocation, the mine would require the plant to modify its process to accept the ashes. In both cases, anticipating this, the non-controlling party will under-invest and the other one over-invest.[8]

In the above model, Grossman & Hart "do not distinguish between ownership and control and virtually define ownership as the power to exercise control". More specifically, they do not focus on the increase of cash flow rights, but rather on the articulation between them and the allocation of residual control. Clearly, the issue of efficiency is subtle, in the sense that *ex-post* productive efficiency will be reached whatever the allocation of rights, due to the availability of renegotiation. But it is the *ex-ante* cost-efficiency that is not granted. Indeed, they argue that "through their influence on the distribution of *ex-post* surplus, ownership rights will affect investment decisions [...] as each ownership structure will lead to a different distortion in *ex-ante* investment".[9] The first-best may not be reached; property rights matter.

They specify that their model departs from the Coasian way of renegotiation, as it is a two-step model in which the incompleteness of property rights makes *ex-ante* bargaining impossible. Indeed, property rights are incomplete in the sense that uncontractibility impedes the specification of all the relationships in the form of specific rights. Residual rights remain. Hart & Moore (1990) concur with this line of analysis, as they "specialise the meaning of residual control rights relative to Grossman & Hart [by supposing] that the sole right possessed by the owner of an asset is his ability to exclude others from the use of that asset". In this case, they adopt a similar approach and conclude that "a person will have more control over an asset's workers if he employs them [...] than if he has an arm's-length contract with another employer of the workers".

8. This arises because, in the model, the choices in the investments are done simultaneously and non-cooperatively, and hence each party puts weight on the non-cooperative outcome in designing the Nash equilibrium of the game theory.

9. This means that *ex-post* they will both organise their production the best feasible way. They may even, if negotiation is free of cost, do the appropriate investment to make the two processes match, for instance the mine will adjust if it is less costly, even if it is the residual rights controller and could force the plant to do it at a higher price. In that latter case, there is a saving and the plant just pays a financial transfer to the mine to balance this. That way, the *ex-post* efficiency has been reached. However, it can be imagined that, *ex-ante* to the initial investment, had the plant been the holder of residual rights, it might have invested in a different technique (for instance even more coal-specific but with higher efficiency on this given coal) investment, then knowing that, if any unknown circumstance arises, it would be able ether to again negotiate if at mutual benefit, or in last recourse, to force the mine to adjust. Not being in such a position, it actually *ex-ante* decides not to go for this specific investment. The control rights allocation changes the decision, thus the outcome. This is in this way that *ex-ante* efficiency is not granted.

For convenience of analysis, let us split the PR models that deal with public organisations or with enterprises under public regulation into two subsets. One subset, in the line opened by Grossman & Hart, relates to the influence of control rights on enterprises under an hypothesis of full cash flow expropriation. Unless otherwise stated, PR will refer to this approach. The second subset relates to models described by some theoricians of the transition, who inspire the World Bank supported reforms. Shleifer and Vishny (S&V) describe the action of politicians vested with control rights, under various allocations of cash flow rights. Shleifer (1995) studies the command economies, for which he argues that political interference leads profit to be de-linked from productive decisions. The mechanism he points out, is the potential *ex-post* expropriation of profit by the State. Indeed, dealing with Socialist Eastern Europe, he argues that "control structures give politicians enormous control rights over all assets, including private assets that are politically controlled through regulation".

Shleifer refers, among others, to Kornai (1992) and Boycko, Shleifer & Vishny (1994). This mechanism integrates a behavioural assumption: Managers in production units anticipate this *ex-post* expropriation and act accordingly *ex-ante*. Shleifer details that "if a complete contract cannot be written in advance between the bureaucrat and the entrepreneur, the bureaucrat can expropriate profits from a business by threatening to shut it down; anticipating expropriation by bureaucrats, entrepreneurs under-invest". *Here the root cause of under-investment is the fear of expropriation. This is the opposite of the SBC analysis, which focuses on the anticipation of expected subsidies.*

Property Rights (1): Modelling the Decision-making Process with Cash Flow Expropriation

In the case of China, Oi (1994) and Jiahua & Yingyi (1998) base their analysis on control rights. Oi argues that, contrary to the classical view, control rights in township village enterprises (TVE) in China are well defined between the local party bosses, the township party bosses and the central government. Also, according to his investigations, well-defined agreements on profit repatriation exist, that explain the relative success of TVEs.

Jiahua & Yingyi (1998) develop a formal model, comparing the effects of various allocations of control rights. They consider the managers, the local government and the central government. Central government focuses on profits, local government on profit plus the local goods it is able to provide (in the model, provision of local goods improves the revenue from projects), and the enterprise on its profit (hence knowing that, under certain conditions, the local government can give it some local goods if it is generating an income). The key hypothesis is that both levels of government fully expropriate "observable" benefits at the end of the game. Indeed, hidden profits exist in the model; they are the "unobservable profits", appropriated by the local managers. Accordingly, their definition states that ownership "provides the owner with the control rights over an enterprise's books and accounts, thereby allowing him to hide and receive unobservable parts of the revenue".

This model illustrates (i) the mechanisms through which inefficiencies arise as a result of allocation of ownership, and (ii) the focus on profit by agents, in the PR approach. Let us recall here that the alternative forms of ownership refer to ownership on control rights only, as the cash flow rights remain the same whatever the structure, *i.e.* full appropriation by the national government of all the observable profit.

Property Rights (2): Shleifer & Vishny Models: Bargaining Over Political Interference

Shleifer & Vishny (1994), as well as Boycko, Shleifer & Vishny (1996), deal with the impact of the allocation of control rights and cash flow rights, on what Shleifer (1995) refers to as the 'Grossman-Hart' style renegotiation. Directing the analysis to cash flow rights partly involves engaging with and discussing privatisation, that is, focusing on the issue of reforms.

Assuming that politicians' utility functions can be expressed monetarily, and with the possibility of bargaining between politicians and enterprises, Shleifer & Vishny compare the effects of various allocations of control rights. Bargaining can take place either through bribes, when politicians have the control rights, or through subsidies, practised when enterprises have the control rights. The two models can be used to make some interesting comparisons. In the model, politicians are not directly concerned with treasury expenditures, whereas they integrate a part of the cost in their utility function, as clarified in Boycko, Shleifer & Vishny (1996). Earlier approaches to political interference in corporate decision-making, e.g. Dewatripont & Maskin (1995), focused on information asymmetries. Shleifer &

Vishny (1994), conversely, believe that focusing on allocation of control rights provides "several new and empirically valid insights".

How is PR Theory Generally Used to Analyse SEBs?

It has been seen that, if savings are realised in SEBs, the budget cannot be retained by the Field for another use. On the contrary, if the operation is improved through better equipment and/or hard work, leading to minimised needs the following year, then a minimised budget will be provided. Further, if operational standards improve in one Circle or Division, then other Circles or Divisions will be – all things being equal – prioritised. Improvements shown by one Circle/Division will then in a sense benefit the other Circles/Divisions. This means that the Field has no actual property rights on its budget: If it saves on the budget, neither does it receive the cash for the following year, nor can it use it for a different purpose. Since property rights, are not in the hands of the Field, advocates of PR theory incorrectly assume them as therefore being in the hands of the Headquarters, which monitor the budget. Then, the classical PR analysis is applied: the Field is described as having no incentive to save, since by doing so, each saving unit is in fact ultimately benefiting other units. This supposedly implies that:

- the SDO has no incentive to cut costs regarding the divisional budget; should he save, another SDO would enjoy the material,
- as cost charged is unknown and ultimately does not depend on the decision to replace but on administered costs, decisions cannot lie on techno-economic considerations. The property right-type of analysis of SEBs therefore assumes that property rights are wrongly allocated in them, as the decision – the control right – rests at the SDO level, while the cash flow right resides at the Xen level within a one-year budget and at the Headquarters as far as the multi-year financial implications are concerned.

Conversely, if one looks now at the revenue side, there is a direct transfer of the cash collected to the Headquarters. There is thus, according to PR theory, no incentive at all for the Field to improve the revenue. Since budget allocation is disconnected from the revenue realisation, this de-links the commercial behaviour from the investment capacity at the Field level. Hence, either due to a wrong allocation of property rights or to the soft budget constraint, nobody in the Field actively cares about the cost, and the financial constraint remains the headache of the unhappy few in the Headquarters. Let us show that this analysis is partially wrong: true, the Field has no PR, but this does not imply that in return the Headquarters or anybody else does. Further, it suggests that "incentives" can easily be put in place, which is wrong (see Part III of the book). Let us rather show that property rights actually do not even exist in SEBs. *This is not a mere casuistic debate, but a core issue. In that context, 'incentives' cannot be compatible with procedure, and, as we will see later, 'privatisation' loses its meaning.*

An Alternative Explanation:
Property Rights as Non-existent in SEBs

Let us here show that the question in SEBs is not so much of the mis-allocation of property rights as that of their very non-existence. Decisions are substituted with processes. This leads to a non-allocation of control rights. Indeed, (i) the separation between technical and administrative sanction, and (ii) the need for further procedure on call for proposals and tender notices, tend to make diffuse what could resemble control rights. Beyond, there are administrative delays, of which unpredictable sorting out does not guarantee if and when paperwork will materialise into action. This fact leads to the non-existence of specific control rights.

As far as residual rights of control are concerned, can it be considered that they recover informal practices such as executive instructions or informal Field agents' discretionary power? One shall first recall that executive instructions are by nature limited in time and in space, due to the paper work system, combined with the absence of integrated information. Therefore, they could at best constitute a very limited form of residual control. But again, the action can easily be counterbalanced by another politician, even promptly afterwards. For this reason, this can hardly be considered an actual residual right of control.

Where are then the PR to be found? For balance in the analysis, one shall discuss the systemic potentiality of executive instruction, which has previously been considered a structuring fact. Does it constitute a control right for the state? That is to say, does the systemic potentiality of executive instructions turn them into a residual right of control? The answer here is again negative. Action might not be taken because of that – and in this sense it is structuring – but no politician or even less the Government can use executive instructions as a guaranteed way to take action. Indeed, the outcomes of such actions would always remain local, the misreporting of agents could hide the non-application, or, simply, any other counter-executive instructions may occur.

Then, could it be argued that agents of the SEBs, using either their informal discretionary power to cover up facts while reporting, or their key position on access to users, abuse it as a residual right of control? Let us show that even considering this, it does not equate to an actual residual right of control. Indeed, their potential action is in essence very limited and fragmented, but beyond this, their power does not go up to obtaining outputs from the system in a guaranteed manner. That is, their action towards the system or towards the users is essentially negative – hiding, refusing or delaying their work –, but they can hardly direct the system to provide positive impacts for them or the users. In that, they can for sure favour some of them in furnishing materials and technical support on time – the part of corruption that corresponds to being paid for the normal job –, but on a necessarily limited manner, due to the system. For instance, they can provide materials with the same limitations of current physical availability in stocks. The demonetisation – *i.e.* the absence of a full-fledged money used as a general equivalent – of the Board hence leads to the very limitation of residual rights of control for the SEB agents.[10]

Ultimately, in granting residual rights of control, the presence of an informal discretionary power does not compensate for the absence of the formal one. What matters in *de jure* discretionary power is the possibility of monitoring and enforcing decisions. In SEBs, the *de facto* discretion allows only passive resistance through paper work, or some corruption. These cannot be monitored according to a cost *versus* benefit criterion, or according to any other monetary, or even technical criteria. Indeed, assessing what one will receive always depends, in an unpredictable way, on the administrative system as a whole.

Cash flow rights similarly remain undefined. Within the SEB hierarchy, the budgetary system is not fixed well enough, as *ex-post* renegotiations can always occur, and as budgets are not actually granted. Then, if there was an internal cash flow, its destination would

10. Unsurprisingly, the limitation of Field power is one major bottleneck for introduction of cash, as interviews show.

not be assigned to fixed parties and internal rights on cash flow would not exist. Beyond the non-existence of cash flow rights, it can even be said that cash flow itself does not properly exist. As most of the relations between the Field and the Headquarters are treated in absence of money (i.e., an equivalent and an inter-temporal reserve), these relations are rather based on physical and local allocations of materials, under a regime of administrative sanction. In essence, no party can be the owner of a kind of administrative sanction. This means that no party can have the guarantee to obtain even a very limited kind of sanction, apart from properly allocating it as a given discretionary power, hence moving out from the administrative structure itself. If one looks now at State-SEB relations, cash flow rights are also undefined. In this case, cash flows do exist; the cash flows into or out of the system. But the rights on them are not fixed, as *ex-post* renegotiation occurs, because the order of paying the suppliers is not fixed either, and because the analysis of subsidies allocation has generally shown that the financial outcomes are supply-dependent.

Hence, property rights do not exist in SEBs. If one follows the example of the transformer repair procedure, the techno-economic paradox can be better explained. The 'classical analysis' is that the Field controls the functioning of transformers and the Headquarters have the cash flow rights. This explanation is wrong. Actually, first, no 'decision' is taken at any level, including the SDO, who only initiates paperwork. Second, whatever the mathematical calculations that are made, no 'cost' is computed as this concept is not valid in SEBs. Thus the issue of ineffective allocation of property rights is simply misleading. By now using concepts internal to the SEB, what happens is that the question does not occur in this substantively cost-related manner, but rather procedurally and on technical concerns. Property rights cannot help in understanding the way SEBs are run. The question of their usefulness in the reform process will be detailed accordingly later. Suffice it to say here that one consequence of their lack of explanatory power is that, where property rights where to be actually established and 'well set up', for instance by fixing actual budgets and decentralising them, the behaviour of the agents would still be tuned towards following the remaining procedures in the absence of change in general evaluation criteria. The concept of property rights cannot serve as a cognitive structure of the Indian administration.

Let us sum up here by saying that, as far as property rights are concerned, they are not wrongly allocated, but they simply do not exist.[11] Indeed, there is no fixed discretionary power, hence there are no control rights at any level, including the State Government. As Grossman & Hart (1986) define ownership as the power to exercise control on residual rights, property rights are missing in SEBs. Cash flow rights are not really defined even for the Government, as the suppliers remain to be paid and the focus is not explicitly made on this aspect. Besides, obviously, the Shleifer & Vishny (1994 & 1996) models are even more radically irrelevant, as they assume a well-established allocation of rights, with implementing power, for two distinct entities that are the politicians – the State – and the enterprise, which is not at all the case here.

Ultimately, in their analysis of public organisations, SBC, PR, and S&V deal with the relationships between an enterprise and the State. They cannot fit for an administration.[12] Ultimately, all these theories integrate at least implicit behavioural assumptions. Indeed, agents are

---

11. In the demonstration, an important issue in analysing public organisation lies in the definition itself of property rights. Shleifer replies to the classical argument that they are not defined in "command economies". For instance, in studying the shareholding in Russia, Shleifer (1995) refuses to consider that property rights are missing as the shareholders have no control rights, which is the 'common pool approach'. Instead, and furthering the arguments of Hart & Moore (1990) on human assets, he suggests that "a more fruitful way [...] is to view control rights over [...] assets as belonging to the managers". According to him, there is a "joint ownership", with a veto right for each agent. Hence, property rights analysis, by specialising the definition of ownership, allocates property rights in public organisations. The argument raised by Shleifer finds a fitting reply here. This argument has already been partially discussed in the previous analysis, as far as a kind of residual control has been searched for in the Field agents' informal discretion. But it has been said that this veto helps only partially in understanding the actions taken. Indeed, it conveys a negative explanation as well as a negative power, that is accepted as a concept to analyse SEBs only if it relates to a cognitive structure on how the decisions will be taken according to the allocation of property rights. But all the descriptions of SEBs have primarily shown that, even if there is a systemic decision-making, there is no allocation of the decision-making power. And second, none of this is ultimately related to any cost. No 'manager' controls any 'asset' of any sort, and decisions arise through materialisation of the paperwork. The idea of Shleifer, however tempting it might look, does not fit with SEBs.
12. In addition, models of SBC and PR are directly applicable to intra-enterprise relations, between different hierarchical levels. SBC, PR, and S&V all consider the same stylised fact: the de-linking of profit from productive decisions, but by putting different stresses on alternative mechanisms in enterprise-State relations. *Ex-post* subsidies, *ex-post* expropriation, and *ex-ante* subsidies respectively depict situations where the State is held up by the enterprise (SBC), the enterprise is held up by the State (PR), or both play at par (S&V). In spite of the differences in the explanatory mechanisms for de-linking profit from decisions, some strong similarities emerge. Indeed, when looking at the objectives and criteria of agents, it appears that profit always emerges as the main explanatory variable – possibly under a form adapted to the model, i.e. reported profit, hidden profit, or political profit.

not only aware of the mechanism (qualitatively but also quantitatively, since they know the limits they can extract from each other), but they also integrate them in their behaviour, up to the point of relying on them to make their decisions.

3.3. Conclusion

The previous Chapter identified the organisational characteristics of SEBs, and it showed that they lead to inefficiency, by making it rational to rely on procedures articulated on a paperwork system rather than on an inaccessible computation of costs and benefits. The current Chapter has shown how all these characteristics are actually consistently derived from the administrative nature of SEBs, whose functioning is based on external discretionary power of the Government and multiple heterogeneous objectives. The administered system derives from a vision of the electric sector as a mono-technique, which would fit to an electric sector to be built, but faces irreducible problems in a mature power industry. In this context, not only are costs *not* used in the functioning of SEBs, but also they are *not* a relevant analytical concept, since they do not relate to decision, neither as an *ex-ante* parameter, nor even as an *ex-post* indicator. Similarly, all cost-related concepts are irrelevant while describing and understanding SEBs. Further, Soft Budget Constraint theory fails to analyse the SEBs in their positive work. The issue of property rights theory in SEBs is particular, since neither specific nor residual rights of control exist, in spite of the existence of some limited informal discretionary power which does not grant such a control right. Also, cash flow rights do not exist as an entity, since they are not even considered separately from the technique. Hence, property rights do not exist in SEBs. It is not so much a case of inefficient allocation as one of sheer non-existence. SEBs are not inefficient just because they know they will get subsidies nor on the contrary because they fear they will not get them, but for a much more structural reason: as administrations they are not primarily meant to be cost-effective.

More systematically, all these theories have their ground in substantive rationality, where SEBs rely on procedural rationality. However, a clue to what could be missing in the above analysis is given by Williamson (1999) who, quoting March & Simon (1958), points out that "the tendency of members of an organisational unit to evaluate action only in terms of sub-goals [can result in] conflict with the goal of the larger organisation". Williamson adds that "the conflicts to which they refer are entirely of an instrumental (as against strategic) kind: Individuals and groups are narrowly focused on the tasks to which they have been assigned". Procedural rationality is the first leading cause of decision-making under several circumstances that occur in SEBs, and the attention paid to profit by Soft Budget Constraint, or the most common forms of the Property Rights theories, is not only overrated, but truly misleading in understanding SEBs at (paper) work. Similarly, analysis of reforms cannot remain unaltered by this radical inadequacy of the classical analytical tools to SEBs.

Part II

Reforms and 'Enterprisation' of SEBs

4

They Have Changed the Name, but the Shop Remains

The Reforms of SEBs: 1991 to 2003

The reform of SEBs has become a subject of public debate in India. Several government reports, like that of the Ministry of Power (1993), Mohan (1997), Government of India (1998), Quraishi (1998), and Ministry of Power (2000), are among the major ones to point out the need for reforms. Taking stock of the failure of limited reform, a consistent reform scheme has been promoted by the Government of India, with the support of development agencies, in the forefront of which stands the World Bank. This scheme is called structural reforms, since it goes beyond the earlier cosmetic or limited attempts. The aim of this Chapter is to discuss the problems which are expected to be solved through each specific goal of the structural reforms, namely, corporatisation, de-integration, and the setting up of Regulatory Commissions. The Chapter discusses, in particular, the effects of these reforms on the administrative nature of SEBs. It shows that the so-called structural reforms have not led to the internalisation of a cost-based decision-making in SEBs. In addition, it demonstrates that, they have not radically altered the administrative nature of the system. The Chapter actually adopts a stand on the reforms promoted by the Government of India till 2003.

These (reform) have crystallised recently into a new Electricity Act (2003), which extends the logic of the 'structural reforms' and puts them in a competition-oriented framework. We discuss the Act in Chapter 5, within the context of the debate it generates today and with the help of the concept of 'enterprisation' which we introduce in next chapter. Beyond the structural reforms, the World Bank also argues that some degree of privatisation is required. The Bank makes it a condition for its financial support. For the World Bank, the structural reforms are hence a transition phase to usher in privatisation. The analysis of the recourse to the private sector is left for Part III of the book, which provides a broader framework to do so. So is the scenario for the World Bank reforms, and similarly for the recommendation of the N.K. Singh Committee Report (2004).

4.1. The Pointlessness of Corrective Actions: The Cosmetic Era, 1991-96

We have described the system as producing a self-enforcing rationality. From within, such a system will not spontaneously evolve towards a focus on efficiency, even limited.

4.1.1. Opening of Generation to the Private Sector

In the context of economic liberalisation,[1] the Government of India from 1991-92 onward has allowed private investment in generation, in order to bridge the so-called investment gap in the power sector. The principal modalities have been to authorise foreign investments up to 100 per cent of each project; and to give imports authorisations. This was subject to two conditions: the promoter of the project must engage to a minimal level of 11 per cent of the total cost – and at least 60 per cent of the investment should come from financial sources other than Indian financial institutions (See Government of India, 1995 and Chandran, 1998). Under these conditions, taxation is to be relaxed over the first five years, and then discounted by 30 per cent over the following five. A 16 per cent return on assets is granted, subject to a 68.5 per cent achievement in Plant Load Factor (PLF).

According to Mohan (1997), 58 per cent of the power sector investment had been expected to come from the private sector between 1995 and 2005. At the outset, it has been done under bilateral agreements between independent power producers (IPPs) and State Governments, through contracts arranged like Memorandum of Understanding (MoU). In this scheme, SEBs were to be the clients of the IPPs. This bilateral MoU route has led to a lack of transparency, bribing and administrative inefficiencies. A competitive bidding process has then been adopted, and is still in use today. However, purchase tariffs based on a cost plus system (repayment of operation costs, plus a benefit equating 16 per cent of the invested capital) are

1. Ensuing the 1991 payments crises. However, a vivid debate on private sector participation had already taken place in India over the 80's

not credible, given the financial position of SEBs that are unable to face the financial implications of such a tariff structure (the case of the ENRON project in Maharashtra, when the company withdrew from its engagements, exemplify this).

During the Eighth Plan, only 2.7 GW have been installed by private companies, not quite matching the 20 GW gap initially envisaged, as reported by the Planning Commission (1997). The Ninth Plan has also not proved more successful. Indeed, the Planning Commission (2001) indicates that "capacity addition in the private is expected to be 6,735 MW, which is about 38.3 per cent of the target of 17,589 MW". In other words, from 2.7 GW in the Eighth Plan, to 6.7 GW in the Ninth Plan, the private sector has broadly confirmed its lack of interest. Worse, the public sector has declined in-between and, for the Ninth Plan, over the total target of 40 GW addition, only 52 per cent is likely to be reached. Most of the projects are still under feasibility studies, and face difficulties in closing their financing. All have been substantially delayed.[2]

In order to balance the financial risk incurred by private investors, some financial tools have been designed, like the development of escrow accounts and credit letters. Escrow accounts are bank accounts opened by SEBs, in which the payments of major clients are directly credited. These accounts are dedicated to paying the generators. Credit letters are issued by banks to guarantee the debts of the SEBs, ultimately under State Government guarantee. Such tools, even if they are useful, do not solve the economic fundamentals of the power sector. Without reforms, global resources remain limited. Therefore, they do not solve the global problem of the SEBs' lack of creditworthiness. Worse, SEBs are shunted through the escrow account mechanism.

They have primarily benefited public undertakings like NTPC, whose officials have reported in interviews that the rate of payment through these mechanisms has reached 93 per cent in 1997-98, as compared to a one-time payment previously limited to 40 per cent in 1992-93. This has ultimately materialised into a tool of administrative monitoring of Centre-State financial relations.

The logic of this reform was to bring private money in generation which, Chapter 1 has shown, is not the main issue. Second, it was

2. See, for instance, French Embassy in India (1998).

intended to 'harden the budget constraint', implicitly assuming that SEBs are operating under an SBC mechanism. However, putting such a constraint in a situation where the Headquarters, even if they want to focus on budgets, are not able to enforce policies (due to paper work), will not solve the problem. Further, as long as the system remains, no budget constraint can be decentralised to the field. Anticipating this, investors do not commit to projects of new plants.

The simplistic and naive mindset at that time had been that, if SEBs generate power, the problems of the power sector would be solved. The more opportunistic political consensus may have been that recourse to private investment under remaining unsustainable scenario could anyway help in (i) getting World Bank loans, (ii) pushing the capital cost burden away for a lesgislative tenure or more, (iii) allowing pocketing some part of the contracts' money. This had thus to be complemented by measures which would ensure profitability for the investors; the 'counter-guarantee principle'. This idea was followed during all the early nineties. In terms of paradigm, the surprising fact is that, though the economic reform of 1991 stated explicitly that public sector planning of the electricity sector had failed, the initial mindset was still embedded in the former paradigm. This paradigm is the centrally planned 'mono-technique' perception of the power sector, described in the first part of the book (also, refer to Ruet, 2001a). Thus, though it had the merit to question the system, the policy was a resounding failure since the additions to capacity in the Eighth Plan and the Ninth Plan have been the lowest in contemporary history. This has been so because the institutional system for private investment was just not created, which is now accepted by the architect of reforms, Manmohan Singh. As Y.K. Alagh stated in interviews, "a part of the problem had been very poor understanding of the meshing of technology and economics and organisations at the lowest levels of the system". Put in other terms, the impact of the organisation-derived procedural rationality on constraining the technical choices and thus the cost-inefficiency of decisions had been unaddressed. This is only in 1995, Alagh recalls, that "the impractical idea of guaranteeing tariffs for private investments was given up" and that "draft power purchase agreements and tariff schedules were issued both for thermal and hydro-electric projects". Similarly, "a procedure was laid out for international competitive bidding and for private investment in rehabilitation and maintenance". As coming sub-sections detail the next step (the turning point being the Chief Ministers Conference at Jaipur in 1996), of 'structural reforms', has emerged and developed from 1998 to 2003, to be generalised by the Electricity Act (2003).

4.1.2. Incentive Schemes in SEBs

Incentive schemes have been put in place in some SEBs, to improve the cash collection. Also some more classical administrative measures had been put in place. For instance, in order to reduce transformer damage, a target of 18 per cent has been set in Haryana[3]; any additional progress above this target would be shared at a 5 per cent level with the Division agents. Similar patterns apply in case of revenue improvement. However, field inquiries show that these measures have proved ineffective. Indeed, these measures are based on the idea of allocating a part of the cash flow rights to the agents, implicitly assuming that they already have control rights (discretionary power) in transformers operation, which is not the case.

No further discretionary power has been given to Field Officers with regards to the budget, nor the right to anticipation in it, which is a *sine qua non* condition for efficiency. Only paper work has been initiated, and no property rights have been granted and these incentives have never been taken seriously. However, when asked to suggest an explanation for the failure, interviewed Government and Headquarters' officials stated that Field agents do not have enough motivation to do so, reiterating that more coercive measures are required. This indicates enough that the administrative functioning of the system has not been analysed as such. On the contrary, an administration-type solution only is proposed. This practically illustrates how the assumption of the existence of incorrectly distributed property rights is misleading in the analysis. As long as absence of discretionary power is left unaddressed, these incentive schemes cannot work.

What about incentives in revenue improvement? The same radical limitations occur. Vigilance wings exist in almost every SEB, and rotating teams have been experimented in some SEBs, like Haryana, Andhra Pradesh and Orissa, on local scales and for a limited period of time. Local results have proved encouraging, but the same organisational problems remain. As long as the administrative

3. Against a present realised level of around 30 per cent.

procedures remain the same, JEs and SDOs are in practice not allowed to install meters, despite the paper work officially requests them to do so.

Limited or corrective actions do not alter the very nature of the system, and cannot lead to the implementation of techno-economic improvements. Let us now analyse the results of 'structural reforms', which include large modifications in the structure, the control on and the regulation of the power sector. With local variations, and provided they are accepted by the concerned State Government, the schemes have begun to be applied in some States. The two main goals of the reform are:

- to give control of the financial, technical and managerial process to the SEBs and
- to rebuild their financial creditworthiness through the fixation of more viable tariffs, subject to actual achievement of technical and management improvements.

The first goal is to be achieved mainly through 'corporatisation' of the SEBs, complemented with the setting up of independent Regulatory Commissions, to target the second goal. This scheme is being promoted by the Government of India. It further supports the State Governments which are willing to undertake it. This scheme was, however, not made compulsory, since the power sector is a concurrent subject of the Constitution of India. The Government of India is also of the view that de-integration is useful. For each concerned State, the term structural reforms will henceforth relate to the corporatisation and de-integration of the SEB, accompanied by the setting up of a State Electricity Regulatory Commission. These measures become mandatory after the enactment of the Electricity Act, 2003.

4.2. Post-1996: Corporatisation and De-integration of SEBs

4.2.1. The Wish for Structural Reforms (1)

As revealed in the account of Ministry of Power (1996) after the Chief Ministers' conference organised at Jaipur in 1996, and as recalled in Chandran (1998), various reform possibilities were offered to State Governments. These minor to major changes, revolving around 'unbundling' or 'de-integration', have been as follows:

- The SEB remains vertically integrated, but is 'corporatised' (*i.e.*, its status is changed, as will be detailed later).
- The SEB becomes a network organisation, and competition is set up in generation.
- The SEB keeps control of transmission and the existing generation, while new plants are independent of public ownership and the distribution is privatised.
- The SEB ceases to exist, a transmission company is set up, competition is installed in generation, and distribution is horizontally de-integrated.
- The SEB ceases to exist and becomes a holding company. A transmission company is set up, as well as Zonal Electricity Boards, authorised to locally deal in generation and distribution, in which independent producers can participate.

As can be seen, this set of reforms opens space for private operation in some segments of the power sector. It constitutes a framework for State policies, which are, however, not forcibly committed to any of the models or even to undertake reforms. Practically, some States have engaged in reforms, along the lines of the five models (see Annex).

'Corporatisation' refers to the change of status, from Boards to entities under the Company Act (1956), that is, judicially speaking, to a status of companies. The basis of each reform, then, is corporatisation, and the actual difference between the five classes of options is the degree of de-integration and subsequent re-integration that is authorised, as well as, the degree of competition, supposed to provide a financial incentive. We have shown that so-called incentives do not positively affect SEBs. Ultimately, in interviews, reformers reckon that competition is not the crucial issue.[4] For this reason, let us focus on how far the corporatisation and de-integration alter the administrative system. Actually, effective functioning of unbundled

4. It is, in this sense, interesting to note that, at a time when competition in infrastructure is promoted worldwide, it is hypocritically used in India, even though in a different context. On the public side, reforms are undertaken by States for the sake of new loans and by the Government of India for the sake of reinforcing its hold over the States. Off the record, World Bank officials are aware that the problem is more organisational and basically went to "break the monolithic system". Aiming at de-integration, they justified it with the dominant concept of competition in infrastructure.

utilities has been very limited, and, at an earlier stage, mostly concerned the States that had engaged into a World-Bank style reform (Orissa, Andhra, Haryana). Till 1998, Government of India was blocked by the Electricity Act 1948, and, after 1996, started preparing the bases of a new Act, that materialised finally in two steps: 1998 and 2003.

4.2.2. The Aim and Means of Unbundling

The following is a detailed explanation of the distinction between what I will refer to as 'legal corporatisation' (which is the simple change of status of SEBs from Boards into the judicial status of Companies, under the Company Act of 1956), and the process of corporatisation as seen by the reforming agencies (more structured and oriented around subsequent organisational changes).

'Corporatisation' is the modification of the judicial status of the SEBs, namely to move them from Boards (*i.e.* the administrative bodies) to companies, ruled under the Indian Company Act, 1956. This involves accounting rules that clarify the financial results before subsidies, as well as provide knowledge of the exact level of subsidies really transferred. Corporatisation is also intended to provide a formal independence in management towards the State Government. For instance, both the Orissa and the Haryana reforms included the designation of some Directors outside the Government entities, appointed on professional merit. They also include signature of corporatisation agreements between the organisations and their Government, to delineate their respective roles, rights and obligations.

In addition, corporatisation as understood by the World Bank, also involves balance sheet restructuring and information system enhancing, restructuring of reporting, training, investment in new capacities, and in maintenance. The World Bank (1996)[5] specifies that these reforms include training and consultancy for (a) system operation, (b) maintenance, (c) finance and accounting (d) metering, billing, and collection improvement, (e) human resources, and (f) environmental management. This is mainly intended to be achieved through the implementation of modern techniques; for instance, new softwares and hardwares, new accounting systems, including profit centre and cost centre accounting, information system, internal audit.

5. World Bank Report No. 14298-IN, Annex 2.5 & 4.1.

Technically, legal corporatisation is done through a transfer of assets – properly speaking of equipments, since we have seen that SEBs do not have 'assets' - and liabilities from the SEB to a new incorporated organisation, *via* the State Government. The balance sheet restructuring does not take place within a single organisation. On the contrary, the process articulates two formal steps. First, the equipment and the liabilities of the SEB are taken over by the State Government and the SEB ceases to exist. In the second step – though simultaneously in terms of time – the State Government grants assets and transfers liabilities to the new organisation. Typically, the level of assets and liabilities comes from the revaluation made by consultants. Regarding assets, the evaluation is based, under political arbitration, on homogenisation of the accounting values of similar materials, or portion of land. But evaluation on assets also has a long term structural impact on tariffs. Indeed, the general scheme is, under the responsibility of Regulatory Commissions, to make the tariffs progressively based on the principles of payment of costs plus a guaranteed rate of return on assets, as theoretically required from the Electricity Act (1948). The valuation of assets, then, will have two consequences on tariffs: first, it will affect the level of capital depreciation, to be progressively covered by the tariffs, and it will affect them through the rate of return principle. At the time of revaluation, a compromise has to be found between the tariffs faced by the consumers and the financial viability of the SEB. Under the corporatisation process, the political arbitration balances these financial viability issues, in order to limit the future pressure on tariffs.

Regarding liabilities, an important part of them can generally not be attributed to identified users, because of lack of records. Receivables are then identified with users if possible, and erased if not. Dues are compiled, and subsequent rescheduling of debts is made. Once the revaluated amount of liabilities is fixed, its allocation between the State and the new corporate entity is made. This again is fixed after some political arbitration, and is determined by their respective ability in managing them and on the expected impact in a privatisation process, or even on the will of the State to give up with this burden. Under the World-Bank style corporatisation process, the information system is also reshaped by consultants. For instance, in Haryana, the number of reports has been reduced from 177 to 70 (30 at the Field level) according to consultants. Technical and commercial information have been put together in the same reports.

Worldwide, support for de-integration in the power sector is based on a theoretical idea. It is agreed that transmission is a natural monopoly. However, generation is competitive and distribution is only a local natural monopoly. Thus, both generation and distribution do not need to remain horizontally integrated. They also have to be separated from transmission to avoid a distortion in competition, and ultimately the power sector has to be vertically de-integrated. This vision rejects a former conception stating that, for technical reasons, a vertical integration between generation and transmission provides a higher efficiency through better co-ordination. This new paradigm, on the contrary, argues that such a structure leads to inefficiencies through the absence of competitive incentives.[6] In India, however, interviewed reformers agreed that de-integration of the former SEBs into generation, transmission and distribution units is mainly intended to provide transparency. The classical argument of the promotion of competition is not the leading one in the case of SEB. What is targeted instead is the issue of creating information to isolate the most inefficient segments, which would require the most rapid reform.

4.2.3. The Result

Let us examine the impact of corporatisation and de-integration, based on the experiences of Orissa, Haryana and Andhra Pradesh.[7] Box 4.1 recalls the main steps of the reform in each of these States.

An Allocation of Discretionary Power Yet to be Made

In Haryana, generation had for some time been placed under the direct supervision of the Power Secretary, appointed as the Chairman.

---

6. For an exhaustive presentation of the techno-economics of the power sector and its needs for co-ordination, see Joskow & Schmalensee (1983). Classically, as discussed in the work of Joskow (1995), the analysis of de-integration in the power sector must discuss the trade-off between co-ordinative and competitive efficiencies. Theoretically, from an integrated power sector, de-integration leads to the need for some co-ordination procedures and specification of contracts between de-integrated companies. Due to network externalities (Joskow & Schmalensee, 1983), co-operative co-ordination is necessary, and market pricing is not enough. The former administrative co-ordination – which used to be done by various ministries and secretariats – will have to be replaced by Grid codes and bilateral contracts. The writing, dynamic modification and the operation of these contracts, lead to transaction costs (see also Glachant (1997).
7. Based on field investigation conducted from August 1999 to April 2000.

Box 4.1

Structural Reforms in Orissa, Haryana and Andhra Pradesh SEBs (Achievements by December 2000)

Orissa SEB was incorporated into two separate organisations, OHPC (Orissa Hydro Power Company) and Gridco (in charge of transmission and distribution) in April 1996. Thereafter, in November 1997, four zonal corporate entities were incorporated as subsidiaries of Gridco regarding its distribution activity. These companies, Wesco, Nesco, Cesco and Southco, (respectively, Western, Northern, Central and Southern Electricity Supply Company of Orissa) have been given Managing Directors during March 1998. The four zonal companies have then been divested – privatised – at 51 per cent. Wesco, Nesco and Southco have been sold off to the BSES (Bombay Sub-urban Electricity Supply, a private company based in Bombay) in April 1999, and Cesco to the American Company AES in October 1999 (the latter finally withdrew in 2001).

The Haryana SEB was incorporated into two separate organisations in August 1998 – Haryana Power Generation Corporation Ltd. (Haryana Generation Company) and HVPN (Haryana Vidyut Prasaran Nigam, in charge of transmission and distribution). In July 1999, the distribution activity of HVPN was transferred to two zonal corporate entities, UHBVN and DHBVN (Uttar Haryana Bijli Vitran Nigam and Dakshan Haryana Bijli Vitran Nigam, in charge of Northern and Southern Haryana respectively). They had applied for licenses to the Regulatory Commission. UHBVN was meant to be divested – privatised – at 51 per cent, by the year 2000, and DHBVN at the latest by year 2002. But this process has been stopped further due to a State Government change, after September 1999.

Andhra Pradesh SEB was incorporated into two separate organisations, AP Genco (Andhra Pradesh Generation Company) and AP Transco (Andhra Pradesh Generation Company in charge of transmission and distribution), in February 2000. AP Transco received licenses on transmission and distribution from the APERC on January 2000. Four Zonal Distcoms (Distribution companies), have been incorporated in April 2000, with no license and working as subsidiaries of Transco, since privatisation is their ultimate goal (initially by December 2000, then postponed *sine die*).

Generation thus obviously remained for long under the discretionary power of the State. The supply continues to be based on the need for continuity of supply, under official control by the State Government. As far as the network is concerned, UHBVN has been visited for inquiries in August 1999 and March-April 2000. On these two visits, the procedures put in place by HSEB were still applied, the characteristics of the budgetary system were unchanged and the paper work system was still in place. No internal delegation of discretionary power had been put in place. Executive instructions remained. Field inquiries revealed that there was no new decision-making system in place compared to the HSEB. In distribution, the sole change subsequent to corporatisation had been the already discussed downsizing and integration of the reporting system. However, in a context which is largely unchanged, there is no more discretionary power to use this supplement of information. Illustratively enough, inquiries have focused on the several meetings between the Field and their Managing Director (MD) or Chief Engineer over these few months. Field officers have disclosed that "all and everything is being discussed and solved during these meetings". However, when asked for the practical results in terms of decision the answer was that "no decisions had been taken." After corporatisation, 'resolving issues' still means gathering of several hierarchical levels and endless discussion on the paper work goes on.

If one now looks at the results of the so-called de-integration between HVPN and UHBVN (transmission and distribution), for instance, the impact is not much. By August 1999, the MD office of UHBVN had been installed in a different building from the Headquarters of HVPN. However, this office had not been granted the necessary staff to process all the files and reports linked with the paper work system. This was accomplished by the staff of the Director Operations at the Headquarters (HVPN) level (this remained the same in April 2000). So, the creation of the MD post under the de-integration process mainly consists of bifurcating the post of Director Operations into two MD posts, equivalent of Director Operations for two distribution zones, plus a Director Operations in transmission. As such, no power has been actually transferred to this Directorial level, and the initiation of paper work remains collegially in the hands of the Chairman, assisted by the Directors. As a result of investigation, we presented a proposal of discretionary power allocation through the reform of the budgetary system (further discussed in Chapter 5) had been presented to the MD of UHBVN by August 1999. He showed interest, but confessed and confirmed more explicitly later, when he was no longer in charge, that this was still dependent on the HVPN Chairman. Moreover, such a reform was still dependent on the State Government itself. The 'MD' was not a MD.

Also, the way sub-stations are operated is illustrative of the absence of an actual separation between HVPN and UHBVN. Sub-stations are the places where the voltage is transformed from 132 kV to 33 kV. According to the transfer schemes, they belong to HVPN. However, they are operated by following the technical orders of the local SE in charge of distribution, who belongs to the UHBVN. The reporting of the substation (HVPN) is done to the SE (UHBVN), who sanctions it and transmits it to the Headquarters of HVPN. Thus, as far as technical operation is concerned, the separation has not been actually made between the transmission and the distribution 'companies'.

Let us now look at the financial arrangements made between HVPN and UHBVN. De-integration assumes the clarification of the financial links between the two entities. It means a measurement of the supplied quantities, plus the financial arrangements regarding their payment of these quantities. In fact, in a case of simple accounting unbundling (separation of the balance sheets) without de-integration, these issues are reduced to the accounting allocation of budgets and collected revenues. The measurement issue can be considered as solved, since meters have been installed along with the World Bank loan for reform. Yet, the issue of setting financial rules has been addressed in a wholly piecemeal manner.

The first thing to be noted is that they are resolved through negotiations at monthly meetings, under the arbitration of the Power Secretary. That is, compared to the previous solution, the arbitration that used to be, most of the time, 'internal' to the SEB, has become the concern of the State Government, but not appropriated by the so-called corporatised utilities. The second aspect is that HVPN goes on receiving the full collected amount but UHBVN has to deal with its necessary expenses. For these, they still have to go through the classical system of paper work demands, arbitrated and sanctioned at the HVPN Headquarters level. Practically, the Field is still granted physical means under the remnant classical procedures. Arbitration is still dependent on the Headquarters, and driven by the continuity of supply. The sole difference is that the stores now formally depend on the UHBVN 'Headquarters'. However, this difference is only formal, since the decision to buy materials to fill the stores actually depends on the goodwill of the 'HVPN Headquarters'. Finally, the so-called UHBVN 'Headquarters' are no more repositories of decision-making power than are the Circles in the classical system. It can be said that the so-called de-integration does not actually lead to the existence of two distinct organisations with fixed financial relations.

To sum up, the Haryana example shows that corporatisation neither provides a discretionary power separate from the State Government nor an internal one. Actually, the Power Secretary becomes even more present. Further, the so-called de-integration only adds a new hierarchical level in the former system, without altering its nature. Let us detail further the so-called de-integration. It does not provide either a separate hierarchy or control rights, or separate cash flow rights. It only provides separate accounting, that is an unbundling rather than a de-integration. For example, the ambiguous monitoring of the 132 kV to 33 kV substations in Haryana shows an ongoing confusion. More graphically, as an Officer declared: "these are not reforms; they have changed the name, but the shop remains".

In Orissa also similar issues have arisen. For instance, interviews had confirmed that till the privatisation of distribution (April 1999, the date of privatisation of the Southern, Western and Northern zones, and October 1999, the date of privatisation of the Central zone), classical procedures were still in use in the two companies visited, Nesco and Cesco. In addition, as far as allocation of funds is concerned, the zonal 'companies' have remained under the discretion and operation of the transmission segment, without even being initially granted a separate operation license. No separation in the tariff was made between transmission and distribution. The fund allocation also was fixed from the Headquarters. This regime had lasted up to April 1999. Additionally, although the 'Headquarters' of the zones had been located outside Bhubaneshwar[8] (the State capital), interviewed Nesco officers reported that "orders stopped coming from Bhubaneshwar when the privatisation took place". Consequently, prior to privatisation and despite 'corporatisation', Gridco and its zonal parts were still functioning as administrations.

To sum up, the legal corporatisation is only a judicial change; once achieved, direct executive instructions remain. The procedures and the paper work also remain. Corporatisation as defined by the World Bank brings something more: it mainly provides an information system, which allows benchmarking and can bring transparency. It makes available managerial techniques based on cost efficiency objective. However, there is no assurance that they will actually be used, and in

8. Except for the Central zone.

practice they are not. It brings some cash flow rights as well, but which remain inarticulated with would-be control rights. The attempt of de-integration neither materialises in locating the decisions nor in setting up cash flow rights. All in all, corporatisation and so-called de-integration do not alter the administrative nature of SEBs.

4.3. The Regulatory Commissions Act (1998): Structural Reforms (2)

Regulatory Commissions (RCs) are being progressively set up. The RC Act (1998) provides them some powers, at the expense of the CEA, and theoretically at the expense of the States.[9] The RCs clarify the procedure of tariff increase. The Act provides strong guarantees for independence, as operations have proved up to now. RCs have to balance between efficiency and profitable operating conditions for SEBs. Practically, they seem to opt in favour of consumers. Their functioning is actually based on the implicit assumption that SEBs operate under Soft Budget Constraint. However, it has been seen that this whole assumption is wrong, and, practically, their existence does not lead to clarify the process of allocations of subsidies. RCs set the tariffs, but then, regarding their revenues, former SEBs remain under the discretion of the State Governments. In particular, the financial transfers between the organisations issued from the SEB are still administratively monitored by the Government. This is understandable from the previous analysis, since SEBs are not moved by financial pressure, nor are able to diffuse the pressure down to the Field.

4.3.1. Setting up of Regulatory Commissions

According to the Regulatory Commissions Act (1998), each State has the legal possibility of creating a State Electricity Regulatory Commission (SERC). Its role is to determine the accurate level of tariffs, setting profitable (on a cost plus basis) operating conditions for the operators, provided they achieve actual improvements (loss reduction, quality improvement) for the consumers. However, it is the choice of each State Government whether to attribute some other functions to the SERC. Besides tariffs, their role can range from that of a simple designer and controller of minimum technical standards and minimum information requirements, to a dispute

9. Reinforced by the Electricity Act, 2003 as we shall see.

adjudicator, or to a strong regulator of investment approval and licensees control.

Provisions in the Act on SERC commissioners' selection and removal assure a reasonable autonomy *vis-à-vis* both Central and the State governments, industries and consumers. The commissions have all the powers necessary to design and enforce their orders. Tariff orders in Orissa (where the first Regulatory Commission has been established) have proved to be transparent procedures, which are further confirmed through other States. The 1998 amended version of the Electricity Regulatory Commissions Ordinance[10], gives a framework within which a Central Electricity Regulatory Commission (CERC), and State Electricity Regulatory Commissions (SERC) can be built. It applies to the whole of India, except Orissa and Haryana. These States had already passed their own reform Acts[11]: the Orissa Electricity Reform Act, 1995 and the Haryana Electricity Reform Act, 1997. The full Ordinance title, "An ordinance to provide the establishment of a CERC and SERCs, rationalisation of electricity tariffs, transparent polices regarding subsidies, promotion of efficient & environmentally benign policies [...]" clearly shows that the points to be solved are both financial and managerial.

The Scope of the Central Electricity Regulatory Commission

The CERC is mainly dedicated to inter-State matters, tariff regulation, and dispute arbitration on centrally owned utilities or companies involved in several States (see Box 4.2 for further details). It can be seen from the box that the CERC has become a powerful organisation in tariff concerns in the Indian power sector. However, technical regulation is not subject to its regulation, and remain in the hands of the CEA, and new capacity approval remained with the CEA till 2003.

It was agreed over interviews that one of the main roles for the CERC in future would be the tariff regulation of the emerging bulk

10. The initial version was passed by the Parliament of India and then published in the Gazette of India, on 25th April 1998.
11. Respectively in the Orissa legislative assembly on the 28th of November 1995, in the Haryana assembly in 1997, with the assent of the President of India on the 28th of February 1998.

Box 4.2

CERC Functions

According to Section 13 of the Electricity Ordinance, 1998 the CERC main functions are to:

- "regulate the tariff of generating companies and transmission utilities owned or controlled by the Central Government,
- regulate the tariff of generating companies (involved in generation and sale in more than one State),
- regulate the inter-States transmission (...),
- promote competition, efficiency and economy in the (...) electricity industry,
- aid and advise the Central Government in the formulation of tariff policy which shall be fair to the consumers and facilitate mobilisation of adequate resource for the power sector,
- (...)
- arbitrate or adjudicate upon disputes involving generation companies or transmission utilities (mentioned above)."

Source: Electricity Regulatory Commissions Act, 1998.

power market, as far as the interconnection is progressing in India. But not much has happened in this at the time of printing (the Power Trading Corporation has shown tremendous growth, but on a niche segment of supply, see Chapter 7).

The Scope of the State Electricity Regulatory Commissions

As far as SERCs are concerned, they are devoted to their respective State utilities, and to all matters specifically concerning the generation or supply in the State, whether they involve a private company or a national public company. Their basic functions are tariff determination for network activities and tariff regulation for generation. However, it depends on each State Government to attribute some other functions to the SERC. They include the possibility for the SERC to deal with all the coordination needed for the development and operation of the power system (for further details, see Box 4.3).

Their basic functions deal with setting efficient tariffs and procurements. No explicit rule for calculation is defined, but Section 29.2 (c, d, and e) gives some guidelines to the SERCs for tariff setting. Sub-section (a) specifies that "the tariff (shall) progressively

Box 4.3

Functions of SERCs

According to Section 22 of the Electricity Ordinance, 1998 the SERCs main functions are to:

- "determine the tariff for electricity, wholesale, bulk, grid or retail (...)
- determine the tariff payable for use of the transmission facilities (...)
- regulate the power purchase and the procurement process of transmission utilities and distribution utilities, including the price at which the power shall be procured from the generating companies, generating stations, or from other sources for transmission, sale, distribution and supply in the State
- promote competition, efficiency and economy in the (...) electricity industry".

In addition, "The State Government may (...) confer any of the following functions upon the State Commission, namely to:

- regulate the investment approval for generation, transmission, distribution and supply of power
- aid and advise the State Government in matters concerning electricity generation, transmission, distribution and supply in the State
- regulate the operation of power system within the State
- issue licences for transmission, bulk supply, distribution or supply of electricity and determine the conditions to be included in the licences
- regulate the working of the licensees (...)
- require licensees to formulate perspective plans and schemes in co-ordination with others (...)
- set standards (...) relating to quality, continuity and reliability of service
- promote competitiveness and make avenues for participation of private sector (...) and also to ensure a fair deal to the consumers
- (...)
- aid and advise the State Government in the formulation of the State power policy
- collect and record information (...), to collect and publish data and forecasts on the demand (...)
- (...)
- adjudicate the disputes and differences between the licensees and utilities and to refer the matters for arbitration".

Source: Electricity Regulatory Commissions Act, 1998.

reflect the cost of supply of electricity at an adequate and improving level of efficiency". This means that not only does the SERC have to determine economic tariffs, but these tariffs can be granted to suppliers only in good and improving management conditions. This is consistent with sub-sections (d)[12] & (e). Sub-section (e) declares that "the interests of the consumers are safeguarded and at the same time, the consumers pay for the use of electricity in a reasonable manner based on the average cost of supply of energy".

The general meaning of the Orissa and Haryana Electricity Reform Acts, (1995 and 1997 respectively) are consistent with the Ordinance. Both argue – they have exactly the same sections on these topics – that the Commission shall "promote efficiency, economy and safety [...] including and with particular regard to quality, continuity of service" (Sub-section 11.1, d) and "keep in view both the interest of the consumer as well as the consideration that the supply and distribution cannot be maintained unless the charges for electricity supplied are reasonably levied and duly collected" (Sub-section 11.1, e).

This shows that the Regulatory Commissions have been designed both in the Ordinance and in the Acts as a tool to resolve simultaneously the two linked aspects of the situation: the tariff and the quality issues.

The Independence of State Electricity Regulatory Commissions

In the mind of the reformers, the central tool to allow independence to the electric sector is an independent Regulatory Commission. Initially, in an earlier version of the Ordinance, it was proposed that setting up of SERC would be compulsory. According to officials interviewed, this has been excluded, for fear that some politicians may lose a part of their power. The establishment of a Regulatory Commission in a State was thus initially dependent on the goodwill and commitment of the State Government.

This commitment has to be credible, meaning that, once the Regulatory Commission has been established, its independence has to be guaranteed through institutional mechanisms. In their analysis of the performance of private utilities according to the way the

12. Sub-section (d) specifies: "the State Commission shall be guided by the factors which would encourage efficiency, economical use of the resources, good performance, optimum investments and other matters that the State Commission considers appropriate for the purposes of this Ordinance". The 'other matters' hence allow large argumentation powers to the SERC to justify its tariffs with respect to the utilities.

regulation is done, Levy & Spiller (1994) focus on judiciary independence and the manner in which regulation is made, arguing that "for legislation to provide regulatory credibility it should make specific the process by which regulatory decisions are to be taken" and that "otherwise regulatory discretion will be unchecked".

In the Indian context, the Commissions need to strike a balance between social subsidies, profitable tariffs, and quality improvements. Therefore, this independence will not only be from politicians but also from companies, SEBs, and even from several categories of consumers. In this respect, the background and the methods of selection of the commissioners, as well as, the way decisions are accepted and enforced, are of central importance for the success of reforms. The SERCs are composed of three persons, with qualifications in engineering, finance, commerce, economics, law or management (Section 17 of the Ordinance).[13] In India, these qualifications are expected to be found in civil servants, or people from governmental positions, or from public companies.[14] The question of independence has all the more to be examined. The State commissioners are selected after a Selection Committee proposal, whose composition is fixed by the ordinance (Section 18). It is composed by a former Judge of the High Court, the Chief Secretary of the State, and a member of the CEA. It gives two names for each member, and the concerned Government makes the final choice. After they complete their term, the commissioners are ineligible to hold positions under the Governments for two years, or to accept any commercial employment in the electricity industry. They cannot represent anybody before the commission (Sections 6 and 19). They can be removed only on grounds of misbehaviour that must be proved in the High Court (Section 20). These provisions on their selection and removal assure the minimal personal independence of each commissioner towards both Central and State Governments, industry and consumers.

Let us now look at the decision-making and the enforcement of the commission decisions. According to the Ordinance (57, 58, 59),

---

13. The Orissa & Haryana Acts specify that at least one commissioner shall be an engineer, and at least one shall be from the disciplines of economics, commerce, accountancy, law or administration.

14. In Orissa, one commissioner is issued from the finance planning in the central defence ministry, one from the former Orissa SEB, and the last one is a civil servant.

"State Government may make rules to carry out the provisions of the ordinance, the state commission may make regulation consistent with this ordinance and the rules thereunder to carry out the purposes of this ordinance, every rule [...] and every regulation [...] shall be laid [...] before House(s) of State Legislature".

The Regulatory Commission Ordinance prescribes, in Section 12, that "the Central Commission shall, for the purposes of any inquiry or proceedings under this ordinance, have the powers as are vested in a Civil Court (...)", and the same for SERCs in Section 23 (see Box 4.4). This is of course also granted in the Orissa and Haryana Acts.

Box 4.4

The Powers of CERC and SERCs

The Central as well as State Commissions have the power to:

- "summon and enforce the attendance of any witness and to examine such a witness on oath,
- discover and produce any document or other material object as evidence,
- receive evidence on affidavits,
- requisition any public record,
- issue commission for the examination of witnesses,
- any other matter which may be prescribed".

Source: Electricity Regulatory Commissions Act, 1998.

The commissions also have the power of seizure, as "they may seize any [...] document or take extracts or copies" (Section 45). Section 46 deals "with punishment for non-compliance of directions given by a commission". Thus, it can be seen that commissions have all the judiciary powers necessary to design and enforce their orders. However, in practice, the staff and general means they have at their disposal remain limited. Especially, in interviews, some SERC Commissioners have acknowledged that they are not in a position to conduct technical counter expertise.

4.3.2. *Regulatory Commissions and the Administrative Nature of SEBs: The Possible Role of the Commissions in Reforming SEBs*

The main function of a Regulatory Commission is the tariff setting. It shall issue tariffs that ensure financial viability for power companies, provided that they achieve minimal progress requirements on their efficiency. According to the 1998 Ordinance, the Regulatory Commission has a great latitude to ask for such requirements. In SEBs, this could lead to major pressure but without the means to withstand it. Indeed, the way a Regulatory Commission allows a tariff increase can be very demanding in terms of information and results. Let us practically study the Orissa experience, where the OERC has been the first Regulatory Commission to issue orders. In this process, it has proved to be largely independent on the tariff issue, and has exerted high pressure on Gridco. On the annual tariff setting, it rejected the demand issued by Gridco and asked for an improvement on the losses (see Box 4.5).

Box 4.5

OERC Statement on GRIDCO's Proposal for Tariff

On December 1996, Gridco gave to the OERC details of calculation of estimated revenue requirements for the financial year 1997-98, based on expected energy sales, and supply cost and a 17 per cent return on equity. This was to be the basis of a tariff proposal.

This proposal has been rejected mainly on the grounds that no substantial improvement in losses has been noticed.

The OERC argued on

- "undue high percentage of system losses,
- artificial revaluation of assets,
- profit calculated on fictitious capital,
- [...],
- basis of forecast that has not been made clear".

Gridco thus did not obtain the required tariff increase.

Source: OERC, Order No. 9, March 12, 1997.

Finally, Regulatory Commissions provide strong constraints. SEBs have to issue affidavits for tariff settings. If they are found to be wrong after Regulatory Commission enquiries, SEBs managers can be prosecuted. This gives an incentive to keep information updated, as has effectively happened in Orissa, Haryana and Andhra Pradesh, thereby placing transparency on losses. Such enhanced information, made available through corporatisation, is giving weapons for argument to both SEBs officers and State Governments. As subsidies are booked, and procedures and annual targets given by Regulatory

Commissions made more transparent, SEBs are in a better position to ask for subsidies and financial support from their shareholder. Invoking the Regulatory Commission directives, managers can more easily argue against day to day interference. State Governments can use the Regulatory Commissions to make SEBs face their responsibilities. So, there could exist some window for reform under public ownership, based on the strategic use of Regulatory Commissions. However, *as long as the general framework of functioning of SEBs does not evolve,* these potential tools are not fully used. Setting-up of Regulatory Commissions, if not complemented with radical reforms in SEBs that allow to implement cost-benefit decision-making, weakly remains rooted in inadequate 'SBC approach'.

The Electricity Act (2003) confirms and by many respects extends the role of the Commissions, and its likely consequences are discussed in the next Chapter. But, if the success of Regulatory Commissions till date has to be assessed, it comes through as important but limited one. Prayas (2003), out of a survey of the decisions taken by the Commissions till 2003, mentions that they have managed to create a public awareness in exhumating some figures from the SEBs that give an idea to the general public about the level of the situation. Their success in bringing transparency to the SEBs has however been severely limited because of the structural organisation of SEBs.

Ultimately, the vision set up by the Uttar Pradesh Electricity Regulatory Commission, might well summarise the role SERCs can have in reforming the sector. Following the analytical framework set up by Ruet (2001), UPERC (2001) mentions that "one is compelled to observe that success of electricity reforms (in Uttar Pradesh) cannot be ensured until the (reforms are) coupled with concrete measures toward altering the organisational set up of UPPCL, UPRVNL, and UPJVNL[15] to make them responsive to commercial needs of electricity supply". Siding with the recommendations made by Ruet (2001), the UPERC (2001) discusses the possibilities for the commission to "explore options to inject formal discretion in the operational and financial decision-making in the working of licensees". Measures along this line are generalised and amply discussed in Chapter 5.

---

15. The unbundled parts of the UPSEB.

Impact of RCs

Finally, one last line of concern from the overall architecture comes from the fact that ERCs are administratively dependent from their respective Ministries of Power in day-to-day functioning. Rao (2004) recalls that these are the "Officers in the Ministry of Power who actually deal with expenditures of the CERC. Thus even expenditures authorised by the Chairman of the CERC have to be submitted to ministry officers".

However, six years after the 1998 Act, and one year after the 2003 Act, one can go beyond the judicial lecture only, and assess the real functioning of ERCs regarding improvement in the efficiency of the sector. The best analysis, as well as, maybe the best source of information, comes from Rao (2004), who has been the first chairman of the CERC. He points some major progress due to the functioning of the CERC and SERCs. He mentions that the CERC "issued the first-ever consultation paper on bulk tariffs and a series of papers on risk and return in electricity, depreciation norms, etc., which were then incorporated in a major order on tariff norms and principles. The CERC also imposed a charge for use of reactive power with a view to bringing voltage levels under some control. Similarly, some SERCs have attempted to estimate costs of serving different consumers categories and determined tariffs for each. They have used performance-based tariff regulations to target efficiency improvements, especially on reduction of T&D losses". His book however concludes on a more pessimistic line on the real impact of ERCs till date, and he states that "however, these measures have had little effect since SEB losses continue to be high", recalling that till today, "there is nowhere a calculation available about (India's electricity sector's) rupee turnover".

Going into the specifics, Rao (2004) states out that "over the first five years of existence, the functioning of the RCs has not been smooth". "A notable exception might have been the CERC, for which its first Chairman testifies that "in the five years since the inception of the CERC, the central government has not issued it any policy directives". He recalls however that, "the relationships between SERCs and their State governments have not been as peaceful". Actually, the Prayas (2003) survey quotes many dysfunctionments, especially in Himachal Pradesh, Madhya Pradesh, or even the case of

Tamil Nadu where no chairman was appointed for years, or Karnataka where the Government instructed the Transmission corporation (created out of the unbundling of the Karnataka SEB) to hold up the implementation of a KERC order, without even referring to the KERC and, Rao details, "against the letter of the law". These vagaries are attempted to be corrected by the New Electricity Act, 2003 (which we discuss more extensively later on in the book), that provides for an institutional recognition of a Forum of Regulators, chaired by the Chairperson of the CERC and composed by the Chairpersons of the SERCs. It is hoped this will provide coordination among SERCs. However, more importantly, the Act provides for SERCs to follow rules set by the CERC in a binding way as far as generation and transmission is concerned, and involvement of the chairman of the CERC in the selection of SERCs members and chairmen. However, if the latter element may provide a larger independence in selecting the SERCs, it may not provide them the means of their functional independence towards State Governments, especially when some of them do not hesitate going "against the letter of the law".

Now, if one looks in detail on the effectiveness of ERCs in regulating the public utilities, Rao (2004) states that "regulating state-owned enterprises by independent regulatory commissions has been found to be less effective than regulating privately owned enterprises. This has been the experience in India as well in electricity both at central and state levels. The enterprise response has typically been of challenge, non-compliance and defiance. Thus all orders of the CERC were challenged by the centrally owned undertakings concerned, in many cases up to the Supreme Court. (The courts upheld all of them.) In many states, the undertakings did not implement tariff orders, and were backed by the state governments". It is in that way compelling to see that the same proposal vests a higher weight with the Government when it comes from a GoI committee than from the CERC: dealing with one of the proposals of the N.K. Singh Committee, Rao (2004) reminds that "the report commands that unallocated central power should be allowed for trading. This was suggested to the Government by the CERC in its order on availability-based tariff. Hopefully, the Government will now implement the recommendation that the CERC made over five years ago".

On another line, we insist throughout the book that the nature of the problem is informational, which Rao confirms in respect to the ability of the ERCs to regulate the tariffs. Table 4.1 shows the amount of fluctuation between proposed estimates by utilities for their T&D losses—that constitute the base of the tariff application filing—and the approved figures by the ERCs. Ultimately, the actual can be anything ranging between what the utility wants it to be (what it declares ultimately cannot be really checked by the regulatory commission, therefore it has a value of truth for as long as the utility wants to declare it as such) to even more losses (as in the case of Maharashtra).

Table 4.1

Extent of Unreliable Information on T&D Losses

(Per cent)

	Year	*Proposed*	*Approved*	*Actual*
Maharashtra SEB	2000-01	27.66	26.87	39.40
Maharashtra SEB	2001-02	39.49	39.49	NA
Uttar Pradesh PC Ltd	2000-01	34.97	29.97	39.47
Orissa	1999-2000	47.00	35.00	45.68
Orissa	2000-01	42.66	34.00	NA
Haryana	2000-01	40.76	35.76	47.71
Delhi	2001-02	46.80	46.80	57.00
Gujarat	2000-01	21.00	30.00	25.00

Note: NA: not available; figures as proposed by the utility and approved by the RC during filing tariff orders.

Source: Rao (2004).

Rao (2004) rightly concludes that "the ERCs decisions on tariffs are invariably based on revenue and expenditure projections that go wrong. They are unable to determine tariffs for more than a year at a time because even one year's projections are unsound". "Regulators have focused on improving efficiencies but with mixed results. They have set high efficiency targets with little basis and no guidelines on how they could be achieved. Only Gujarat has ordered and received results from a study on T&D losses and demand forecasts. Some regulators have ordered staff rationalisation, maintenance of asset registers, and studies to bring transparency across the system. Little data is available on how far these measures have been implemented but SEBs performance does not show any impact." Ultimately, the crux of the matter comes partly from the understaffing of ERCs, where "On an average, SERCs have about 8-10 posts for these key technical, finance, economic, and legal functions. About two-thirds from the technical staff are from regulated utilities" (Rao, 2004). This raises real questions for the possibility of an efficient RC-based regulatory regime, in a context where SEBs have been structures that structurally used to retain information or prevent its creation, where there are hardly any technically trained consuming groups, and where even the regulatory commissions are at the best understaffed or at the worst not as transparent as the spirit of the law would suggest. Indeed, Rao (2004), quoting from the Prayas (2003) survey, reveals that "three SERCs (HPERC, DERC, and MPERC) do not have a library/ reading room, where people can easily access all non-confidential information available. Except the WBERC and the APERC, all other SERCs mentioned that they have not prepared a detailed classified index of all available documents (such as petitions and rejoinders), a necessary mechanism for facilitating transparency (...). Only 10-20 people have visited the ERC libraries in an entire year".

4.4. Beyond Structural Reforms

Ultimately, previous considerations show that neither the change in the status, nor the bifurcating or trifurcating of the activity, specifically help in altering the administrative nature of SEBs. The so-called structural reforms have no impact on this, nor lead to a radical rupture. They do constitute a first step through (i) the setting up of an information system, and (ii) the establishment of some cash flow rights, but SEBs remain SEBs.

Since the creation of control rights has not simultaneously arisen, structural reforms have practically turned to be problematic for SEBs. The earlier processes of negotiation have been suppressed while the SEBs have not been given the means to install a discretionary power, either external or internal. This is all the more true for instance for Gridco in Orissa. Indeed, the Government of Orissa has fully suppressed all the subsidies right from the signing of the agreement for the loan with the World Bank. In other States as well, the SEBs and their offspring entities have from then on mainly survived on the disbursement of World Bank, Asian Development Bank, or Power Finance Corporation loans. Practically, this means that these SEBs have been waiting for the physical availability of materials, whose global quantity had been defined from outside, at the moment of the signing of the agreement. The practical composition of the materials to be delivered has as well been partly defined externally from the SEB-derived organisations, by consultant teams, in agreement with the lending agencies and subject to its authorisation for further disbursements.

Finally, the process of undertaking new works has not been determined internally by electric utilities but has remained subject to a form of external discretionary power. Under the absence of control rights, the SEB-derived organisations are ultimately deemed to depend on lending agencies loans the same way they used to depend on State Government subsidies. The basis of the negotiation has apparently changed but in fact its nature remains the same. Indeed, the core of the approach is supposed to be based on financial targets and not on continuity of supply. But, at least in initial stages of the reform, due to the lack of information, the practical monitoring by the World Bank or ADB can only be based on the establishment of new procedures, regarding the information, the computation of costs, and the hierarchical relations. That is, the negotiations are ultimately dependent on the ability of the Headquarters (helped by the Government) to show their commitment to the reform and to initiation of the right processes. This is, in turn, exactly what used to happen in their earlier negotiations with the State Government. *The terms and the vocabulary have changed, but the structure of the procedural environment has remained.*

As a result, it can even be argued that the vision of the electric system as a mono-technique remains unchanged from the point of view of Headquarters. Indeed, in absence of control rights and in a context of information building, with respect to the World Bank loans, the actions linked with the enhancement of the system, its expansion, or its maintenance can hardly be disentangled. But, if the loans are considered by reformers as "a way to pay the unavoidable costs of the transition", as a World Bank official declared, then these three kinds of actions should be shown separately. Indeed, enhancement of the system, the need for which resulted from the former system, can be related as an unavoidable cost of the reform, to be supported once and for all.[16]

In addition, although the long term objective is that expansion becomes self-sustainable, it can be understood that under the present circumstances, in the short run, a part of the sustaining of the growth shall be included in the loan. But, as far as maintenance is concerned, it is doubtful if this ever-going activity should be related to a one-shot loan. It should rather arise from self-generated funds. Only from this separation, the cost *versus* benefits approach can emerge. Because of the ongoing confusion between enhancement, expansion and maintenance, almost every problem is still tackled through new works, under the mono-technique paradigm. Practically, partly because they have remained in the Headquarters, but also because new reporting systems have not been made operative in decision-making, when consultants leave the floor, the reform process does not endure.

Reformers and Consultants have failed till date because they have considered a bounded rationality as the element to eliminate, instead of focusing on the importance of the procedural rationality. Techniques have been improved, tools have been given, softwares and training have been delivered and information has been made available. The framework is in place, but the driving principle is missing. In this respect, the very term 'transition' used by officials, shows how far actual changes are different from the *radical change* which is needed.

4.5. Conclusion

To sum up, even after structural reforms, the former procedures remain; internal discretion is still unavailable, there are still no rules for subsidies allocation, and there are direct executive instructions. Only in the case of the generation activity, the need of a power purchase agreement has contributed to fixing the rules of income generation. Yet, organisations issued from SEBs are still not enterprises. Moreover, there is no 'hardening of the budget constraint' through the setting up of Regulatory Commissions, as the concept of budget constraint itself is not valid, and *there is no 'reallocation' of*

16. Although it has been seen that a part of it would have a reasonable profitability under assumptions of established property rights.

Property Rights through attempts of de-integration, as there were no Property Rights earlier. Property Rights have still to be created, and the focus on costs is yet to be integrated in behaviour.

Therefore, the so-called structural reforms as envisaged by the Government of India and enforced by some States do not lead to any substantial change neither of the organisation nor of the administrative nature of SEBs. The next Chapter places the need for reforms in a more theoretical framework, that we name 'enterprisation'.

5

A Concept for Radical Reform: 'Enterprisation'

The question of efficiency is alien to the functioning of SEBs. This Chapter deals with the changes that have to occur in SEBs if they are to be held accountable to efficiency demands. We define the concept of 'enterprisation', which is a radical change of the nature of the organisation. What enterprisation shall recover in the case of SEBs and how it relates to the creation of property rights is then discussed. Practically, since enterprisation recovers a whole set of measures and initiatives to be enforced and monitored, the feasibility of these measures within the public sphere is to be discussed.

5.1. A Radical Transformation: 'Enterprisation'

The issue in SEBs is to shift from a state of 'no management' to 'actual management'. But this is hardly feasible in the present structures. A radical moving out from the administrative system is needed if the question of cost efficiency is to be addressed.

5.1.1. 'Enterprisation': A Definition

By nature, an administration does not focus on costs. Enterprises do. Therefore, SEBs formally and practically have to be turned into enterprises. For this, what kind of a target does reform attempt to reach? What does it include as a process to reach this target? Let us for that deal with what we call 'enterprisation'. 'Enterprisation' is a concept that has been coined in the study of post-socialist countries (Hirschhausen 1994, Bomsel 1995). It starts from the fact that, in the socialist systems (here we extend the concept to administrations like Indian SEBs), (i) production can circulate in the public sphere, under the form of flux of energies and raw or processed materials, or information, with a physical coordination of these flux *which is not a monetary coordination*. As well, (ii) the principal function of socialist industrial networks and units (including plants) is not production, which is only a means to reach administrative targets (Hirschhausen, 1994, quotes targets such as territorial control, social welfare, political control among others), sometimes an accessory parameter, or even a mere by-product of the administrative activity of these units (see Bomsel, 1995). SEBs, though at a lesser geographical scale, and less connected in a network of other 'socialist-type' units, thus function the same way. Money, costs, do not exist in socialist units, and their essentiality resides in political coordination and arbitration, through an administrative machinery. When economic concerns take over from politics (the end of the socialist regime), money becomes active, flows through the networks of units, and destroys the political procedures of control, according to Bomsel (1995). Hence the *productive* collapse[1] of the post-socialism, because production was not based on its own rationality, but on administrative monitoring that ceased existing.

What is the equivalent in SEBs? Let us have a 'thought experiment': the day the political control/support on SEBs is released, they have to coordinate with their suppliers (NTPC, IPPs, others) through money (costs and benefits) only, which they are structurally incapable of. This is not an issue of management only, this is an issue of structure. From this day, they have to rely on their networks and generation plants, which will be 'activated' as assets only if they build commercial assets from scratch, that is, if they build 'clients' from their 'users'. Otherwise, the value of SEBs is nothing but the price of materials on second-hand markets and their competencies, productive organisation is valued at zero. This is again what has happened in Europe after the end of socialism. Technically, socialist units have collapsed because costs have suddenly appeared, materialised through their inductment in decision-making (intermediate goods acquired a cost, transport as well, cost of social functions started being measured). In SEBs, the State has a key role in settling disputes through its administrative circuits. For instance, an illustration of this comes from the political bifurcation of Madhya Pradesh, with the creation of the State of Chhattisgarh, in 2000. Generation units are located in Chhattisgarh, while the major consumption is in Madhya Pradesh. The bifurcation of the State led to meter and price the transfers between two entities which used to be

1. And not *economic* collapse. In post-socialism, socialist production initially collapsed due to the birth of economy (see also Giraud, 2000).

parts of the same administration. This has resulted in a major crisis for months with heavy power cuts even in the capital, Bhopal. After some months, the administrative system has defined new channels, new circuits, and finalised arrangements less based on costs, than with the political arbitrage of the Central Government. This temporary crisis is interesting, because the system has ultimately always remained 'administrative'. It has never really been envisaged that actual massive financial transfers would flow from Madhya Pradesh to Chhattisgarh, and administrative solutions have been looked at. The crisis has then been a temporary moment of adaptation of the administration to a new situation. But let us imagine what would happen with a sudden real and lasting break in the administered-control of the sector. Such an example is, though again limited by the existence of financial safeguards, the Orissa privatisation, where the Central zone has been bankrupt in 2001, after two years of privatisation. In that context, structures inherited from the public socialist-inspired system have to be radically and structurally transformed into enterprises. Their 'enterprisation' amounts to the target and a *process of their industrial capitalisation*. That is, *building of economic assets from their mere physical equipments*, and *building of commercial assets from their users*. This is structurally impossible in present SEBs' organisation, where costs do not exist.

In other words, and to serve as a *definition*:

- *enterprisation of SEBs amounts to their proper capitalisation through building of assets, that is, the accumulation of capital through their production;*
- *as a corollary, their re-organisation around cost as a central concept is a pre-requisite.*

A practical corollary of this is the suppression of the existing administrative procedural rationality and hence of the present techno-administrative procedures. The former analysis has proved that, beyond 'interferences', the real aspects to be suppressed are the structural organisational features of the Indian administration in SEBs.

The general question becomes (i) how to enterprise SEBs, and (ii) who can do this. The present Chapter technically focuses on the first issue while next part of the book will show that it is unlikely to happen in a purely public environment, and therefore, it is inefficient to rely on pure public solutions to do it. The third part of the book will deal with the private and public-private ways.

5.1.2. Enterprisation in the Post-Socialist World

As there are many possible types of initial organisations (and various environments), there are also many types of enterprisation. In Eastern Europe, enterprisation mainly occurred by suppressing the polyfunctionality of the combinates, that is, isolating their productive functions from others and reconstituting contracts around the productive equipment; in Russia, it happened by bringing consumers markets to them; in China, by creating appropriation and different rules around some parts of the former communist structures, that is by creating some new enterprises alongside 'danweis' (the Chinese term for production plants), with different control rules (see Huchet & Richet, 2000). The enterprisation process is specific to the type of goods that are concerned (the type of the future market) and, moreover, to the type of initial administrative system (see Hirschhausen 1994 for East Germany, Bomsel 1995 for Russia). In case of SEBs, this detailed process has then to be defined, which is a normative work, based on the experience of the first reforming States. *As a concept, enterprisation not only refers to an administrative starting point and an enterprise ending point, or in other words it not only refers to a target, but also to the process to shift from the initial to the final point.*

5.1.3. Enterprisation and Creation of Property Rights

Reforms based on 'reallocation of property rights' are misleading and deemed to fail, it has been seen. However, using the concept of property rights within its right field of application as far as SEBs are concerned (how to 'create' property rights) can be operative. An analysis, aiming at defining from which point property rights start existing, can provide a good criteria to discern when the process of enterprisation is starting. Indeed, the process of capital accumulation and of asset building will start only from well identified property rights. The building and specification of property rights is the precursor to enterprisation. The sole presence of, and indeed the creation of property rights is hence an indicator of potential enterprisation. Once the transformation from an administration to an enterprise has conceptually occurred, then only the classical issue of property rights efficient allocation occurs. Of course, in a reform process, the two questions of the existence of and of proper allocation shall be treated simultaneously. It is only in their conceptualisation that there is an interest in separating them. This is in order to stress an aspect that may risk being neglected. Indeed, *in current reforms, creation of property rights is taken for granted under the influence of the common misleading enterprise-based analysis of SEBs.* Once this point is acknowledged, the two aspects have practically to be considered jointly, putting in place right from the beginning an efficient allocation of property rights within the new structure.

However, more dynamically, one will also recall the fact that the new structure will be the heir of the former one, and that some transaction costs will occur along the path of transformation. In this situation, the creation of property rights should also take into account the characteristics of the previous system, and the transformation should be based on an approach in terms of 'remediability', as advocated by Williamson (1994) or Lotter (1995). Williamson states that, in the remediability standard, "an existent condition is held to be efficient unless a feasible alternative can be described and implemented with net gains". We will have to keep this in mind while framing a system of allocation of power.

Creation of property rights, combined with the remediability theory, can therefore become a positive tool for enterprisation. If in SEBs (as in socialism) 'property rights do not exist', in enterprises they have to.

5.1.4. Corporatisation, Commercialisation, are not Enterprisation

Corporatisation, it has been seen, does not alter the administrative nature of SEBs. That is, it does not turn them into enterprises, because it does not allow them to capitalise, nor to build assets. What we call the 'World-Bank style corporatisation', that is the legal corporatisation supported with training programmes and capacity building, goes a step further. It does pave the way for future creation of property rights, but does not actually create them, and hence does not enterprise SEBs.

Indeed, the World Bank policy combines corporatisation with de-integration between the generation and the network. This has an impact on fixation of subsidies and on the financial relations between the newly created generation and network organisations. As far as subsidies are concerned, the result of the reform process in Andhra

Pradesh, Delhi and Haryana has resulted in the setting up of planned monthly financial transfers from the State Governments to the SEBs and then to the transmission or distribution segments. The aim has been to progressively reduce and ultimately do away with the subsidies, as World Bank (1996, 1997 & 1999) indicates. This measure has thus structurally allowed a space for the creation of cash flow rights, as it has guaranteed minimal subsidies. It is however limited due to the fact that the rest of the financial concerns remain subjected to the classical procedures. Expectations on increase of the tariffs and improvement of the efficiency have not materialised. A second limitation comes from the fact that the creation of control rights has not simultaneously arisen. Another point is the way disbursements of loans are made by the World Bank. They are phased, and depend on milestones achieved, whose evaluation ultimately remains under the discretion of the Bank. Moreover, the disbursements are clearly earmarked to specific issues (consultancy, new equipment...). In practice, disbursements are directly made to the consulting teams, the material suppliers and so on. In a way, this also follows a path from which SEBs' internal discretion, therefore, capacity-building, is absent.

Likewise, power purchase agreements have been signed between the generation and the network entities, contributing to fix clear rules and hence cash flow rights. However, this has been done in all the three 'World Bank' States by fixing cession tariffs on the basis of a 16 per cent rate of return. Indeed, this practice, initially reserved for new private projects and meant to attract them, has been extended by the Central Ministry of Power to all the generation entities. But here again, firstly, these cession tariffs are not always actually paid and delays do appear, similar in manner to what happens between SEBs and Central Undertakings (like NTPC). Secondly, in the absence of control rights, this has contributed to make the situation more difficult for the network utilities. The network segment has to formally bear the impact of the prevailing tariff structure. As a Gridco (Orissa) official declared, "we have been forced to sign power purchase agreements and so, the day Gridco has been incorporated, it has started short of cash".

To conclude with the presentation of the concept of enterprisation it must be understood that it is a far more radical change compared to 'commercialisation'. This latter concept is sometimes advocated in the economic literature, and should not be misleading. Commercialisation refers to the unbundling of 'profit centre' units, and the subsequent establishment of stringent procedures to bill and collect. This does not convey any concept of the creation of property rights and does not provide the discretionary power to locally improve the service, incorporate special schemes for consumers ready to pay them, or only to set-up priorities or locally link improvement in the collection with technical improvement in the quality of service. In other words, this does not open space for capitalisation on consumers, or enterprisation.

5.2. Enterprisation of SEBs

Let us now be specific on what enterprisation of SEBs will mean.

5.2.1. Enterprisation of SEBs as a Target

Generally speaking, the objective of enterprisation should be to change SEBs into *organisations basing their decision-making on cost efficiency without external discretionary power*. Compared to many productive sectors, the power sector is characterised by some amount of natural monopoly in network. In this context, a power enterprise refers to an organisation that is able to base its decisions on cost *versus* benefits, *under a distinct and transparent regulation*. The analysis conducted up to this point serves to highlight what has to be changed in order to break away from the classical system. Broadly, *enterprisation of SEBs would comprise a modification (de-administration) of the procedures, a change in the evaluation criteria for the agents, while simultaneously putting in place a discretionary power within the structure, and a budget allocation-cum-decentralisation.*

Indeed, according to the delineating definition of administrations and enterprises, the primary radical change that has to occur is to institute cost as a central concept and criteria for behaviour. This will be the *sine qua non* condition to the perception and appropriation of the concept of efficiency by the agents. Towards this aim, a true budgetary allocation has to be put in place, evaluation of the agents has to be based on cost related results. Subsequent training has to be done on the very possibility of using this budgetary allocation, to make costs structurally in-built in the organisation.[2] This measure

2. It is only after this radical change that the issue of the opportunistic behaviour on budget (that is, the question raised by the soft budget constraint approach) can be raised. In addition, it is only after this actual allocation (that is after this step towards creation of cash flow rights) that the question of incentives can be asked, through a property rights approach.

only will enable officers in general and Field Officers in particular to build on assets from the equipment and from the users they deal with. It needs to be stated, however, that this is not enough and this condition is far from being sufficient to enterprise a SEB. Indeed, as long as executive instructions remain, and as long as the discretionary power is not properly allocated, the system will not be radically altered. In other words, the measure of allocating budgets remains insufficient to the extent that executive instructions can then expropriate the benefits of the decisions that are taken. After budget allocation, property rights are still not properly established.

So, complementing the establishment of a budgetary allocation, and in support of making central the concept and the use of cost, two necessary conditions must be fulfilled.

- First, *discretionary power has to be established*. This partly means that at least a minimal budget must be locally allocated. Conversely, setting discretionary power means putting in place an allocation of decision power, identified at few levels of hierarchy, and ideally for most of the common decisions, within a single hierarchical level. In this scenario, creating cost-based information is an accompanying reform and making it used in decision-making is a necessary structuring condition. Simple improvements are already available with limited further information at the Field level, for instance regarding transformers. Also, once the focus has been shifted to costs, then it becomes rational for the Field to put in place new procedures on information that will be efficiency driven, provided they are given the means and the power to do that.
- Second, *executive instructions have to be replaced by policy directions and regulation*. The difference between them has been sufficiently dealt with in Chapter 1 and further clarifications here are unnecessary. However, this issue raises many questions about the feasibility of moving from a regime of executive instructions to a well-policed one. These questions open space for a discussion on the public or private nature of the sphere in which the enterprisation shall take place, as well as on the regulation or on the possibility of plan contracts within the public sphere. Therefore, a detailed discussion on this is provided in coming sections and Chapters, which will present a more elaborated framework for analysis.

5.2.2. *Enterprisation as a Process: The Example of Financial Discretionary Power*

At this stage, the discussion of the enterprisation of SEBs needs to be further substantiated, in terms of process as well as the practical issues needed to be solved. What follows is a proposal regarding the establishment and decentralisation of formal discretionary power within the SEB, especially regarding financial responsibility.[3] Rather than constituting a full *vade mecum* for practical enterprisation, this is an illustration of the way the concept of enterprisation can be operationalised in the context of previous systemic analysis.[4]

Rationale and Method

The Circle level seems to be the most indicated as the first step to allocate financial discretionary power.[5] This would allow the Field to acquire property rights based on the results it achieves. Each Circle would be more accountable as long as a techno-economic approach becomes available. Put in place jointly with a system that fixes actual upper limits of expenditures and lower boundaries for revenue collection.[6] Let us consider a loss-making zone (refer to Figure 5.1) for the proposed mechanism. The so-called budget of year N+1 is derived from actual expenditure of the previous year (for all Divisions in a given Circle), plus an applicable increase to establish the new so-called budget. From that level, let the Headquarters allocate a fixed part in cash to the Circle. Two methods for this are possible. One way is through 'direct allocation'; Headquarters should start giving cash

3. This scheme is based on a proposal we made to the Government of Haryana for the distribution in the Northern part of the State, operated by Uttar Haryana Bijli Vitran Nigam Ltd, a corporate company created from the restructuring of the former Haryana State Electricity Board. This proposal has been made further to a Field study sponsored by the Power Secretariat of the Government of Haryana, and examined in Ruet (1999c).

4. Compared to precious works on enterprisation, by Hirschhausen (1994), ours enters into the 'black-box' of decision-making. Where Hirschhausen had described the ultimate recourse to (unstable) political arbitrage in a Soviet system, we underline the lines of regularities and the structural direction of decision-making in the Indian system. This specification is what allows us considering enterprisation as a process that articulates to the structure of the organisation.

5. A practical reason for decentralising at the Circle level is that experience, seniority, accounting and computing resources are higher at this level.

6. It would constitute for the Headquarters a guarantee for the respect of a financial constraint, which in interviews appears to be a limiting factor on the will to implement decentralising measures. Of course, pure zonal profit centres are hardly expected to be a viable solution (because of an uneven mix of consumers, and the present global financial situation). Hence, this decentralisation would be limited, while being progressive enough to accompany the necessary learning process.

allocation to the Field, regardless of initial improvements in revenue collection. The other way is through 'bound allocation', by waiting for initial revenue recoveries. In Figure 5.1, this cash portion is hence represented in the two sections of the budget. A discussion of their respective pros and cons follows.

Figure 5.1

A Proposal for Budgetary Allocation-cum-Decentralisation in SEBs

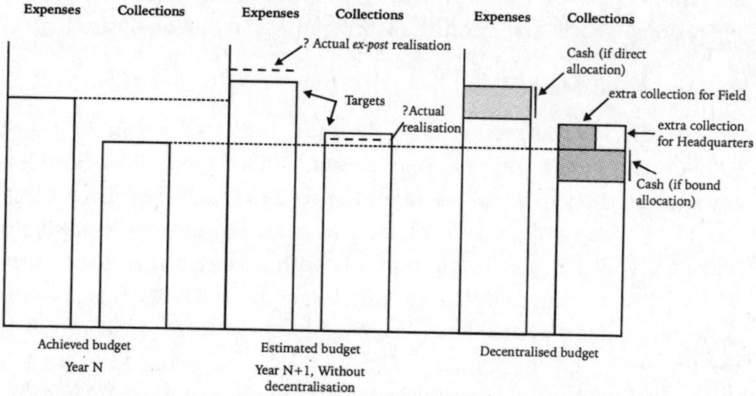

The cash allocation has to be done according to a given timetable. To start the reform, it could concern the lines of credit corresponding to the investments, maintenance, and repair of transformers, as they constitute a crucial point. Let the Headquarters authorise the Field to use:

- either this cash in these transformer-related fields, irrespective of the share between them, *i.e.* to divert from previous use within these budget lines,
- or to use a limited part (up to a fixed limit, say a few per cent) of this cash for any input purchasing.

This creates property rights for the Field: it will be able to use the cash, as it wants, when it wants. For the Headquarters to be sure to control the total budget, it may fix the maximum limit on it, *i.e.* for the book currency budget part. This, in turn, solves the concerns of the Headquarters related to the budget constraint of the Field (on Figure 5.1, the level of expenses is fixed and cannot be higher).

However, this can be balanced by personal incentives on wages to comply with these limits. As far as revenue is concerned, let the Headquarters specify a minimal revenue collection, based on feasible targets, for instance previous achievements. To be credible, the Headquarters can make their cash disbursement subject to completion of a given timetable in collection. Above this level, let the Headquarters allow the Field to retain, as an property right, a part of the extra realisation for its own cash account (this measure can be additional to a personal incentive scheme), let us say on a 50-50 basis, to be simple. These changes once made, incentive schemes become effective, since the latter are associated with an environment where property rights start existing and render incentives credible.

What is to be Expected from this System?

This system, at least, allows the Headquarters to put the budget under control. As far as the Field is concerned, at a first level of analysis, no additional budgetary resources will be provided, but a higher flexibility will be made available to reach an increase of the revenues. In particular, if a very limited part of the cash is allowed to be spent on materials like additional cars, computers, or meters, there is a way to fulfil recurring demands of Field officers to improve the revenue, and to allow them to show their abilities as managers. Combined with the financial incentive to implement some managerial practices, which experiments have shown to be efficient (rotating meter reader teams, for instance), this should allow them to improve the collection, and hence to cope with the associated budget constraint. Further, this allows to locally capitalise the distribution equipment and build assets on users.

At a second level of analysis, the partial decentralisation of cash at the Circle level (unlike at present, when the budgets are specified Division-wise) provides some additional flexibility. This mutualisation of the cash portion – or this local centralisation – results in temporarily affecting the cash, specifically in some zones. This will allow better use of the cash where the investments are the most needed (the Field being expected to have more information regarding this data than the Headquarters). It can also be argued that, given the present high level rate of damage in some States, or more generally speaking, the low level of collections, completing the enhancement of some specific zones is better than dispersing the efforts.[7] In the case of transformer repair, the resulting higher income (manifested by a lower number of transformers to be repaired in these zones, hence resulting in a higher number of transformers that can be replaced in other zones) could be used in other zones. As far as the Headquarters are concerned, this reform would help them decentralise the burden of the financial constraint.

Practical Issues to be Solved

- Setting a system of actual budget allocation implies the implementation of a budget constraint. This has to happen in the framework elaborated below:
  (i) A transparent and synthesised information system is in place, allowing both managerial tools for the Field and control tools for the Headquarters.
  (ii) A coordinating committee between the Field and Headquarters is established, to follow the monitoring of the budget constraint.
  (iii) Training of the SE and the Xens is organised, with accounting support from the Headquarters.
- In particular, corruption might occur. Under this system, the money would not be easy to divert directly to personal accounts, as there will be some control. However, a mechanism needs to be in place, to ensure that managers do not enjoy it physically, by buying unnecessary inputs. This percentage allowed for inputs purchasing might either be introduced after a while, or could be under the control of the monitoring committee through specific reports on their final profitability.
- *A priori*, direct allocation shows a higher commitment of the Headquarters to the Field, but the bound one offers an incentive to make collection faster. A mix of both, or initiating the reform with direct and then replacing it with bound allocation, could be the optimum.

---

7. Indeed, overloading is high. Dispersing the investments would locally reduce the overloading duration, but in peak hours, overloading would still be there. Hence, burnings would go on, at only a slightly reduced rate. Instead, treating some areas as a priority would result in the suppression of the burnings in these areas over period 1, the spare funds being invested in a second zone with concentrated investments over period 2.

- The introduction of actual budgetary allocation must not end up giving disincentives. One needs to take into account the fact that unexpected events can occur, like a heavy monsoon or a drought, for instance. If that happens, the pilot zone shall of course benefit from comparable help to the other zones.
- The introduction of cash at the Circle level also implies the introduction of cash in the store and workshops, with guarantees given on timetable and costs, and/or authorisation to purchase from the private sector in case of non-compliance with the commitment (under the *ex-post* control of the coordinating committee).
- As far as annual renegotiation is concerned, in order to maintain the incentives, some guarantee that the improvements achieved by the Field will not be expropriated has to be given.
  - (i) The growth of the total budget shall be comparable to the growth of the total budget of the whole Board.
  - (ii) The share of the cash part in this total budget shall remain at least constant, conditional to efficiency improvements.
  - (iii) The new minimal limit for revenue collection shall increase, but shall remain inferior to the actually reached level; this will ensure that the Field enjoy a part of the extra revenue it managed over a longer period, thereby strengthening the incentives.

These guarantees should be given for a period of at least three years, while this process is broadened to cover the entire area. The sole risk is that, over this period, the pilot zone achieves big improvements while the situation remains unchanged in other zones; hence, the money kept would be potentially better used in these other zones. This risk is very limited. First, it relates to a positive context, where improvements have been achieved. Second, the number of profitable operations and improvements is enough to ensure that money coming from initial improvements will still be profitable in new ones. Third, the profitability in zones where actual improvements have not been initiated is only potential, and the incentive given to these zones by such an example is higher. Fourth, in this context, the Headquarters receive more cash than in a business-as-usual scenario, which can be used for other areas (assuming that they will have actual property rights on it).

A Discussion on the Scope of Creation of Financial Discretionary Power

The possibility of starting such a scheme within a system that would remain the same in other respects has already been discussed, by pointing out the need for a specific monitoring committee. But another limit has to be studied. Indeed, the proposed scheme jointly addresses an expenditure issue – the repairs on burning of transformers for instance – and a revenue one – collection improvement. The point up to which they are linked or are separated has to be discussed. The stake is that, if they are not linked, then one would be tempted to look at easier schemes to allow collection improvement. Let us argue that they rather constitute a minimal package.

First, if the will is to generate and spread out a costs *versus* benefits behaviour, then direct earnings indicate more than indirect earnings through savings on burnings. Likewise, if the Field accepts this scheme for reducing the transformer burnings and builds it in his behaviour, the access to additional sources of income may speed up the process. In return there is an incentive on improving the collection. Thereafter, allocating discretion and accountability on transformer repairs is profitably complemented with allocating discretion on collection. Improvement in collections is, in this respect, simultaneously a catalyst and a by-product of improvement in operation.

Also, allocation of discretion in collection cannot be started solely. Indeed, even if actual discretionary power is allocated in implementing improvement measures, there is no incentive in collecting more *per se*. If the additional income cannot be used at the Field, then additional collection is useless. Similarly, the Field being concerned with technical improvements, in the proposed scheme, it can consider the financial parameters, an indirect way through which it is able to improve the main technical parameter.

Another way to put it, is that, for the Field, it should be project-oriented. In that perspective, an accompanying measure can be thought of at the project level. Such organisational mechanisms can be completed with banking mechanisms. Let us again take the example of distribution transformers. An 'enterprisation-though-decentralisation' mechanism, to be credible, has to create the local information, centred around the technology-cum-procedure improvements. It has to create the economic and financial information linked to the project. In that context, everything linked to the project is identifiable, and a banker can come into the picture, an idea that we owe to discussions with Y.K. Alagh (be it a public banker in the first stage, like PFC). Then, as Alagh states, "the repayment of the principal and debt servicing is clearly identified by a banker, this kind of policy reform should go hand in hand with the reform of the State Electricity Boards as a whole". In the terms of the book, the financing aspects are integrally part of the enterprisation process. The combination of both SEB-level and project-level reforms relates to margins available at the local level, through catching local markets dynamics.

If one needs to show, these proposals we had raised earlier (Ruet, 2001) may not be unfeasible, for UPERC (2001) finds some credit in them. It states that "to internalise techno-economic considerations in (UPSEB's) decision-making, (...) SDOs, JEs, and Linemen working in UPPCL could be given some control over finances and could be given some incentives to cut transformer burnouts". It of course specifies that this mechanism "has to be carefully designed by the commission to avoid unwanted micro-management of the licensee by the commission", but that "some interference by the commission into organisational matters of the licensee, at least in an advisory capacity, may be desirable". We subscribe to the additional point the UPERC has, of bringing the RC into the mechanism.

Though having been long thought as 'unfeasible' by many, such a similar measure has been implemented by the State of Madhya Pradesh in 2003, in the Indore (the economic capital of the State) Distribution Circle. Especially, direct budgetary hand on operation and maintenance as well as right to disconnection of consumers has been granted. This has resulted in recovering arrears from the HT consumers in a first step, as well as from the LT consumers since then. The indicators of results are provided in Table 5.1. Details (in Hindi) can be found from MPSEB (2003).

This discussion between bound and direct allocation keeps in mind remediability. The direct form corresponds more properly to a full allocation of property rights, while the bound version is a form of property rights limited to specific rights, the residual rights of control – meanwhile created – remaining in the hands of the Headquarters.

Table 5.1

Commercial Improvement of Distribution for Indore City Circle, from Year 2001-02 to 2002-03

Units Sold (MU)	+15% (495.66 to 570.6)
Input Units (MU)	+8% (897.5 to 966.8)
Billing (Rs. crore)	+23% (19.64 to 24.17)
Collection (Rs. crore)	+28% (17.94 to 22.88)
Rate of collection	+5% (0.91 to 0.95)
Per unit Realisation in Rs.	+45% (2 to 2.9)
Energy Loss Improvement	+8% (46 down to 38 per cent)

Source: Madhya Pradesh Paschim Kshetra Vidyut Vitaran Company Limited, MPSEB.

5.3. The Concept of Enterprisation and Analysing the Debates on the Electricity Act (2003)

A new Electricity Act (2003) has been enacted, which replaces the Electricity Act, 1948 (as well as the Act of 1910) and the Regulatory Commission Act, 1998, extending the provisions of the latter, and breaking away with the SEB-based organisation of the latter, to promote a competition-based sector in the future.

The main features of the Act revolve around:

- de-licensing of generation (and the end of restrictions on captive generation); this materialises in the suppression of the need for CEA techno-economic clearance,
- granting of open access (traders/sellers of electricity may use the networks of the utilities/network companies by paying a regulated charge); this is to come in effect immediately as far as transmission is concerned, while the SERCs are given one year for proposing modes of gradual open access in distribution,
- corporatisation of remaining SEBs within a year, and unbundling since the newly formed State Transmission utilities will be prevented from trading electricity,
- granting of multi-year tariffs, in order to reduce the so-called regulatory risks, and
- empowerment of the inspection powers of the Regulatory Commissions.

The Act is seen by its inceptors as a way to force unbundling and promote competition, by authorising consumers to shift from the incumbent to the generator or trader of their choice, and, true enough, the Act is indeed ambitious. On these aspects, Shahi (2003) mentions that "the Act empowers the regulatory institutions to oversee that the utilities function efficiently". He adds that "determinants of efficiency, like norms for availability-based tariff (ABT), will ensure that those who fail are adversely affected while those who improve gain financially. For example, if the distribution licensees gradually reduce the technical and commercial losses, the power tariff for consumers will fall". Two dimensions are hence present in the Act: strengthening the regulator as well as developing competition. On a similar line, Haldea (2003a) mentions that a notable facet of the new Act, "following universally best practices", is the open access system, under which a set of customers can get together as bulk consumers and purchase power either directly from the generating company or through intermediaries such as traders and distribution companies. If one looks closely at the Act, competition is supposed to come, among others, from section 39(1), details that "State Transmission Utility shall not engage in the business of trading in electricity". Section 39(2) (d) specifies that it will provide "non-discriminatory open access" to distribution licensees, generating companies, consumers. This ensures a legal compulsion to unbundled SEBs (according to the Act, it is to be completed after a year, starting from the Enactment).

However, the ambition of the Act, with the ability to implement it in a phased *versus* rapid manner, is precisely what is debated in India. The debate actually revolves around two lines: the feasibility of competition in line with the today achievements of the regulators, and the (unavoidable question of the) role, merits and dis-merits of the private. For instance Godbole (2003), despite he agrees that "the most important element of the reform strategy contained in the Act is of unbundling of SEBs", however argues that the Act "raises a number of new issues which are likely to pose serious problems in the coming years". He specifically argues that, given section 172 (that provides a possibility that the State Government, with the sanction of the Government of India, continues the function of the SEB as the Transmission utility), and also section 131 (that gives margins for vesting the property of SEBs in State Government), it is clear that "no final date has been for the abolition of of SEBs and this decision has been left to the State Governments". Godbole indeed argues that, politically, the Centre will unlikely terminate a SEB if the concerned State does not wish so. Equally, Subba Rao (2003) argues that "in a way, the Electricity Act, 2003 being a forward looking legislation, may have run quite ahead of the available infrastructure and system capabilities. Proposed innovations like open access and power trading will require many technical pre-conditions. There has to be enough capacity in transmission lines as well as inter regional connectivity. Without these pre-requisites for moving energy from surplus to deficit areas, open access may not actually materialise. These considerations will also apply to open access in distribution systems". He adds that "it may take a while to design and create technical pre-conditions on ground such as needed hardware, capacities, systems, codes, energy accounting methods and computerised monitoring devices for operating the provisions". Ultimately, he states that the regulators "are still fledgling organisations". Others, like Kapil Sibal, Member of Parliament and member of the Standing Committee on Energy, even fear that the Electricity Act, 2003 will help perpetuate private monopoly in the power sector and discourage competition.[8]

Here there is a risk to enter in the realm of the sole ideological debate, for the Act lacks a history by now. It is true that the Act does open a considerable scope for competition, which will be much welcomed in the future. The current debate in India actually revolves more around the way to introduce it in a phased manner, many arguing that it is premature to generalise it right now. Such arguments are difficult to clinch out univocally, but, working on the fact that there is a general consensus that long term issue is competition, we argue that the framework set in place in this book allows shedding light on several issues linked with today's phasing of reforms. Especially, one needs to discuss (i) the generalisation of the structural reforms in a context where (ii) competition, that is to say, incentives, may then be activated, where (iii) the role of the regulator is enhanced, but also where (iv) the bankruptcy risk may be increased and articulate a specific manner with the debate on privatisation. We will

8. This latter argument is more extensively dealt with in Chapter 7, in line with the debate on privatisation.

discuss the three former points in respect to enterprisation in this chapter, while we leave the discussion of the latter (not the least important) for a more consistent framework, in Chapter 7.

5.3.1. Competition Needs Regulation, Based on Information, through the Pre-requisite of Enterprisation

Generally, the setting up of competition is envisaged through establishing of open access. However, competition should be disentangled between two levels: generation as well as distribution. Haldea (2003b) details that "once you have open access, consumers in south Delhi, say, can decide if they want to buy power from BSES (Bombay Suburban Electric Supply) that has the monopoly for the region right now, or from some other company, say Y. Naturally, competition between BSES and Y will lower prices, the same way competition between BSES and Tata Power has driven down tariffs for high-tension consumers in Mumbai (Bombay)". This statement articulates differently whether one considers generation or distribution.

In generation, there may be competition if bulk consumers can choose between different providers of energy. But, as Morris (2003) explains, as of today major economic distortions continue in terms of costing of energy. Captive plants, new plants, old plants, unallocated capacity, all face different rules of pricing, still to be either harmonised or liberalised, but in a converging way, with similar rules for all generators. Morris also underlines more cynically that, in the long run, the risk is that opening up may be necessary to bring the SEBs to collapse, and then to reform. However, if SEBs have to be turned bankrupt, this poses several problems. What can happen if SEBs massively collapse?[9] This scenario is quite likely, when the Act authorises most of the customers (hence those who cross-subsidise others) to desert for other generators, like for instance Central PSUs. In a context where SEBs would remain with the subsidised consumers mostly, how can one dream that the size of the private will be enough to cover such a collapse, several authors or practitioners like Godbole

9. In a different context, after the collapse of the Soviet system in Eastern Germany, all the 'Combinates' had to be restructured. Hirschhausen mentions that, true, most have been ultimately 'privatised' after sheer restructuring (which saw anyway a large drop in production), but at the net cost of 900 million DM (450 million Euros), when the reformers had initially expected sales for a net positive value of 2,600 million DM. The 3,500 million difference had been the ineascapable cost of enterprisation.

(2003), Sagar (2003), recall? For instance, Godbole specifies that "it is unlikely that private sector will have the capacity to take over the whole electricity business from SEBs even during the next two decades". This is how Godbole calls the Act a "halfway house" as well as in "anxiety to (...) be unduly futuristic". Actually, one might have to remain on a more transitory mode, and in this regard, it is interesting to notice that Haldea (2001) minds the necessary transition by proposing a gradual competitive system where the existing sources "would not enter the competitive market, and would continue their supplies as per existant agreements. Only new capacity would be subjected to competitive markets to begin with; and competition would thus be introduced at the margins".

Further, others like Phadke & Rajan (2003) state that "except for the increased role of the Regulatory Commissions in retail rate setting (...), there are issues of concern in several of the other provisions" of the Act. Their concern is more particularly with the fact "in developing countries it would be even more difficult to instil competition and mitigate the exercise of market power. Factors like the small size of markets with large centralised power plants, a tight demand-supply situation with low reserve margins, and virtually no real time demand response mechanisms in place will increase the potential to exercise market power in the generation sector substantially in a developing country market". Dealing for instance with the sole 2,000 MW coal plant of Chandrapur in Maharashtra, they mention that "the existence of this large plant is sufficient to make the Maharashtra electricity market highly non-competitive during the peak periods".

But, more structurally, one can wonder on the empowering capacities of 'incentives' and 'pressures' on SEBs to reform themselves? Indeed, and maybe first of all, they *already* are virtually bankrupt! Their Rate on Return on assets (RoR), which has mandatorily been of 3 per cent according to the Electricity Act, 1948, has dipped from an already abysmal (-) 19.6 per cent in 1996-97 down to a catastrophic (-) 44.1 per cent in 2001-02. True, SEBs are 'under-capitalised' (we know what to think about the concept of capital in their case), but still, they are just burning their resources. This present situation means, *inter alia*, that SEBs have not been sensitive to 'incentives', which is not a surprise if our thesis is correct that the concept of budget constraint is not operative in the analysis of SEBs.

In other words, competition is to be seen rather in a framework where, in future, private companies (or public-private partnerships) will be established, and cannot come before enterprisation of SEBs. Let us put it in a different wording: Phadke & Rajan (2003) state that their "central argument is that the successes of reforms in India will depend critically upon the existence of some sort of restraining or disciplining mechanism in the sector, in the absence of which current efforts will likely result in a transition from inefficient public ownership to profit-gouging monopolies or oligarchies". They add that, in India, "in the absence of either effective competition or regulation, whatever benefits privatisation has to offer may never reach the common people". Godbole (2003a) gives an illustrative example: in Maharashtra, the private companies Tata Electric Supply Company and the Bombay Suburban Electric Supply have "not filed their annual revenue requirement submissions before the MERC though over three years have elapsed since the setting up of the commission".

Beyond these measures affecting generation, the Act stipulates that, in terms of distribution, several licenses can be granted for the same zone! This distinction between specific distribution (the operation of the local monopoly network) and supply (the competitive commercial use of this network) is, according to what we have described on the level, accuracy and reliability of information, largely premature in India, and this in no way can help enterprising SEBs.

In other words, and as many authors now recognise, the most important developments in the power reforms in India have revolved around the Regulatory Commissions, justly empowered by the new Electricity Act (2003): the much acclaimed competition can come only if credible and empowered Regulatory Commissions have developed capacities to assess the SEBs or their heir entities or the private companies to come. Here lies the credibility of the reform. The Act provides these measures to empower the commissions, and the years to come will tell if and how the Commissions effectively build these capacities. But still, regulation will revolve around its capacities to generate and check data in a dynamic process. As we have detailed, and given the present shape of SEBs, this data building is part of the enterprisation process, and this sheds light on Subba Rao's (2003) call for "technical pre-conditions". Here may actually be the political wisdom of the Act (along with its manipulability), where the section 172 entitles delaying the final unbundling of SEBs.

5.3.2. *The Act as a Window for Early Bottom-up 'Market' Initiatives: Enterprisation Through Local Markets: No 'islanding', but a Kick-off Effect*

The issue of imposing cost-based decisions at the local level can also be addressed through "helping those who help themselves", following the expression coined by Y.K.Alagh. One way of addressing the problem, is to harness the great vitality of decentralised markets and integrate them with the growth process in the core areas of distribution networks. Organisations and communities which foster limited and well focussed areas may be targeted (see Alagh, 2001). Practical experiments have been attempted with some success, since 1998. Among them is the much discussed 'Tatkal Scheme', developed initially by the Rajasthan Electricity Board, further followed by Gujarat, and then Haryana.[10] This consists in giving rapid connection for tubewell consumers having expressed their willingness to pay the full cost. In most of the SEBs, applications for tubewell connections have been pending, the power utilities alleging 'lack of resources'. The potential of this scheme is therefore important: Indeed, Alagh (2001) considers the number of potential applicants in Rajasthan for instance to be at around 18,000 in each district, while there are 60,000 pending applications in Haryana. The Gujarat Electricity Board reports having electrified 29,200 applicants by the end of March 2002 under a 'Tatkal Scheme', and 61,000 by September 2002. *Tatkal* connections are all metered, with consumers having agreed to commit to a minimal tariff (Rs. 1.4 per unit in Rajasthan for instance). Similarly, one should promote schemes where a village or industrial estate promise to pay the price of electricity, and then provide the facilities urgently and regularly to them.

In other words, new projects on sub-systems of the power economy should be promoted. This concept of 'islanding' is therefore a constitutive part of an enterprisation strategy, and complements the macro-economic and organisational reform of the entire system. Now that the Electricity Act (2003) is in place, such strategies can easily be implemented within its framework.

---

10. In Haryana for instance, consumers to be connected with a cable of not more than 20 metre length from the nearest LT pole are required to pay Rs. 10,000. Those who fall within 90 metre of the nearest LT line, would pay Rs. 20,000.

On this point, the argument of this book in favour of tying-up with the private sector, can be declined as follows. First of all, the various schemes described as part of the enterprisation process, such as allocating a financial discretionary power to the Field, or building-up an information system that Field officers can effectively use, concur in locally complementing the 'Tatkal Scheme' or any islanding measure. Indeed, farmers show a willingness to pay but, for it to sustain, the SEBs have to provide a reliable power. This reliability has to be both in terms of guarantee of supply over time (no power cuts) as well as in quality of supply (voltage). For that, it is necessary that the organisation is able to buy or produce more energy to fill its commitment towards the *Tatkal* consumers. Beyond, it can be ensured only through a better information and metering at the local level. Second, the pursuit of quality also implies local power to monitor the supply according to the load at the 11 kV distribution station.

Let us here reframe in this vision the way reforms are practically implemented in SEBs. If reforms are seen by today's reformers as a way to create small entities to be privatised as quickly as possible, then what becomes important is to give some global visibility to supposedly hurried investors. Balance sheet restructuring then becomes a priority. If it is felt as well that substantial improvements cannot diffuse in the public structure, even through granting and decentralising of discretionary power, then the reform of the reporting system can be effected with a Headquarters oriented top down approach only. This is what happened and what can explain that, sitting at the Field level, Superintending Engineers have barely met or seen the armies of consultants doing the job, while the Xens and SDOs have not met them at all. On the contrary, if the need to enterprise is understood, these reforms will also target the lower levels of the decision-making, and not be designed at the benefit of the sole Headquarters. This can in other words explain how the practical implementation of structural reforms has till now taken the form of solving bounded rationality instead of addressing procedural rationality.

5.4. Conclusion

SEBs are administrations. In that context, reforms should not implicitly suppose that a cost-based behaviour is possible. They rather should create the conditions and the structure to enable such a behaviour. Otherwise, these are deemed to fail. If not tackled, the strength of techno-administrative procedures combined with the absence of discretionary power for the Field officers simply impede any change. *Thus, a radical change in the nature of the organisation is needed, and SEBs have to be turned to actual enterprises, or 'enterprised'. As a normative target, enterprisation shall simultaneously address all the structural and mutually enforcing characteristics previously identified. Namely, enterprisation shall target the suppression of the discretionary power of the State, the allocation of discretionary power to the Field officers, the replacement of the procedures and the paper work with a cost-benefit analysis, based on a sound and integrated information system.* In spite of the toughness of these simultaneous tasks, as a process, some pragmatic lines for enterprisation are exemplified in this Chapter, through a proposal of creation cum actual decentralisation of some budgetary power.

Similarly, a precious impetus of enterprisation can be found in the creation of presently missing property rights. In that respect, the creation of property rights is a tool for the process of enterprisation and the existence of property rights is an indicator of its completion. Analysed with the concept of enterprisation, the so-called structural reforms can be evaluated as such: reforms have not enterprised SEBs, and have not attempted to do so. In detail, enterprisation of SEBs must (i) create cash flow rights for the organisation as a whole, (ii) separate these cash flow rights among various circumscribed units within the organisation, (iii) create specific rights of control for and within the organisation (that is, limit the executive instruction from the State as well as decentralising power to the Field hierarchy), (iv) allocate on certain domains and issues residual right of control to the Field. The last part of the book now assesses the respective roles of the public and the private sector in this enterprisation process yet to be carried out.

Part III

Reforms Analysed through 'Enterprisation'

6

From Charybde: Public Reform Without Reform... to Scylla: Private Reform Without Privates

Both ways of enterprisation of SEBs, based either on public-control or on private-ownership, have risks. In a public reform, the State Government might accept a low pace in the elimination of non technical losses, which would lower the revenue of its SEB. The assumption that public reform will be less efficient than private parties in tackling with losses is indeed a conservative assumption. Privatisation, on the other hand, can also present difficulties. In non-enterprised SEBs there is asymmetric information between the seller and potential buyers, as well as total inexistence of information on some key parameters (list of assets, physical condition of these, level of energy losses...). In that situation of radical uncertainty, investors may make a very low bid, even if they are told by the reformers that "India is a big market"...

Despite of blatant inherent risks in privatisation, the World Bank supports it in several States, arguing that it is a pre-condition to success. However, there are *ex-ante* technical difficulties in the valuation of what is not an enterprise. That is, in the valuation of an organisation which, by nature, has not built the cost-based information to be used in such an exercise. *Ex-post* as well, the use by the private investor of property rights, which had not been earlier adequately defined, can turn out to be a headache. This is confirmed by the Orissa experience of privatisation of distribution while the 'Delhi model' has faced under-bidding *ex-ante* and renegotiation *ex-post*. In a similar context, privatisation would not even be conducted to its term in Andhra Pradesh or in Kanpur (Uttar Pradesh), and remains simply unthinkable for the mass of the Indian hinterland. More theoretically, there is an issue in understanding how it is possible to 'privatise', *i.e.* transfer the property rights, of an organisation where property rights do not exist.

6.1. Are Pure Public Solutions Credible?

Proposals for reform within the public sphere are unlikely to create property rights, thus, unlikely to enterprise the SEBs. Kikeri, Nellis & Shirley describe the reforms that have been attempted throughout the world "short of ownership transfer" (that is, in absence of privatisation). Namely, they involved "(a) exposing SOEs to competition (...); (b) (...) instituting hard budget constraint, (c) increasing the autonomy of managers from government interference in day to day operational decision-making and from non commercial goals". The previous discussion of Soft Budget Constraint theory enables us to foresee the in-built failure of this set of reforms for SEBs. However, public reforms in some cases attempted to go beyond, as they aimed at "(d) developing institutional mechanisms, such as contract plans and performance evaluation systems, to hold managers accountable for results". Let us analyse them.

6.1.1. Not Addressing the 'ownership': Memorandums of Understanding

Taking the example of Romania, Djankov (1998) elaborates on isolation programmes, supposed to "Harden the Budget Constraint". They combine re-organisation and funds to pay wages under tough bankruptcy procedures. But Djankov points out that their implementation includes rescheduling of debts, turning them into equity, and setting up "severance packages for workers" through special funds. Ultimately, isolation programmes are seen by many reformers as a means to access to extra funds, as they believe they are "perceived (by managers) rather as a sanatorium than as a jail". Empirical analysis shows that the 'State Owned Enterprises' (SOEs) under isolation programme have statistically done worse than others in a "control group". Actually, extra subsidies only help the organisation to survive longer, but do not alter the decision-making. Dealing with the adequacy of the World Bank reforms with the field situation, a State Power Secretary stated in the interview that "beggars can't be choosers". This gives an idea of the real level of commitment of the administration when the World Bank asks for corporatisation as a precondition for loan disbursement. Finally, the failure of isolation programmes (or of corporatisation programmes) is rooted in their inability to tackle the enterprisation issue, and not in SOEs' opportunistic behaviour.

Let us discuss the family of 'performance contracts', and more precisely the form in which it materialises in India, *i.e.* the Memorandum of Understanding (MoU). Galal, Shirley *et al.* (1995) state that performance contracts "define the relationships between the government and government employees managing a state-owned enterprise". Within the performance contracts, the MoU is the "signalling" form of the French *plan contracts* (Trivedi, 1992)[1]. Signalling is a process whereby various targets are weighted and a synthetic indicator is calculated based on that. According to Trivedi (1992), "the MoU system is founded on the concept of eliminating day-to-day interference by managing enterprises by objectives and not by procedures". A MoU is a written contract between the public organisation and the Government, specifying objectives and targets to be met. In Trivedi (1990), it is detailed that "once performance targets are set, public enterprise managers must be left free to manage within the agreed parameters". Experiences of contract plans/MoUs have been very successful in France and in Korea. But Vernon (1992) underlines the difficulties of implementation, due to problems in making clear the manager-minister relationship, while Trivedi & Gopal (1992) show that, broadly, MoU are only complements to various other performance improvement systems[2], that Iyer (1992) demonstrates as having been deceptive in India.

Empirical work has been done on contracts between the Governments and the 'SOEs'. Shirley & Xu (1997) have reviewed 14 of them throughout the world. They admit that governments have various objectives, "often conflicting", and sometimes contrary to certain economic objectives. In the latter case, contracts may be viewed as setting both economic and non-economic targets and leaving scope for other sources of enhancement within this set of constraints.

Surprisingly, all the elements of the administered system are pointed out, but *its very consistency remains unaddressed*. In the same line, for instance, Nellis (1991) only points out that, in India, "the first batch of MoUs was incomplete" and that "for example, none of the MoUs dealt with the non-commercial objectives of enterprises or

1. These contracts have long been successful in France with the public power company EDF. But EDF was an enterprise, not an administration.

2. Like management by objectives, zero base budgeting, performance budgeting and so on.

financial compensation for those activities". Here the concept of enterprisation helps going beyond the limited current analysis.

Indeed, the number of objectives listed in the MoUs is very large (usually over 20, for a single organisation). They are also subject to frequent amendments (4 out of 12 surveyed organisations faced suppressions and addition of some of their objectives). Most of them regularly face an annual change of more than 20 per cent in the weightage given to the key targets. For instance, Shirley and Xu report that Indian Oil had seen its "financial objective" fluctuating from 20 per cent in 1989, to 12 per cent in 1990, and 40 per cent in 1992. This actually manifests the variable political equilibriums, and in fact *portrays the actual administrative practices*. Contracts in this case just happen to write out what was previously unwritten in the 'pure administrative system'. MoUs do not attempt to enterprise, either through perennity of targets, nor through addressing the internal organisational hindrance.

Then, statements like those by Trivedi (1992), for whom "if Government is serious about reducing day-to-day interference, MoU can be as effective as, if not more than privatisation", have unfortunately turned to be naive in SEBs. More generally, Mishra (2000) shows that in India, the "policy of imparting greater autonomy to efficiently functioning public enterprises" has been deceptive, since "the much professed autonomy remains to be conferred". It is evident that plan contracts applied to SEBs the way it has been done previously, for instance, with NTPC or Indian Oil, would fail. Hence, the empirical evidence proves that the MoU route will not by itself bring progress, since the MoUs in themselves do not actually create control rights. Progress towards enterprisation would ultimately depend on the willingness of the government to cope with the implications of its own previous commitment[3], but previous experience has not shown satisfying formulas, and credible guarantees remain to be designed.

6.1.2. Decentralisation Schemes and Profit Centres as Unsecured Tools

Going beyond the MoUs, and on more recent lines of proposals, some authors, for instance Ranganathan (1997) or IMI (1999),

3. In a different geographical context, Ramamurti (1991) recalls that "It would appear the contract plans were adopted in Africa more to discipline government than SOEs". This illustrates well how far the issue of the commitment of the government is central in this scheme.

support decentralisation of power in the electricity sector.[4] IMI advocates for (i) "commercial accounting", with an integrated and computerised system and with primary accounting set at operational units, as well as for (ii) responsibility accounting, either in the form of cost centres or profit centres. The actual difference between the two concepts is that in cost centres, only the direct costs are to be recovered, whereas in profit centres, direct costs plus depreciation costs (or costs of capital) are to be recovered. Ranganathan & Gupta (2000) give more details on whether to use one or the other. Indeed, they conceptually disentangle support activities from operating divisions. They state that a "decentralised organisation structure with responsibility and accountability at lower levels", has to be promoted, and emphasise that "this is achieved by incorporating a responsibility centre system in the organisation in terms of cost centre for support activities and profit centre for operating divisions". These accountancy issues are a new measurement system, that needs being operationalised in decision-making.

Both Ranganathan (1997) and IMI (1999) base their proposals on a necessary delegation of authority. How does this proposal of decentralisation lead to the creation of property rights? As long as the paper work and the following of procedures remain, the setting up of these control rights is not credible. However, in details, the issue of cash flow rights is unclear in these proposals. For instance Ranganathan (1997), in the very similar context of Nepal Electricity Authority, proposes a transition process, during the first phase of which, a unit becomes a cost centre, and then a profit centre in the second phase. And he states that only "the branch managers who make surplus in phase one and profit in phase two will be rewarded with budgetary discretion". In other words, property rights cannot be created straight away. It is difficult to imagine how SEBs can *make* surplus and then benefits in the absence of a radical change, by the sole setting up of a measurement system. And indeed, practical experiments prove deceptive in that respect, as Box 6.1 illustrates.

Ranganathan (1997) discusses the sustainability of external property rights. He recognises that the proposed scheme "makes an assumption, *i.e.* the top management, represented by the Board, has

4. Ranganathan's proposal is in that case designed for the Nepal Electricity Authority, but as far as organisational characteristics are concerned, they are very close to the situation in SEBs.

only one objective viz. achievement of business efficiency and that there is no political interference on the firm's top management in pursuing this goal". The administrative nature of SEBs of course proves this to be hardly expectable.

Box 6.1

Profit Centres in Kerala

Profit centres have already been set up in Kerala. The key element of the Kerala State Power Policy, announced in August 1998, is indeed the restructuring of the KSEB through profit centres only. There are now three profit centres: generation, transmission and distribution, which itself has three distinct units covering the three geographical regions: north, central and south. This new structure has been set up further to drafting action plans suggested by a cross-section of over 120 KSEB employees from different categories – see SNC Lavalin (1999). However, field inquiries conducted in December 2000 and again in December 2003, showed that no actual change in the paper work has occurred. The concept of profit centres, in place of setting up managerial tools, has been turned into a mere accounting system, hardly measuring physical inputs and outputs. As far as the external discretionary power of the State is concerned, nothing has changed.

If one wants to fully analyse the chances of the public sphere in reforming, one could imagine that a MoU combined with a decentralisation scheme may be an alternative process for reform. However, the earlier remarks on the risks linked with the sustainability of reforms also apply to such a scheme. Thus, all said and done, MoUs and decentralisation schemes only are not credible. Indeed the example of allocation of budgetary power given in Chapter 5 has largely detailed the number of guarantees to be given and of rights to be created beyond the mere changes of information system and cost computation procedures. Still, even with this, these rights remain at the mercy of the administrative arbitrary in the public sphere.

Accumulated empirical evidence as well as analysis show that the attempts of reform under pure public control, if not deemed to fail, are not credible enough, at least not enough to convince the funding agencies or to credibly represent the users' interests.

6.2. The Privatisation of What?

The World Bank supports privatisation of distribution, in which some States have already engaged (Orissa, Delhi, and, in some areas,

Uttar Pradesh – the city of Kanpur), while others have either at some point of time considered it (Haryana) or still consider it (Andhra Pradesh). The World Bank states that the sole structural reforms do not lead to a substantial change in the way SEBs are operated. On this the present book agrees, but based on a different analysis. The World Bank further binds its assistance to the commitment for privatisation. Consequently, it sees all the structural reforms as a first step, prior to 'privatisation' of generation and distribution. This book then strongly departs from the latter causality and from what it considers a too simplistic view, for actual difficulties to privatisation do exist, and must be underlined.

6.2.1. Valuating what, 'privatising' what? : Property Rights and Privatisation in Orissa

Difficulties emerge in privatising un-enterprised SEBs. In World Bank-style reforms, structural reforms prepare privatisation. Especially the argument for de-integration is not the classical one of competition, but rather practical considerations on the optimal size for privatising. However, after structural reforms, SEBs and their heir entities have still not been enterprised. That is, property rights have still not been created. From this point, what does 'privatisation' actually recover? Quotes are used since, by definition, the concept of privatisation refers to a transfer of existing property rights, from public to private ownership. In the case of un-enterprised SEBs, a problem emerges in knowing what the term refers to, since property rights do not exist. For instance, one does not 'privatise' an administration in the sense that one cannot acquire rights over an administration. Privatisation has then to be a *process firstly including the creation of property rights* as well as their selling. If creation of rights is not clear enough before the bidding phase, then, estimating the value of the property rights becomes difficult. There may be derived risks of (i) under-bidding and (ii) inefficient selection of the investor, not to mention the un-ending negotiations over unclear property rights. As far as practical experience is concerned, let us discuss the examples of the distribution in Orissa, and Delhi.

What is 'Privatisation of an SEB'?

After the structural reforms:

- As far as cash flow rights are concerned, at the level of the whole former Board, they are only partly created, through the *ex-ante* fixation of subsidies by the State. But the way dues to other public undertakings will be paid is still not clear, nor the power to claim payment of bills from users. At the distribution level, actual de-integration has not occurred and the rules for revenue sharing are not fixed. If fixed, then the former rule applies, that is, the direct transfer to the Headquarters.

- As far as control rights are concerned, they are not created, since neither the former Board as a whole, nor any of its heir units are protected from the discretionary power of the State.

Just after the privatisation of a distribution company, cash flow rights have definitely to be established, and discretionary power must rest within the hands of the company. The issue of internal allocation can come later. This means that the privatisation process has to create and secure these rights.

Regarding the cash flow rights, subsidies have to be fixed in advance at the distribution level. Tariffs and intermediate tariffs have to be fixed accordingly by the Regulatory Commission for each segment of the power sector. Any scheme for payment facilities that might be envisaged must be fixed at that time. In that respect and with these provisions, the privatisation process can help to enterprise SEBs by rendering necessary these clarifications and hastening these measures. But in practice, this clarification always partly occurs at the very moment of the take-over. Indeed, in Orissa for instance, even though the three (up to four) zones were already privatised, the negotiations on payment facilities to the transmission part – Gridco – took place till the last minute for Cesco, the fourth Company. Moreover, the discussions on the timing of disbursement went on for months later. Indeed, interviews confirm that the Government of Orissa has finally allowed Cesco to use its payment facilities toward Gridco at a higher pace than expected, while allowing the three other companies (taken over by the same investor) to cross-use their respective payment facilities. Regarding the control rights, the exact rules regarding the specific rights are solved along the privatisation process – and sometimes expeditiously referred to Acts and Bills without jurisprudence, as UHBVN (1999) illustrates. From the moment of the privatisation, residual control rights are supposed to be in the hands of the new managers. But, since this was not the case earlier to the privatisation, interviews confirm that the new managers have constantly to make their rights reckoned by politicians.

Thus, privatisation is seldom a transfer of property rights, but consists in their very creation or germination, as long as some of them have to be further consolidated. In that respect, *the buyer does not only buy, but he also builds. In other words, he does not buy direct property rights, but rather the right to establish property rights*. *Ex-ante,* the investor has no way to know at which rhythm these rights can be created, nor how easily they will be secured. Let us detail the practical implications on a bidding process.

Valuating What?

Privatisation can work if there are investors willing to take over. In trying to valuate a generation or a distribution activity, an investor will look at the anticipated benefits he will generate. If the job expected from the private investor is to turn un-enterprised SEBs into enterprises, this has to be profitable. This profitability is the expected reward of the private investor's work. Here is the privatisation deal, between a State Government aiming to give off this job, and an investor aiming to have a fair return. During the bidding process, the value attached by investors to an SEB will be the sum of the discounted expected profits. Due to incomplete enterprisation, there is low information regarding the level of actual improvements to be expected in organisation, management, human resources. This leads to difficulties in valuation that cover technical – how to do – as well as financial aspects – which level compared to an enterprised body.

Let us be very clear at this stage. We do not refer to the much discussed 'business risks', nor to the 'regulatory risks'. True, an investor has to make assumptions and design anticipations on the growth in demand or related matters, the investor has to focus on expected tariffs, subsidies. The tariffs issue relates more generally to the category of all the regulatory risks, and is classically treated by the economic theory.[5]

Conversely, on the question of expected improvements, there is a radical uncertainty about the very possibility of these improvements,

5. Though the theory proposes multi-year tariffs schemes, not yet applied by Regulatory Commissions in India. In practice, this issue is far from negligible, as Rao (2004) shows.

and not only on their level. That is, the investor knows that he will have to enterprise by himself an organisation in which he has simply no way to determine the possibility of changing the behaviour. For example, in pre-bid conferences, both in Orissa and in Haryana – see for instance UHBVN (1999) – many questions have focused on evaluation of losses, on kinds of information to be shared and level of access to data during site visits, and guarantees for payment of public bodies bills, guarantees of support from the State Government. At a later stage in the privatisation process, in interviews, investors have insisted on the uncertainties in managerial functions: legal ability to sack the agents caught red handed being bribed, practical possibilities in improving billing and collections, with regard to the support of the Government and Courts. The ability to make users pay, call for police if necessary, in other words, to do what Government structures did not manage to do, all this can not be codified or measured, or found through any auditing.

Further, the situation is worsened by the fact that, were all these property rights granted, *internal allocation of residual rights of control on selected issues has still to be implemented by the investor*. Obviously, given the ongoing prevalence of the paper work, right from the take over, the management does not have the possibility of making its decisions internally enforced. The different strategies implemented in Orissa are illustrative in this regard. In Cesco, the Central company taken over by an American company (AES), new teams, parallel to the former hierarchy have been put in place in order to conduct 'raids' against unscrupulous consumers. These consumers, were disconnected during field interventions by these teams and then offered to be regularised. This took place along the new discretionary power of the teams, out from the existing procedures, which are deemed to disappear. Simultaneously, several officers of the former hierarchy were proposed to join the new one. Conversely, in the three other zones, taken over by an Indian company, BSES (Bombay Sub-urban Electricity Supply, a private company based in Bombay), the strategy relies both on making the procedures on revenue collection actually applied by the existing hierarchy and on new techniques (conversion of distribution to high voltage, or delivery of bulk to clusters of villages). What shall be highlighted from these experiments is that, at the time of the take over, nobody can be sure of whether the selected strategy will work and within what timeframe. Five years after privatisation, energy losses have reduced at a very slow pace, setting a discouraging example for further investors. This arises simply because the actual potential in training agents to new techniques cannot be evaluated *ex-ante*. Here again a radical uncertainty emerges from the un-enterprisation of SEBs at the time of privatisation.

Therefore, whatever the openness of the information system to bidders prior to the bid, these elements are not attainable except through subjective perception. This may lead the bidders to lower their estimation of the value of the SEB to be sold, compared with what it would have been with higher information. Indeed, all the bidders could underestimate the real value of the SEBs and make a depreciated offer to the States by integrating a big prime risk. This is the main bottleneck of private reform on short term. Hence, many investors could be discouraged to invest, and those going on could take a high premium, as the Orissa case shows. Indeed, in Orissa's privatisation of the distribution, no foreign bidder initially made an offer and no bid was initially made for the central zone. This shows *ex-post* either that the risks have been considered as too high by foreign companies (Indian companies accepting these risks) or that Indian companies value them differently (appreciating them differently in the present conditions of the privatisation or being more confident in some *ex-post* renegotiation). This mechanically lowers the bid level, and anyway, actual bids by foreign companies were a target of the reform promoters, at least to put a pressure on the selling price. Likewise, the case of Delhi, is really illustrative.

6.2.2. Privatisation of Distribution in Delhi

The Government of Delhi and the Delhi Electricity Regulatory Commission (DERC) have taken into account Orissa's experience, to limit the risks of failure of the bidding process. The Government has that way given, formal and secure guarantees on all the subjects that could be contractualised or guaranteed in compliance with the regulation. This has amounted to a very clear specification of some property rights where feasible. Still, the unknown margins of improvement have led to a dramatic under-selling of the three distribution 'companies'.

Indeed, whereas the distribution losses in Orissa had been initially estimated to be at around 38 per cent (and considered as such by the

OERC) when it finally soon appeared to be 46 per cent, and ultimately 51 per cent, the Delhi Vidyut Board (DVB) and the DERC have been transparent and have acknowledged a 54 per cent level for the Capital. Besides, the Government of Delhi has secured a 'no-risk' situation on this point for the investors. Indeed, the call for bidding has focused on commitment to reduce *aggregated technical and commercial losses* from their initial level. That is, they have committed on a reduction objective, not on a final level objective. No revision of the initial level due to unproper estimation could then impact the investor, only evaluated on the actual improvements it will have achieved. Besides, all unserviceable liabilities have remained with the Government[6]. Post-privatisation subsidies have also been designed, in order to secure cash-flow rights. The Government has designed a guaranteed scheme of subsidies to be versed, to last over ten years on a decreasing basis. And lastly, as far as cash-flow rights are concerned, a Government fund has been created to take care of initial losses, over the first five years. It is supposed to be considered as an advance on early losses, as against future benefits. It has been provisioned with an amount of Rs. 2,600 crore, *ex-post* extended to Rs. 3,500 crore (in 2003).

In these circumstances, one can consider that most of the classical 'regulatory risks' are covered, through adequate establishment of property rights, while the business risks are nil in a city which is the capital of the country and which enjoys a steady economic growth. Still, the results have been deceptive. Initially invited to commit to a total of 20 per cent reduction in aggregated technical and commercial losses over five years, the investors have finally made a bid for 17 per cent only, with, in any case, a very low number of bidders (Tata Power and BSES only). More important, if one believes (so do the reformers) that DVB has 'assets', and that they have a 'value', then one could have expected a bigger offer. These had been estimated at Rs. 23.6 billion (Rs. 2,360 crore), by the rating company SBI Caps. The sale of 51 per cent of their shares has brought Rs. 4.81 billion (Rs. 481 crore) only, that is a 'depreciation' by a steady 60 per cent (refer to Table 6.1) and is nothing compared to the financial help the Government is giving.

6. This is not at all marginal, since, up to the Rs. 231 billion of liabilities of the DVB, Rs. 200 billion have been declared as 'unserviceable' and kept with a holding structure of the Government of Delhi. The remaining Rs. 31.6 billion have been assigned as the book value of the 'assets' (source: TERI, 2002).

Table 6.1

The Privatisation Income in Delhi

(Rs. in billion)

Zone	*Investor*	*Valuation by SBI Caps, for 100 per cent of the Shares*	*Purchasing Cost for 51 per cent of the Shares*
North & North-West	Tata Power Co.	9.2	1.88
South & West	BSES	11.5	2.34
Central & East	BSES	2.9	0.59

Source: Powerline Vol. 6, No. 9, June 2002.

This example clearly shows that, however well engineered, a quick privatisation of a non-enterprised SEB will always lead to a major drawback: the under-value of selling the newly created property rights. Whatever compared to the initial value of unserviceable liabilities, or to the funds put in place or the subsidies to be given, the income generated through this way of reforming cannot be an argument enough to justify it[7]. This ultimately proves again that, when the private sector is brought to power management, its managerial capacity should rather be targeted than its investment capacities. Indeed, even the investments put in these companies by the private (sector) further to privatisation are not substantial. For instance, TPC has announced a Rs. 380 crore only (Rs. 3.8 billion), which the State would have been in a financial position to do. This is in reverse to be seriously balanced with the request in 2004 from the private utilities for the State to provide an additional financial help that could amount to a Rs. 2,000 crore (Rs. 20 billion) for the next couple of years. This question will be fully addressed in the last chapter of the book.

However, and without entering in details, since several States or several cities in some States are on the path of privatisation, this also opens another question. What is the capacity of sole Indian companies to absorb a substantial part of the Indian SEBs? Hence this questions the sustainability of a high rhythm of privatisation on the scale of the country. If at all privatisation was the solution, it could no longer be feasible for the late-comers.

7. Even consulting fees are huge: in Orissa, they have earned Rs. 306 crore, Kannungo (2002) Reports.

In tune with us, Rao states that "privatisation should not replace state monopoly with private monopolies. This is the case with privatisation both in Orissa and Delhi. This can be avoided if distribution wires remain a neutral natural monopoly while small supply circles related to each sub-stations are privatised."

Dealing with the 'Delhi Package', that initially had envisaged a multi-year tariffs principle as a guarantee for investors, but where this principle had been wiped out by the Delhi ERC, Rao (2004) puts a comment that is right in pragmatic terms (we totally subscribe to the principle of a multi-year tariffs, as last chapter of the book discusses) but, the least to say, paradoxical in principle. He states that "a clear lesson from the Delhi experience is that the regulator must be a part of the reform planning process but cannot have a veto on it". Arguing that "a multi-year tariff structure is necessary", he states that "once the package has been widely discussed, the government should use its policy direction powers if the ERC does not cooperate". This example clearly illustrates the ambivalence and the paradox of any regulatory system set through an 'independent commission', if stakeholders with technical and financial analytical capabilities are not numerous and active enough in the regulatory debate. Indeed there is obviously no lasting objective criteria through which one could disentangle between policy directions 'for the good' or 'for the wrong'. Now, what in the specific case of Delhi the government could do—and what it did—is to secure and subsidising fund to be used later to cover initial financial deficits of the utilities; this is in full accordance with the letter of the Act. However, on a more general plane, the only long term issue of such debates lays is the availability and involvement of trained stakeholders as well as efficiency-aware regulators. Rao himself implicitly agrees with this, when he refers to "a need to provide funding for developing a consumer organisation in each region with the necessary expertise". This might be one way of bringing the much needed information. Having made clear the difficulties of a privatisation process, let us evaluate the grounds on which it is anyway supported by the World Bank, to see how the concept of enterprisation will help improving the debate in last chapter.

6.3. Redistributive Issues and the Political Economy of Privatisation

Having shown that both public reforms and privatisation have technical drawbacks, let us specify further what are their respective redistributive impacts. Especially, their technical drawbacks translate into redistributive concerns. This allows to shed some light on the political economy of the privatisation choice, and therefore to discuss the World Bank position.

6.3.1. Redistributive Issues

Let us analyse the respective effects of public and private reforms on redistribution between the various stakeholders. To do this, we first indicate the redistributive effects of a successful reform, whatever the mode of enterprisation. Then, from their respective bottlenecks we derive the short-term and long-term redistributive consequences of various types of reform.

Redistributive Effects of a Successful Reform

Let us define what would be a successful reform, either public or private, as compared to a 'business as usual' scenario. Let us distinguish three categories of stakeholders: the benevolent State, supposed to target poverty alleviation programmes[8], the consumers and the private investors. The consumers may be sub-divided into (i) industrials & commercials paying a tariff higher than the average cost of supply, (ii) residentials & agriculture paying a subsidised tariff and (iii) stealers of electricity which cut across categories as surveys show.

In a business-as-usual scenario, the average cost of supply would remain high or increase, essentially due to the high level of non-technical losses. Tariffs distortions would remain, which would lead several of the most profitable SEBs' clients to turn to captive

8. This category is taken to represent the welfare in India. In models focusing on OECD countries, the category of tax-payers represents the welfare. In India, the tax-payers are not directly representative as a category of people, since fiscal evasion is high. The category of the poors, targeted through the poverty alleviation programs of the State, also has the advantage to correspond to the marginal use of the Governments budgets. Indeed, reforms in the public sphere are designed to make available additional resources in poverty eradication programs. World Bank (1996, 1997, 1999) also considers the poors as the major beneficiaries of the power reforms. Besides, since political feasibility matters, there is a clear interest in including a category that has proved being able to demonstrate in the streets regarding reforms, for instance in Andhra Pradesh in Summer 2000.

generation. Therefore, SEBs financial situation would worsen, to be supported by public finance.

Let us now examine the impact of a successful reform, defined as able to (i) substantially cope with technical and non technical losses in the short run, and (ii) to be cost efficient in the long run. From now, short term efficiency improvement will then refer to the mechanical effect of sharing the same costs between a higher amount of billed energy, while long term efficiency improvement will refer to a decrease in generation and supply costs, through organisational measures and investment. In such a successful reform, whatever public or private, in the short run the average cost of supply is expectable to stabilise since the 'loss consumer'[9] will be targeted (or even to decrease, but let's take a conservative view). This comes from a trade-off between the mechanical effect of energy losses improvement, and the higher cost of new investments and operation charges. Power sector financial results would improve, due to gains from theft-fighting and short as well as long term efficiency improvement measures. Therefore, subsidies could decrease and public finances improve. Thieves of energy would then definitely lose, as non-technical losses will be addressed.[10]

Success of the reform is defined as managerial improvements, and so has little to do with tariffs level. However, a convergence in tariffs is expectable from regulatory commissions: low tariffs would increase, leading to initial financial burden for farmers and residentials. A part of the gains in efficiency can be passed on to industrials. Actual tariffs will ultimately depend on political decision according subsidies to some users to facilitate the transition. Therefore, only signs of variation and not precise levels can be given for redistributive effects (Box 6.2). This indicates who would mechanically be the winners and losers of a reform, notwithstanding compensation for losers through subsidies. In the long term, gains in efficiency in several fields are expectable, and average tariffs could therefore decrease, at given

9. We owe the concept of 'loss consumer' to discussions with Sanjeev Ahluwalia. Assumption of political economy, however, remain ours and we shall bear alone the critique.

10. This assumption should actually be refined: among users who benefit from 'non-technical losses', many actually show a willingness to pay if quality of service improves. Indeed costs attached to low quality (damaged equipment or coping strategies) overbalances the amount of cross-subsidies (See TERI 1999, World Bank 2001).

amount of subsidies. Then all consumers as well as the State/poors and/or shareholders (according to the type of reform) could benefit from the reform, depending on appropriate tariff-orders. Results are summed up in Box 6.2.

Box 6.2

Redistributive Effects of a Successful Reform

Successful reform (either private or public) *versus* non reform:

Short term	- thieves of electricity	--
	- farmers, residentials	-
	- industrials	+
	- State/poors and/or shareholders	++
Long term (with efficiency effects)		
	- all consumers	+
	- poors and/or shareholders	+

Now, comparison between public and private reforms, based on their respective bottlenecks, can take place. Assumptions and recalls on regulation are initially pointed out in coming subsections.

Private *versus* Public Reform, on Short Term Redistributive Effects

Let us compare the redistributive effects, with public reform taken as a reference, and the private one as a variant. As a framework, let us consider the regulatory process as fixing objectives in losses reduction over a period. Tariffs are set so as to ensure a return allowing profitability, provided the costs are under control. If the regulatory objectives are not reached the power companies will immediately bear the cost. This implies that in a public-oriented reform the State – and ultimately the poor – would bear it, whereas in a private-oriented one, a private company would do so. Private reform, in large part designed to solve the risk of low political commitment, is also a transfer of risks from poors to shareholders in case of reform failure or delay. Enterprisation under public reform is more probable than private one to lead to delays in losses reduction. Of course, stealers of electricity are bigger losers in a losses reduction scenario. Hence in private reform they lose more than in public one;

the relative redistributive effect is negative (negative sign in Box 6.3) on them in private compared to public reform.

Box 6.3

Redistributive Effects of Private versus Public Reform in the Short Term

Private *versus* public in the short term

Hypothesis: the losses reduction is higher in private reform:

- thieves of electricity	-
- all paying customers	0
- State/poors	+
- shareholders	+

Let us show that the delay cost of public reform would be, in the short term, passed on poors and not on paying users. In the short term, energy losses targets – and hence tariffs – will be based on the levels the Commission believes to be attainable. They will therefore be independent of the nature of the licensee. Then redistributive effects to various categories of paying consumers are the same in both reforms. Redistributive effects on paying consumers are neutral towards the type of reform – hence the '0' in Box 6.3 – on the short term (apart from the quality and reliability of supply). Then the cost of such a delay in losses reduction in public reform (as compared to a private one) is borne by the SEB and so, in this case of public reform, by poors, because of the conservative assumption that *the marginal use of budget by the State is for poverty alleviation programmes*.[11] This effect tends to give to the poor better redistribution in private than public reform. Similarly, since the State derives an income from the privatisation, and if the hypothesis that the marginal income of the State goes to the poor, then they also benefit from this in the short run. Hence the '+' in Box 6.3. In case of private reform, the category of shareholders appears. Under the efficiency and regulatory assumptions made above, they have a benefit in private reform; hence the positive sign. Then, the short-run redistribution is

11. 'Marginal' here does not refer to a low level of expenditure. It refers, in public economics, to the fact that this is the last budgetary post, once all other expenditure are met. These programmes are made only if there are *margins* for them. In reverse, once all other budgetary posts are covered, additional revenues directly benefits the marginal expenditures, all things being equal.

favourable to the State (and the poor) in a privatisation scenario. Actually, the decision will depend on the political economy and weight given to 'thieves of electricity', as well as 'loss consumer.

Private *versus* Public Reform on Long Term Redistributive Effects

Let us now compare the redistributive effects of reforms in the long term, with the public one as a reference. For that, let us first analyse the expectable tariff regulation process in the long term. Tariff revision will have to be based on the previous actual achievements, and the level reached will expectedly be used as a basis for the new objectives. In other words, targets and estimation of what is feasible are expectable to be somehow readjusted after a while, to take into account what has actually been done. Therefore, if the hypothesis that public reform will need more time to reduce losses is correct, to provide manageable situation to corporatised SEBs, improvement targets will remain after a while somewhat lower in public than in private reform, and tariffs higher. Thereby, a part of the delay cost will be passed on to consumers, and no longer to poor, as would be the case on the short term. Then, in the long term, at a given level of subsidies, poor are neutral to the type of reform ('0' in Box 6.4). Consumers would therefore pay a higher price in public reform; hence a higher redistributive effect the in private one ('+' in Box 6.4).

Box 6.4

Redistributive Effects of Private versus Public Reform in Long Term

Private *versus* public in long term

Hypothesis: private long term efficiency is superior to public one

- all consumers	++ or + (depending on actual selection of the most efficient)
- poors	0
- shareholders	+

The State is in a different position. In case of enterprisation through privatisation, the expectable cost of under selling of SEBs would in the long run be ultimately passed on the State. This effect is to be balanced with higher efficiency. The total redistributive effect on them is therefore unknown *ex-ante*; it depends *ex-post* on actual delays and under bidding respectively attached to public and private reforms. Therefore, in the long run, choice between prior enterprisation through public reform, which is time consuming, and early privatisation is linked with the trade-off 'delay costs *versus* low bids'.

On the long term, after a prior substantial losses elimination, reduction in all costs (investment, operation, management...) can besides be expected from the power sector. In the present agency relation with the States, public sector is expectable to delays. Assumption can then be made that a private reform could be more efficient in reducing these costs. So, by and large, a part of the delay cost will also have to be passed to consumers in public reform. Here again this assumption is conservative.[12]

Let us now consider the problem of selecting the most efficient investor. For that, let us look at the final offer that will be made, *i.e.* the highest bid. Let us recall that potential bidders face (i) incomplete information and (ii) asymmetries of information among them. Previous sub-section has detailed that there is thus no guarantee that the most efficient would be selected, as would happen with the same level of information and the same subjective evaluation of risks among bidders. In turn, the consumers benefit will be affected in the long term, being all the more positive if the most efficient is selected among bidders (combined with the above '+' for consumers, it leads to '++' or '+' according to this selection).

To sum up, corporatised SEBs are incompletely enterprised. To that are attached potential discretionary power from Governments in case of public reform, and incomplete information that grows important in private reform. Considering the present situation, the cost of public *versus* private reform is linked with the risk of delays in efficiency improvement. The consequences would, in the short term, be delays in reducing losses, to be paid by State/poor, and in the long term, ongoing low general efficiency, which would be passed to all consumers.

---

12. Here we do not discuss public-private partnership solutions, left for Chapter 7.

Thus cost of private *versus* public reform is linked with incomplete and asymmetric information due to incomplete enterprisation. This may lower the bid, incurring immediate cost for State/poor, and possibly lead to not selecting the most efficient investor, occurring long term costs for all consumers.

The respective technical limitations of both types of reforms in offering credible paths to successful results, ultimately translate into related redistributive drawbacks, which are seldom taken into account, when Governments often engage into reform for the sake of extended loans. Besides, surveys show that benefitors of the 'non-technical losses' are widespread across all categories of consumers. Even if all face however costs that overweight those benefits in the long run (damage of equipment due to voltage fluctuation, cost of power cuts-coping strategies), the short term stalemate is politically less risky.

6.3.2. *The World Bank and the Political Economy of Privatisation; 'SEBs are mummies'*

Pro-privatisation reformers target the soft budget constraint they identify in public organisations. These organisations are designated as State Owned Enterprises (SOE), and hence implicitly analysed as enterprises. Actually, the various reports on which reforms are based, (World Bank 1996, 1997, 1999) implicitly analyse SEBs as enterprises.

Let us illustrate how the concept of enterprisation articulates with this. Coming back to the will to lower the size of the organisations in order to sell them, let us refer to what an official stated in the interviews. He graphically elaborated that "When economists come from Washington with nice theories and arguments for efficiency through competition, I keep quiet; then I bring them to the Headquarters of (this) SEB, in the office of Mr X; before entering, they notice how far a mess the files make, documents and archives, lying in fallen piles, on old shelves, sometimes on the floor; then they understand that the point in India is something else". Needless to say, the point is that only privatisation 'as fast as possible' can bring these bodies back to the normal and net situation. In the same vein, an official told me off the record: "SEBs are mummies; they must be cut into pieces and privatised". However dramatic and illuminating such a scene may be for the touring economists, it is argued here that, on this particular issue, for instance, an analysis based on the study of the paper work can be more valuable.[13] At a more general level, we believe that one can be more 'analytic', and that the concept of enterprisation offers such a possibility.

Strictly Speaking, the Need for Structural Reforms is not induced by Privatisation...

The structural reforms (corporatisation, de-integration and setting up of Regulatory Commissions) are sometimes presented as deriving from the need to attract private investments. For instance, the Government of India (1998b) argues that "to attract private capital in the industry, structural reforms in the industry would be required".[14] Interviews have effectively shown that private investors are asking for some autonomy guarantees. Nevertheless, in the official diagnosis, two facts have been pointed out: the State Governments are structurally involved in the day to day running of the power sector and the SEBs have *ex-post* been inefficient. Assuming that this diagnosis is correct, it cannot be agreed that the structural reform motivation is derived from the single equipment financial needs. If we follow its own logic, then the structural reforms are needed anyway if there is a will to address the efficiency issue, and if privatisation is no longer to be a political alibi.

Let us examine separately the two justifications given for privatisation: private investment needs and managerial improvement. It can be read in Government of India (1998b) that "Need for additional resources for system upgradation would need private sector participation in distribution", which is only a matter of quantitative justification (on the basis of the investment needs compared to the available public investment capacity). But this document is also expecting "private sector to bring in efficiency in management of operations", which is now a qualitative argument. The answer to the

13. The apparent disorder of the archives, although unarguably kafkaesque for an external observer, does not prevent SEBs agents locate the necessary files. Hundreds of uneducated helpers have acquired after years a close knowledge of the structure and have become the depositories of the local mechanics of the system. In this regard, the paper work analysis allows to precisely characterise the knowledge of the helpers. They know the order, and they are able to find the files that are useful for the administrative processing of the paper work. They do not know and nobody knows – because the system does not know – how to find information that is useful for managing, which is what the external manager, and to a lesser extent, the touring economist would look for.

14. The example has been taken from the Government of India, but this assertion can be considered as 'common assumption' among the officials and in public debate.

first argument has straightforwardly been given right from Chapter 1, showing that the analysis on quantitative aspects is misleading. The focus falls then on qualitative aspects, on knowing if enterprisation is accessible without recourse to privatisation, or if the latter is compulsory in exclusion to any other alternative model, as management contract or any public-private partnership for instance. In other words, the point is to find out whether it is only privatisation that can provide such improved efficiency.

... and practically Power Finance Corporation does not address the question...

Practically speaking, as far as the Government of India is concerned, it has no constitutional right to impose nor to promote any specific mode of reform of the SEBs.[15] This includes primarily the fact that it shall not push the States for the privatisation option. Its funding agency, Power Finance Corporation (PFC), thus only asks for the structural reforms discussed above in order to extend its support. It does not insist on privatisation, or any form of delegation in management. The PFC-style reforms generally corporatise the light way, that is they effect a 'legal corporatisation', as previously defined, or unbundling. The State of Kerala has been looking for a solution based on profit centres with the support of PFC. The issue of the degree of State disengagement in management is generally addressed on a case to case basis, and not in a complete framework.

... while World Bank-style structural reforms are implemented with privatisation as a target

However, the debate on alternative strategies to privatisation is considered as already clinched in World Bank funded reforms. In Orissa, Haryana, and Andhra Pradesh, the State Governments have had to commit on a timeframe for privatisation. Starting from the Haryana loan, the disbursements have been fragmented in phases, actual disbursement being subject to achievement of the structural reforms on previous phases and also on progression of the privatisation process. As appeared from interviews, respecting a proper calendar in issuing standard of qualifications, requests for

15. This is now being proposed as a model through Electricity Act, 2003.

proposals, organising pre-bid meetings to answer the questions of potential investors, organising data-rooms and Field visits have materialised as corner-stones of loan disbursement. As a matter of fact, further to the political change in Haryana State Government which took place by September 1999, the relations between the State of Haryana and the World Bank have focused on respecting of the schedule. Loan disbursements have been delayed and then interrupted following the attempts of the Haryana Government to delay or postpone *sine die* the privatisation of UHBVN. The central role which is given to privatisation cannot be better illustrated than by the statement of one World Bank official. He declared in interviews – off the record – that corporatisation and de-integration are methods to allow for the privatisation of smaller entities, easier to privatise.

This kind of arguments, we believe, locks the debate in favour of privatisation, which Chapter 7 proposes to unlock.

6.4. Conclusion

Both public reforms and privatisation have drawbacks. Privatisation is based on a bidding process. The potential bidders on an un-enterprised body face (i) incomplete information and (ii) asymmetries of information. Thus valuation becomes mostly subjective, based on non-standardised information. In other words, as Veljanovski (1987) observes, in a 'transition economics' context, "privatisation involves more than the simple transfer of ownership. It involves the transfer and redefinition of a complex bundle of property rights which creates a whole new penalty reward system which will alter the incentives in the enterprise and ultimately its performance". *When the initial organisation is not an enterprise, organising these redefinitions and valuating their consequences over such a complex bundle turns to be problematic.*

Each bid will be derived from what the bidder perceives as the expected efficiency in this context of incomplete information, and not from what would be its effective efficiency if selected. In other words, the bid will depend not only on the absolute efficiency of the bidder but also on the information level it enjoys. Thus, the highest bid is not the ultimate criteria of selection since the highest bidder may not be the most efficient in terms of cost reduction. Privatisation loses in this context one of its soundest characteristic as an economic tool: its ability to promote *competition*.

Then, though the World Bank underlines the limitations of structural reforms (as this book does), the causes and remedies the Bank highlights and suggests actually departs in a straight way from our enterprisation-based analysis. Indeed, structural reforms, even in the States whose reform is supported by the World Bank, are shaped by the attempt to target the supposedly bounded rationality. They do not address the nature of the organisation, that they implicitly analyse as an enterprise.

Towards the target of enterprisation, privatisation and public reform are two alternative candidates with their respective bottlenecks. The problem also has a redistributive dimension. Considering the present situation, the cost of public *versus* private reform is linked with the risk of delays in efficiency improvement. The consequences would, in the short term, be delays in reducing losses, to be paid by tax payers, and in the long term, ongoing low general efficiency, which would be passed to all consumers. Conversely, cost of private *versus* public reform is linked with incomplete information due to incomplete enterprisation. This may lower the bid, incurring immediate cost for tax payers, and possibly lead to not selecting the most efficient investor, occurring long term costs for all consumers. Indeed, one can imagine 'theoretical optimal solutions'. For instance: first, a deeper enterprisation through public reform, then, at least partial privatisation to increase efficiency through competition (actual & comparative). The delay cost, if not too high, might be balanced by higher selling price and by increasing the chance to select the most efficient investor.

Addressing the choice between public and private reform is not of immediate concern: provided significant steps toward enterprisation are done, this choice can be postponed. As an official from the CERC did declare, "the issue is not whether to privatise or not; this can be left for later. The urgent question is how to track down the 'waste consumer'".

7

Practical Means of Enterprisation: Management Contract as a Private-Public Hybrid Solution

A quick privatisation leads to a low selling price for the SEB, and therefore a low income for the State (since the investors face uncertainties on the possibilities to enterprise the SEB). Conversely, a delayed privatisation can either bring a higher or a lower income, depending on the success or failure of a prior 'public' enterprisation. Pragmatically, one cannot seriously think that the whole of Indian SEBs can possibly find private takers. Let us examine and model further the way to solve both drawbacks, and discuss the supporting measures the Government of India can take.

7.1. The Political Economy of the 'reformer' State Government

Since the ultimate drawback in public reforms is their low credibility, let us examine precisely how it operates.

7.1.1. The Limits of the Public Reforms

The interest to attempt a public enterprisation ultimately depends on the probability (the credibility) of the State to be successful in it. A simple parameter can be given to assess this. Let us call V_0 the average discounted value the investors would give in a bid for a particular SEB. Let us associate a range of uncertainty σ, due to absence of information. A way to interpret σ is that, in case of a successful enterprisation, uncertainty would disappear, and the bid would bring the value $V_0 + \sigma$ for the SEB. That is, if one imagines that the States first attempts and successes at reforming the SEB initially, a further privatisation would bring the value $V_0 + \sigma$. Let us consider, conversely, that it would bring V_0 only both if no prior attempt is made, or if it fails. Hence σ can also be considered to represent the potential gain for the State, linked to prior enterprisation.[1] These values are of course empirical. However, from Delhi privatisation case, we have established that, if not 'under-estimated', the selling price may easily be doubled. This is far from being a negligible issue.

If this is feasible, then one can be more precise on the redistributive outcomes for various stakeholders. Let us distinguish, apart the State, the future Winners of a successful reform (those industrial and domestic consumers paying their bills), and its Losers (a part of the rural highly subsidised consumers, and all the stealers of electricity, be they industrial or domestic). At the first order, the winners of a reform are the consumers who initially subsidise the others, these latter being the future Losers. Initially, State and Winners subsidise Losers.

After a successful reform, two changes occur. At the first level, managerial behaviour results in modifying the toughness in billing and collecting. In other words, the subsidy transfers change, hence the net transfers for each category. However, in a second stage, technical improvement in handling the operational constraints arises and has to be integrated in the equation. The technical improvement can either help in smoothening the change for the Losers, or be additionally transferred to the Winners, depending on the political economy of the sector. Looked at a graphic way, the technical efficiency improvement measures the benefits of the 'inefficiency consumer', that allow margins in a sustainable evolution of financial transfers. In the current political economy of the power sector in India, the managerial improvements from the system can mainly come from actually charging the Losers for electricity. Since Regulatory Commissions are somewhat reluctant to increase the tariffs, let us assume that the managerial progress is borne by the Losers. On the other hand, even if winners presently highly cross-subsidise the system, it is difficult to imagine that they could enjoy either better tariffs or better financial situation through managerial improvement only. They actually need technical improvement to see a betterment of their situation and become true Winners.

1. A more mathematical way to look at things is as follows: the investor gives the discounted value of the revenues it expects. The discounting factor bears the cost of re-financing itself, which will be, all things being equal, all the more important that the risk is big.

That is, Winners have an incentive in technical progress. Actually, *in the present political economy, they truly become winners only when there is technical progress, which avails a reduction of their bills*. The to be-Winners have thus all the reasons to support a smooth transfer to allow selecting the best private operator possible. Any public transitory measure favouring this should gain their support. Next sub-section will show that this is to be reached through Management Contracts between the State and a private contractor.

Losers, on their own, *a priori* have an interest in public enterprisation. Indeed, *in public enterprisation with a 'reasonable' probability of success, the Losers have a comparative gain with respect to the direct privatisation case, because the higher value of sale will be passed to them and help smoothening their losses. This is why they can hence be a political support for such a reform, which is a counter-intuitive result*. Indeed, if natural losers of a reform consider that it is deemed to happen sooner or later, they have to support the less damaging strategy. Again they have to favour a way that avails technical improvement and that ensures that the most efficient reformer will be selected. This is for them a 'second worst' scenario.

To sum up, a successful public enterprisation leads to a net transfer from investors to State and Losers, and is indifferent to Winners in the short run (then, if successful in the long run, they will in any case benefit from it). This reform is thus politically feasible. All these results stand true as long as the State shows a minimal credibility to ensure successful step of enterprisation prior to the privatisation. Even investors, when interviewed, would prefer paying more in exchange of lesser uncertainties. This very recurring pattern is explained by the load that risk has on re-financing cost. The only relevant question becomes how to design the best credible scheme to ensure this, especially taking into account the potential non-benevolence of the State.

7.1.2. Preventing from the Non-benevolent State

The problem of credibility of reform can now be expressed as the temptation for a government to mimic a genuine attempt of reform, while cashing loans before the end of its mandate. Government face elections and consider the short term as a 'political time'. In other words, discounting future benefits at present time does not reflect their perception of State incomes or of redistributive issues: it can be assumed that whatever happens after elections simply no longer matters. Then previous discussion shall be modified by taking into account a time-bound horizon. That way, any Government has an opportunistic incentive to choose privatisation, even at a low price, in order to benefit from a direct income. With a time-bound horizon, it does no longer consider efficiency improvements to come, but (i) the short run money it derives from loans or privatisation, compared to (ii) the political implications of the redistributive impacts for the respective stakeholders. Moreover, this bias is amplified due to the loans assorted with the commitment to privatise. These loans have not been considered till now in the discussion since they have to be repaid by the State sooner or later, either directly or by the future investor who will then take it into account at the time of bidding.

At the first order, there is thus no need to take this into account in the discussion as long as we consider that the State (the continuity of the State) is the stakeholder. But now, if we consider that a State is potentially made from the discontinuity of successive governments, this element matters. Even if privatisation is a politically risky subject, it vests the possibility to opportunistically phase its timeframe so while leaving the actual privatisation for after the electoral period, as to encashing loans before, and any way being discrete during the campaign about promises made to funding agencies, as had for instance happened in Haryana. Indeed, in Haryana, till mid-1999, the Government was committed to privatisation. It however lost the elections and the new Government initially showed less enthusiasm, to finally renege from the commitment of its predecessor. In Andhra Pradesh, the Government engaged into reforms before the 1999 elections and enjoyed the loans. It got reelected, then courageously kept reforming, but postponed privatisation (arguing on the drawbacks of the model in the neighbouring State of Orissa).[2] In this latter case, the State only enjoys the loans, without any real commitment.

An intermediary optimal solution can even consist in: (i) committing to privatisation and advertising to Winners, (ii) enjoying loans, (iii) phasing the selling out just before (or more likely after) the elections, for the private investor not having the time to substantially alter the living conditions of the Losers, (iv) using the

2. The 2004 election brought a new State Government, whose policy regarding privatisation is to come.

money for 'visible' and 'quick political return' projects in other fields. This opportunistic privatisation scenario is strengthened by the fact that, if the Winners do not correctly anticipate their future benefits in redistributive terms, they will not straight-away support public reform. In this case, the choice of privatisation would occur for the worst possible reasons.

Looked at from the point of view of the funding agencies, some guidelines have then to be defined to take some guarantees. In the Indian federal system, the Central Government might as well find it legitimate to ask for such guarantees. Hence the risk on sustainability of public enterprisation is two-fold: technical, if the public is not radical enough in enterprising, and political since it can be a reversible decision, being subjected to elections. Let us now discuss the practical ways to answer both aspects.

7.2. A Public-Private Approach: Management Contracts

Let us introduce management contracts and show that they should be considered for solving credibility issues and privatisation bottlenecks in SEBs' enterprisation. Technically, they do not necessitate any 'transfer of assets' and thus the valuation problem is not to be faced. Secondly, they allow bringing the private sector managerial expertise and, in an interesting way, they can become an information-building mechanism.

7.2.1. Management Contracts

Let us examine what management contracts exactly recover and how they could be implemented in India. Galal, Shirley *et al.* (1995) detail that Management Contracts "define the relationships between the government and a private firm contracted to manage a state-owned enterprise". Management contracts include attributes which go far beyond the simple contracting out of some technical operations. As far as electricity distribution is concerned, this includes:

- not only technical operation/maintenance/repair of the networks,
- but also preparation of extension programmes,
- and even more the billing/collection/conduction of commercial relationships with customers,

- and the right to re-structure the organisation in order to conduct all these.

Compared to MoUs and decentralisation schemes, Management Contracts involve a private partner, that is, involve its expertise. This is hence not a pure public solution. Similarly, compared to privatisation, it does not imply the tricky valuation process nor a risky financial engagement. Looked at that way, it is an hybrid scheme between public and private attempts at enterprisation.

This kind of contractual arrangement basically recovers all the functions concerned in a privatisation, except that the management of human resources (postings, sanctions), which is more constrained compared to a privatisation. Further, the private enterprise is not the 'owner' in the usual sense of the term of the assets it operates. But still, as far as ownership is concerned, the contractor enjoys well-defined 'specific rights' (in the sense of the property rights theory). Beyond, and within clearly established duties, it enjoys the full discretionary power on these specific rights. Close to management contracts, is the concession system. It is a step further toward privatisation, by allocating more control rights for a longer period as well as, a share in investment. It still keeps the property on assets to the State and allows the whole set of possibilities by the end of the period: indeed, renegotiation, taking over, or privatisation remain available.

In a management contract, cash flow rights are defined and shared between the public owner and the private contractor, since the latter has a contractually defined incentive in benefits or efficiency improvements. A management contract is implemented through a fee, "usually a success fee but sometimes for a fixed fee as well", handed over to the private contractor, as Galal, Shirley *et al.* (1995) mention. They specify that "under this definition, the government does not receive a fixed rent (as it would be in a lease), it is responsible for fixed investments (which it would not be with a concession), and it holds majority ownership, ceding control only via an explicit contract (as distinct from a joint venture in which the government owns only a minority)". According to Ranganathan (1997), the fee is "in return for specified improvement in certain identified parameters like system losses, revenue collection, etc."

All other residual rights (the ultimate property rights) remain with the State. Galal & Shirley (1995) further argue that management contracts "have generally been successful where they were attempted". Girod (1993), points out that they have succeeded in Africa, for instance in Mali. More generally, this kind of reform is now widely accepted as a central tool for the water sector for instance. Management contracts have been signed on water distribution in Burkina Faso (in 2001), Kenya (in 1999), South Africa (in 1999), Niger (in 2001), among others. Similarly, the power sector has already experienced such reforms in several countries in the world : Campbell-White & Bhatia (1998) report that Water & Electricity Management contract have been signed in Chad (in 2000), Mali (in 1994), Guinea (in 1989), Morocco (in 2001), as well as, contracts for Electricity distribution alone in Georgia (in 2001) or East Timor (in 2002). Electricity Generation too can be concerned, as the example of Zimbabwe (in 2001) shows. Also, the case of Ivory Coast, where concession has occurred in electricity distribution, under a context of clarification of the managerial rules bifurcation of the utility, and clarification of the status of the agents, proved successful (Ruet, 1997). Campbell-White & Bhatia (1998) report the same for water concessions signed in Ivory Coast (in 1996), South Africa (in 1992), or Mozambique (in 1999), or for Water & Electricity concession in Gabon (signed in 1997). Dealing with the Guinea example, Ménard & Clarke (2000) detail that "both consumers and the government benefited from reform of the water system in Conakry". They stress out the importance of "strong and stable institutions", of an "independent agency capable of restraining arbitrary government action, regulating the private operator, and enforcing contractual arrangements", and "adequate conflict resolution mechanisms for contract disputes". It is in these lines that we shall discuss the implementation of Management Contracts in India.

7.2.2. *Credibility/Sustainability of Management Contract: In-built Information Mechanisms*

Galal & Shirley (1995), or Ménard & Shirley (1999) emphasise that all "desirability", "feasibility" and "credibility" (or "sustainability") matter in reforms. The previous chapter has suggested explicitly enough the drawbacks of both pure public & private reforms, including on the redistributive aspects. It has thus already answered the issue of desirability of a public-private partnership to overcome these drawbacks. The next sub-section will practically discuss the technical feasibility and the main conditions of a management contract in India. However, let us first discuss the advantages of management contracts in terms of credibility/sustainability, especially compared to less credible MoUs and decentralisation schemes. Let us show that management contracts are sustainable due to the presence of *in-built information mechanisms in them.*

The first element of credibility can be ensured through long term contracts and explicit details of the mechanisms of conflict resolution. Indeed, Galal & Shirley (1995) underline that the "Government and management must be able to demonstrate commitment. Governments can signal their commitment by agreeing to longer contracts and agreeing to explicit conflict resolution mechanisms, including international arbitration. For its part, the management can be seen as committed when the contractor has a reputation to worry about". This reputation issue is valid for a Government as well. Indeed, after a break out of a well-reputed contractor, the concerned government may find that its position is no longer credible toward funding agencies.

In an attempt of enterprisation, the threat itself of privatisation matters, because if the attempt fails, only this solution remains. It can even be noticed, in terms of credibility, that the privatisation is a higher threat in the case of a management contract than in the case of a pure public enterprisation. Indeed, if even a single management contract fails, the private investors will *as well* show really low confidence in privatisation. This constitutes à first guarantee that politicians will not renege. Further, the private contractor is able to discern whether he faces executive instructions or not, *i.e.* whether the State exerts discretionary power on the matters falling in the contracted fields. Then, the implementation of the management contract can be modelled as such:

- As long as there is no external discretion, the management contract lasts. This sends an external signal that the contractor is left free to conduct the enterprisation process (elimination of the paper work, integration of an information system, replacement of techno-administrative procedures with cost-benefit analysis). This therefore signals that the organisation is, most likely, on a relatively higher profile of cost-efficiency and profit, compared to the situation prevailing before the signing of the management contract.

- Whenever executive instructions arise, it can be imagined that a negotiation process occurs, followed by a dispute settlement process if the dispute endures. In that case, if monitored through recourse to a (multilateral or Indian) funding agency, the problem (i) is advertised, and (ii) may lead very soon to the rupture of the management contract. This again sets a signal : this time, that the path is on a low-efficiency trend (see Figure 7.1).

Figure 7.1

Failure of a Management Contract after a Period t

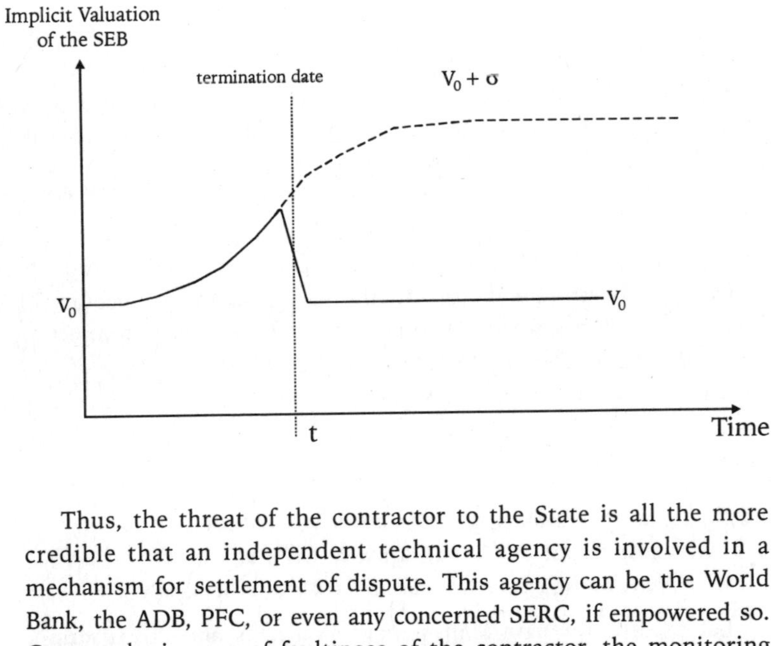

Thus, the threat of the contractor to the State is all the more credible that an independent technical agency is involved in a mechanism for settlement of dispute. This agency can be the World Bank, the ADB, PFC, or even any concerned SERC, if empowered so. Conversely, in case of faultiness of the contractor, the monitoring provides that the advertising on reputation is strong enough to make the reverse threat credible as well. For the supporting agency, the whole process provides information on the commitment of the State.

Under this scheme, the cost-efficiency is thus on a high profile as long as the management contract lasts, and vice-versa: *The sole ongoing of the management contract is the very indicator of the cost-efficiency of the followed path. Hence, failure of a public enterprisation is made more visible under this scheme than under a simple Memorandum of Understanding, because this scheme creates publicly available information.*

On the financial aspects, if the management contract is successful, then the value extracted by the State from its SEB is close to its maximal value, $V_0 + \sigma$. It allows to reveal the maximal possible value of the SEB, and to extract most of it for the State. Actually, what remains is the fraction (1-a) of the additional value σ, where the fraction (a) is the share the private contractor gets as contractually specified. From this, the fee f has to be further deducted every year over a period t. Ultimately, the State gets the following value for the SEB[3]:

$$V = V_0 + (1-a)\sigma - tf$$

Thus, the State compares $(1\text{-}a)\sigma$ to t*f. Since the fee can be nominal compared to the value involved in a capital-intensive industry, and when σ can double the initial value of the Board, the gain is largely in favour of the public in case of a management contract. A management contract has the property to specify the probability that the State is able to publicly enterprise. As long as the contract lasts, this probability increases and is near to 1; whenever it stops, there is strong support for the belief that this probability is actually low. This is with that respect that a management contract is a useful tool for the supporting agency in the monitoring of the reform process. The scheme of *management contract is thus essentially characterised by an in-built informational mechanism which reveals the suppression of executive instructions.*

7.2.3. *The Same Advantages as Privatisation, without its Drawbacks: The Privatisation in Delhi as a Hidden Management Contract for a Private Monopoly*

Let us now compare Management Contracts and Privatisation. Previous chapter has discussed the 'well-designed' Delhi privatisation. It has shown that, even with well-designed definition of cash-flow rights and provision of special funds, the valuation of the infrastructure has been problematic. Notwithstanding with the specific respective merits of privatisation *versus* management contract in the

3. If no discount rate is taken to simplify, which stands true if t is low.

case of Delhi, let us show that the two approaches have lot in common.

Indeed, the financial engineering around the transfer of 'assets' of the Delhi Vidyut Board amounts to isolate financial concerns over the first five years. That is, over this duration, mostly managerial concerns only remain with the private investors. Over this period, the losses will in practice get covered by the Government. It is true that these financial mechanisms are supposed to be an advance on future profits only and, technically, the investors are supposed to enjoy the cash-flow rights (and duties) on deficits. However, the funds that have been secured for subsidies and losses do constitute an advance on treasury, and hence they have an economic value. Ultimately, there is no clear indication that they can not be renegotiated in favour of the investors in the future (see Box 7.1).

Box 7.1

The 'revenue-minus approach' in Delhi Privatisation

The regulator will determine retail tariff increase, and compute the cash-flow to the distribution company based on the expected units realised (i.e. units which get paid for). The units to be purchased from the transmission company would be calculated based on the aggregate technical and commercial loss committed by the bidder. The regulator would also approve the costs of the distribution company, including a 16 per cent return on equity and reserves. The cash-flow to the distribution company, less approved costs, would be the funds available with the distribution company to pay the transmission company. This system moves the cash-flow gap in the system into the transmission company. This gap will be met by the Government of Delhi, on a committed amount of Rs. 3,400 crore over five years, after which the regulator will decide the approach based on the electricity laws.

Source: KPMG

Let us now carefully compare the net financial result (after transfers from the Government funds) for the private party (or, symmetrically, the State). The use of secured funds will allow designing financial transfers from the State to the private, to balance the operating results and make equilibrate results after transfer. In that case, the net financial result will mostly depend on the technical and commercial improvement (evolution) of the private sector, and not on the structural operating conditions (initial level of losses, tariffs, etc.), that is, not on the absolute level of the operating parameters. The whole system can therefore rather be considered as a (mid-term) incentive more than a direct appropriation of gross results by and to the private.

A management contract, on the other hand, would have technically amounted to a full separation of financial risks, and be completed by a reward based on an incentive-scheme. That is, in practical terms as far as this five-year period is concerned, to nearly the same net results as in privatisation after financial transfer. Actually, *over the years, as far as the net financial transfers are concerned, management contracts and a Delhi-type privatisation amount to quite the same for both the State (net debtor) and the private (in the first order, meeting equilibrated net results)*. Box 7.1 more precisely details the way the financial arrangements have been defined in terms of regulation.

This 'revenue-minus approach' (as compared to the classical 'cost plus' tariffs) to which the investors in Delhi get subjected exemplifies the pass-through mechanisms which have been put in place for the investors, the State ultimately remaining the last recourse payer. Again, technically, similar kind of mechanisms are to be implemented in management contracts (though even in a lighter way), and, from this point of view, the financial agreements of a management contract can not be considered as much more complicated to legally enforce than those of a 'well-defined' privatisation (nor are they radically different, *de facto,* when a private owner is isolated from risks).

Further, given the present scenario, subsidies need to be continued for a span of time. In that case, privatising amounts to give the subsidies to the private company, and then to dis-incentivise its efforts on the net result of the company. We subscribe with Haldea (2003), when he mentions that "Privatisation of state-owned distribution companies was first undertaken in Orissa about four years ago. But it was based on creation of private monopolies. Control over the power sector was thus apportioned between chosen private entities and incumbent government functionaries through a chain of interconnected monopolies – public and private. Absence of competition and choice inevitably led to rising tariffs and poor quality of service. The recent privatisation of distribution companies in Delhi is also based on a similar model and the dominant private players happen to be the same in both the states. It is unlikely that the outcome in Delhi would be materially different from Orissa".

Indeed, Haldea (2003b) specifies that "When DVB[4] was being split and privatised, the government had kept aside Rs. 3,450 crore for avoiding tariff shocks during the first five years of 'reform'. But in just the first 21 months of privatisation, this entire sum will be exhausted". *A management contract, in that case, would have allowed earmarking this amount independently from the cash flow of the private companies. We argue here that their (positive) reward would have then been less secured, while incentives on managerial improvements would have been clearer.*

And indeed, if one looks at the achievements in terms of losses reduction, one can find that (i) the time needed to build information system may have been underestimated, while (ii) one can still wonder whether the incentives have been appropriate. Indeed, out of the three zones, the improvement is not much, if not inexistent in some cases (see Table 7.1).

Table 7.1

Aggregated Technical and Commercial Losses in Delhi's Companies

Company name	*FY 2001-02*	*FY 2002-03*
BYPL (North East)	57.2	61.89
BRPL (South)	48.1	47.40
NDPL (North)	48.1	47.79

Source: Powerline, 2003b

To summarise in a graphic vocabulary, Orissa had irrealistically privatised the losses and hence led to a backlash of investors, while Delhi is privatising the benefits and socialising the losses, which may be as untenable in future if the private companies therefore do not have real incentives. The only solution in our view, remains to separate the subsidies from the operation of the sector; for this, only one tool exists, management contracts.

The essential difference in this respect is that a well-defined management contract (the way next sub-section will define its content) would have spared the valuation problem. This is not neutral, and this is on this basis that the choice between them can be made. We will detail this in coming sub-section, after a preliminary presentation of what a management contract shall consist in.

4. Delhi Vidyut Board.

7.3. Practical Implementation of Management Contracts in India

The two practical issues in enforcing a management contract in India are (i) the credibility of the creation of property rights, and (ii) the measurement of its efficiency. Another fundamental question is to know in which circumstances to implement them.

7.3.1. Management Contracts and Control Rights

Here again the Orissa experience shows that the control rights over the manpower are crucial. Indeed, a badly designed management contract failed there in 1996-97. But management contracts are not deemed to fail in general only because one did so.[5] The management contract in Orissa had been uncarefully designed. Indeed, Rajan (2000) details that "Gridco entered into a management contract called the distribution operations agreement, with BSES to take over the power distribution in the Central zone, with effect from October 1, 1996. According to this arrangement, the private utility was responsible for distribution of energy, maintenance of the distribution system, and collection of electricity dues in the central zone. Though the initial agreement was designed to last over a period of three years starting from October 1996, Gridco cancelled the agreement in April 1997, as it claimed that the private utility had shown a negative incentive of Rs. 0.28 crore over the 6 month period between October 1996 and March 1997". On this failure, Rajan (2000) points out "drawbacks in certain contractual provisions in the distribution operations agreement", particularly that "the private utility had to manage the distribution business over 8,000 employees and engineers over whom it had no administrative control".

Practical Provisions to be included in a Management Contract

Lessons can be derived on several issues from this attempt.

Human resources, reporting and making decentralisation credible: First, while the Government would take charge of the payment of present employees,[6] a management contract should be designed with

5. Unless one applies the same logic to privatisation: 'it failed in Orissa... therefore...'. In this book we aim at putting analysis of (i) structural characteristics of economic tools, (ii) modes of implementation.

6. As well as taking care of the general wages revaluation in the public function.

provisions to administratively sanction the faults, at least by posting different people in place of corrupt officers. The contract should not only leave the contractor free to re-organise the activity but also to have power over the human resources function. The contract should clearly mention and specify a right to alter procedures in the following fields: technical studies, maintenance, measuring and reporting systems, billing. Reformatting of reports should similarly be explicitly allowed, and the private contractor should be allowed to draft out human resources policies at progressive conditions for employees. That is, a (limited but granted) percentage of internal geographical rotation could be defined at every level, in accordance with the unions. This could for instance be tuned with presently existing rotation rates, and would not have any regressive impact on manpower as a whole. On the contrary, this would recognise and grant a flexibility to the contractor which otherwise could be contested by unions. It would therefore prevent from future disputes. As long as they would be granted their present earnings, non-performing officers should be removable and replaced with more performing -promoted- ones, with the promise by the State to preserve these promotions in case the contract is terminated (again, a quota can easily be agreed on this at the moment of signing the contract).

Similarly, the contractor should be given the right to add privately financed posts in the hierarchy. Here we think about managers appointed for a fixed term (renewable) under a private law contract and not as a public officer. They would be an integral part of the hierarchy. Some posts like these should be financed through the benefits realised in the management contract, then shared between the State, the contractor, and the financing of specific investments like these posts. These would gather some functions formerly given to the public officers, being used along with the right to propose and finance reward schemes.[7] Such a scheme has been used for some time in Orissa by the private company AES or, after 2003, the Madhya Pradesh SEB. The contractor should also be given the right to invite public officers to join this privately financed type of posts.

Lastly, the contractor should get clear provisions on right to take action against any officer caught red-handed being bribed. Such

7. This can even be financed through a mechanism of benefit appropriation, similar to the one proposed in Chapter 5.

measures would render enforceable and credible the measures of decentralisation as proposed by the book in Chapter 5. An initial financial volume should be secured to set-up an incentives system (now rendered credible by the other guarantees mentioned here).

Similarly, financial discretion should be given to commission a certain level of external support or to temporarily hire external experts.[8] Then to achieve rendering all these measures credible, and for preventing from external discretionary power of the State, all these points should not only be contracted out, but the contract should explicitly mention clear and rapid procedures for conflict resolution. This can take various paths and imply various sets of institutions, not necessarily the Courts. The Regulatory Commissions, for instance could be thought of for serving this purpose.

Though the list of provisions could appear to be impressive, it should be noted here that the prescriptions we make are nothing more than what State Governments are implicitly agreeing on when they engage in a privatisation. The point is only to well describe and specify them. On the other hand, compared to a classical public reform scenario, these constitute more stringent conditions. These are necessary measures we believe to render credible the mutually threatening game and thus the information-building mechanism that a management contract amounts to.

Investment: As far as control rights on investment procedures and choices are concerned, although they are under the responsibility of the government under a management contract, the private contractor should be granted specific rights. Indeed, a full discretion over a given amount of investment would facilitate the implementation of urgent (and often very profitable) measures in a decentralised and prompt way. The remaining part of the investment can be left to the government and be based on a process of negotiation taking place along specified rules. This kind of measures would for instance make possible the implementation of techno-economic gains identified on distribution transformers for instance.

---

8. The Bangalore Agenda Task Force (BATF) has demonstrated this point to be very crucial and instrumental in reforming administrations. The BATF, based in Bangalore, is a Government-sanctioned private association which helps the city of Bangalore in restructuring its administrations and is a very interesting and innovative form of public-private partnership (see Ruet 2002a). It was unfortunately terminated after the Congress Party lost the local elections in 2004.

Commercial Measures: For the job required from the contractor is to ultimately ensure a commercial functioning, it should be left free to design and propose commercial measures as far as it demonstrates that they improve the recovery of costs, without being discriminatory to consumers. Again, as far as practical commercial policies would be concerned, the Regulatory Commissions could be thought of as the proper place to sanction these. This includes single-entry points measures for *Panchayats* or local communities, resident associations, willing to commit on ensuring the payments regularly in exchange of a better quality of service. This could also include straight connection schemes for users ready to bear the costs of connection and committing to a regular payment, for instance. This leads us to an important aspect of management contracts as facilitators in tackling the dynamism of local markets, to give an impetus to enterprisation of SEBs.

Management Contracts and Enterprisation Through Local Markets

The importance of local level measures has been emphasised already. Enterprisation includes tackling the local markets, for instance using willingness to pay for rapid connection.

More generally, organisational innovativeness in private-public arrangements can be fostered through management contracts. For instance, cooperatives, contracted distribution systems, or companies which originally grew for "captive power" for dedicated owners – but started selling to the Grid – have all succeeded. Again, a private manager would have higher flexibility in not only buying the surplus power, but truly co-developing the local distribution networks, as the Coelho Committee (Government of India, 1998b) had suggested. Besides, recent technological improvements allowing decentralisation at the user end, which has introduced the possibility of considerable flexibility at the level of the management of the distribution end of infrastructure products and services.

Alagh (2001) rightly mentions that this introduces a certain degree of complexity in policy formulation for such sectors which simple paradigms tend to miss. He recalls that "two such paradigms which have caused substantial damage in India have been the notion that all infrastructure should be planned centrally (...) or at the other extreme the view that private competition without regulation will allow stooping the public sector investments". The very issue is to get out of the 'mono-technique' paradigm that Part I of the book has documented. Again, it is thought, the concept of enterprisation is flexible enough to give practical clues about that. It allows going beyond ideology.

In that respect as well, let us again underline the advantages of management contracts. The public sector would not be able to do this efficiently in a sustaining manner. The actual failure of Tatkal Schemes has shown this. In interviews, Alagh had reported from a survey of his, that at the time of introducing the Tatkal Scheme in Rajasthan, he had examined the records of 11 kV lines to different villages. This survey showed that "between 8 per cent to 27 per cent of the time, power supply was not being delivered at the lowest level on account of distribution constraints". Further, that "there were no circuit breakers and even the fuses were in some cases of an unacceptable kind, while the operators were generally untrained". Indeed, an administration is not fledged to segregate between its various users, be it to answer their differentiated needs. On the other hand, privatisation would lead to achieve this, but is however facing the already mentioned problems of valuation of the Board. Ultimately, this is typically these kind of local constraints, we argue, that a management contract is able to tackle, by contractually putting these parameters as the key issues to be improved.

Measuring the Contract Implementation

As far as the cash flow rights of the private contractor are concerned, the fee should be both based on a fixed part (to sustain the commitment of the government) and on a success-based part. Here the issue of measuring the efficiency comes into play. Galal & Shirley (1995) indicate that financial performance, productivity, and savings-investment deficit can be thought of as indicators of success or failure of reform. Given the non-integration of the reporting system in SEBs, productivity can hardly be thought of as a parameter in the fee, at least in the preliminary years. Moreover, residual decisions on investment will not depend on the private contractor, but on the Government. That way, the savings-investment deficit would at best measure the "Government efficiency", had this concept a meaning. It cannot serve as an indicator.

The financial performance remains a good candidate for this, and can easily be implemented through a way suggested by Galal &

Shirley (1995), that is, the operating surplus to sales in current prices. In utilities as well, it can be done through the increase of billing and collecting. And, actually, the "revenue-minus" aspect of the Delhi privatisation really fits into this. On collections, the related part of the fee should be success-based. Indeed, this would allow the private contractor to fully establish an internal delegation of control rights based on an incentive system, and hence to fully use the provisions on control rights discussed earlier. A part of the management contract shall even explicitly include provisions for setting up a proper information system, including measurement, metering and so on. The fixed part of the fee would relate to this role of the private contractor.[9]

7.3.2. *Enterprisation through Management Contracts: When to Implement Them? The Difficulty to Replicate Delhi's Case*

Let us be clear : the main argument that we have against the 'well-designed' privatisation in Delhi is that it is costly, and most likely only workable in an urban environment. Therefore it is not a solution for the bulk of SEBs, even if it does enterprise the former Delhi SEB. We consider 'well-designed' management contracts for one can be imaginative on this tool too, for there can be a continuum in practical public-private agreements, and for there is simply no other choice.

Let us detail the question of the respective domains of applicability of management contracts and privatisation. For that, let us first analyse deeper their similarities and differences in terms of creation of property rights. Let us show that the management contract will not *a priori* result in the setting up of cash flow rights for the SEB as an entity, since this is not needed in the design of such a scheme. The cash flow rights between the State and the contractor will be defined, but not the cash flow rights allocation between the State and the organisation-SEB. This point may be reached only under either some

9. This latter provision answers the reluctance shown in interviews by some reformers. These argued that a management contract, in case of SEBs, would have to address the fee issue in a context of unknown level of technical and non-technical losses. However, this is already an issue to face in the scheme of privatisation, to be addressed by Regulatory Commissions in tariff setting. We argue that, in a context of a management contract, this is of less importance, since the owner is still the State, and therefore this uncertainty does not come on the fore, unlike in a bidding process. Also, the completion of the work of establishing an information system can be easily checked through objective and clear criteria, like installation of meters at different levels, restructuring of reporting and so forth.

more or less degraded version of a privatisation (leasing, concession) or through a full privatisation. A management contract would, however result in an initially greater definition of control rights, with all the previously listed items be specified.

The Difference between Management Contracts and Privatisation in Terms of Property Rights Creation

Ultimately, this book argues that, to be credible, a public reform, defined as "short of (cash-flow) ownership transfer" has to integrate most of the elements of a 'Delhi-type' privatisation in terms of control rights, but without 'transfer of cash-flow ownership'. In turn, a credible public reform (through management contract) is quite close to a credible private reform[10] in the case of SEBs.

The relationship between the two measures is as follows. *Though a management contract will remain 'short of cash-flow ownership transfer', it has to include a fair amount of control rights specification to be workable.* That way, it isolates a part of the functions of the organisation to transfer their control to the private. *In the same way, a privatisation, to be attractive, has to isolate much of the financial issues and liabilities inherited from the past functioning and leave it with the State.* It ultimately conducts to also separate this from the rest of the functions of the organisation. At the exception of the future investments this latter part is nearly the same as what management contracts isolate. Credible privatisation and credible management contracts have to deal with the same issues indeed. Then, what is their fundamental difference in terms of property rights creation? *By nature, a privatisation focuses on cash flow rights transfer; it is assumed that control rights will follow, and these are less specifically designed. Conversely, in a management contract, one is dealing more precisely with these control rights, while specification of cash flow rights is limited.* Negotiations on cash-flow are linked to measurement issues, and are simply instrumental in enforcing the contract itself. Table 7.2 describes the level of efforts to be put in designing various types of rights in both scenarios.

10. They are actually so close that, for the general public, the private would be involved through a simple management contract, the reference to the term 'privatisation' would hence appear. However, it is not technically the case, and therefore the book maintains this distinction. This debate is not neutral, but the central argument of the book is that what has to be 'public' in the electricity sector is the way everybody should access it in reasonable conditions; this is not achieved under 'public' management, and the issue of the 'public' ownership of the infrastructure has actually no link to that.

Table 7.2

Respective Focus and Amount of Effort Put in Specifying Rights in Management Contracts and Privatisation

Rights to be Granted	*Privatisation*	*Management Contract*
Cash Flow Rights	++ (the core of the bidding phase)	+ (instrumental in measurement and incentives issues)
Control Rights	+ (assumed to be a by-product of cash-flow ownership)	++ (the core of the contracting out)

Privatisation focuses on transfer and thus creation of cash flow rights. All the efforts and work of the consultants and funding agencies aim towards this. In the case of a badly prepared privatisation, unclear specification of rights leads to ongoing disputes. This is what has happened in Orissa, where the transferred organisation had not been previously enterprised. Conversely, defining a management contract goes through working out detailed claims in specification of control rights. The efforts in terms of consultants' time are now put in these contractual clauses.

A management contract, that way, creates more control rights on the part of the SEBs functions it covers. It may be more limited but, if well monitored, can lead to an in-depth enterprisation of a substantial part of the organisation.[11]

The Political Economy of Management Contracts *versus* Privatisation

As far as a State Government's point of view may be concerned, we have already suggested that, the management contract can even be seen as a preparatory step to privatisation. It allows setting-up some of the property rights that will be valuated in the bidding process. But it must be underlined that it also remains conceptually separate from any privatisation scheme, and may in practice remain a solution of its own. That way, a management contract may solve the bottlenecks of a direct privatisation process or only ensure a public enterprisation, depending on which target it is used for. This balances the point raised by Galal & Shirley (1995), who maintain that "under the

11. This is actually quite close to what has actually happened in the much discussed case of Chinese 'Township-Village Enterprises', though it was informally contractualised in this latter case.

conditions where management contracts can work, privatisation will often offer governments higher benefits (revenue from sale) and lower costs (no need to monitor, enforce and renegotiate the contract)". We argue against this position, that stands true only by considering the sole financial transfers at the moment of taking the decision, but which is wrong by considering the discounted benefit of a higher selling after some years of management contract.

However, Governments are not the only choosers and the analysis of privatisation has detailed enough its bottlenecks, both at the local level (one State may not be attractive or not give enough guarantees) and at the global level (there are too numerous SEBs in India, for all of them could be privatised). Investors matter. Let us then propose a final very simple political economy model, dealing with securitisation of rights under two parameters: the economic income of the customers and the local level of governance.

Law always secures cash flow rights more easily and faster than it does for control rights, because the former are more easily 'appropriated' and identifiable to a party, and more easily defined. In particular, residual control rights are difficult to define and therefore to enforce or to protect on a legal basis. Also, law has emerged to protect private property in the sense of its cash flow rights, whereas the importance of control rights has only recently been stressed out by economists. Thus, all other things being equal, rights derived from a privatisation are always more secured than rights resulting from a management contract. In that framework, private companies consider a trade-off. On one hand, they wish to get the cash-flow ownership for securing their rights. On the other hand, in the case of SEBs, they conversely show a prevention against privatisation, due to unclear definition of the rights they would buy. This trade-off materialises in lowering their bid, which we have already discussed. But thus, how should this be taken into account to decide whether to promote a management contract or privatisation?

The first parameter to take into account, is the capacity to pay of the consumers. It can be expressed through a proxy: the per capita gross domestic product.[12] The higher it is, the more the investor is

12. Actually, what directly matters is the willingness to pay, linked to the capacity of the utility to provide an increase in the quality of the service. Numerous studies prove that willingness to pay is present in a reform scenario; hence what remains ultimately is the actual income of the users.

interested in getting the cash flow rights, at least in the long term. Let us now add a second element and examine how the governance matters in this. Let us here define the good governance as the ability for Regulatory Commissions to independently sanction disputes between SEBs and Governments (and simultaneously the tacit or explicit agreement of the concerned State High Court to leave these matters with the Regulator), and the enforceability of simple penal laws, as in the case of thefts, corruption and police action against power Mafia. That is, as the ability to solve all the disputes on the points related to the management contract. All other things being equal, and given the reluctance to invest in unclearly enterprised structures, good governance does favour Management Contracts, while a low governance does relatively favour Privatisation. In effect, let us consider the case of a (minimal) given interest of a private party for a SEB. If the governance is high, the provisions of a contract can easily be enforced. In this scenario, the private can prefer a management contract and avoid investing in the short run, until the information asymmetry reduces. On the contrary, if the governance is low, the rights have to be truly owned (in the sense law considers ownership) in order to secure them. That is, the cash flow rights have to be transferred, and privatisation is more of an obliged way.

Let us now cross these two parameters, income and governance. Four sub-cases appear in this very simple stylisation (see Table 7.3).

Table 7.3

The Feasibility Domain of Management Contracts and Privatisation

	Low Income (Low Interest for the Investor)	High Income (interest in Catching the Cash-flow Rights)
High Governance: (Relative Push for Management Contract)	Management Contract is Preferable	Both are Feasible: The State can Decide on an Economic Trade-off Basis
Low Governance (Relative Support to Privatisation)	Problematic Situation but, ultimately, at most a Management Contract is Feasible	Privatisation

- When both governance and income are high, everything is feasible once well-defined. The State can choose according to the trade-off described earlier, between early privatisation and higher selling value later.

- When the income is high and the governance low, the Board is attractive and a privatisation is in a sense more secured: this may have been the scenario in Delhi.
- When the income is low, though the attractivity is low, a management contract can bring reasonable income to a contractor if governance is high. In these States, management contracts should be favoured (Andhra Pradesh might be an example of this, though it rather presently wants to privatise its SEB).
- When both income and governance are low, the situation is problematic. If the income is too low, the investor is not even any longer interested in a privatisation, for there is nothing to secure that way. Still, a management contract will remain the only feasible solution, while offering low credibility because of the low governance. On these States, the support of the Central Government will be essential. Orissa is in one of the two latter categories, depending on the assumption made on its level of governance; in both cases, sticking to a well-defined management contract would have been better.

This model commands several remarks. It is a 'second worst' only in the low governance/low income scenario. Otherwise, we argue, it is a matter of a positive choice: both tools have their pros and cons in a real, non-ideological world. This model is designed for a State, however, it can be considered that its recommendations do not depend on the geographical scale of the area it is applied to. For instance, in low-income, low-governance States, a segmentation of the State into several zones may be helpful. For instance, Uttar Pradesh may be considered as having a different background in few cities/urban areas; that way, privatisation of zones like the city of Kanpur, or the private status of the Greater Noida[13] zone can as well be analysed by this model. One State may present a low income, as well as, a low governance, and still, could offer smaller areas that are workable under a private scheme. Further, at a micro-level in rural areas, *Panchayats* ready to behave as a 'single entry point' may be considered as zones of local good governance; then, the agreement can in a sense be formally considered as leaving the management of the local supply to the *Panchayat*. Again, islanding strategies.

13. In the semi-urban fringes of Delhi.

That way, privatisation of relatively more well-off zones even in low-governance areas, as well as, the local agreements with organised communities (whatever their income) makes sense. This proposal should be well understood: it neither amounts to "privatising the benefits", nor "socialising the losses". On the contrary, the present pragmatic situation is as such: SEBs make financial losses while creating social losses (the mechanisms that lead to the losses benefit the richest) everywhere, in both low and high income zones. If the private is able to make both financial profits and social benefits in some zones, this does not mean that "benefits are privatised". This means that the private creates these benefits. They are further shared with the State, all the more that a Management Contract is favoured. Even in the Delhi case, an improved trend for losses is planned. These benefits can further be passed on the other non-private zones, under the form of technical improvement schemes.

General Aspects on Tariffs in both Management Contracts and Privatisation

A detailed study of tariffs options is not the purpose of this book, that rather focuses on structural change, and when anyway several studies exist (see Sinha, 2004; Dossani and Ranganathan 2004, Chakravarty, 2004, or even Ruet 2004). However, it is important to state here, which general tariff framework fits with the reform mechanisms we propose and analyse. Without entering into the details, and since it is clear that the name of the game is about control rights in particular and securing of property rights in general, a multi-year tariff (MYT) assorted with yearly increasing incentive targets (on losses reduction for instance) should be the rule. The N.K. Singh committee, though through a different reasoning, supports this view and states that "the Task Force believes that implementation of performances based regulation through MYT framework is by far the most important structural initiative required to minimise risk for utilities and cosumers, to promote efficieny and to attract investments in the distribuition sector". It details as a recommendation, that "the form of MYT implemented should be clearly defined and preferably be formulaic in design. The approach should envisage little regulatory intervention during a control period particularly in the determination on the revenue allowances". In other terms, securing the cash-flow rights. Now, if we add nothing on the financial aspect, we shall however stress out that this should come in complement to securing the control rights through enterprisation. That way, MYT is complementary to the latter. In other words, the issue of "minimising risk for utilities" implicitly implies that the latter care for it; i.e., that they are enterprised. Indeed, the Singh report further deals with "incentives", which we have seen to be effective only in an enterprised scenario.

This gives ground to a multi-faceted enterprisation scenario, and to the use of local markets dynamics to initiate enterprisation. Enterprisation will not take a uniform shape at different scales, nor in different socio-economic backgrounds. Then, what matters is not a ready-made solution, but the concept, to serve as an analytical tool in practical reforms.

7.3.3. *Possibility and Rationale of Private Public Partnerships through Management Contracts within the New Electricity Act (2003)*

In that context, how can one analyse the enactment of the Electricity Act 2003, in terms of allowing or favouring management contracts? The Act does not mention this possibility, but leaves potentially space for it. Actually, its logic is quite compatible with management contracts, in the sense that a transition will be needed between the present situation and the implicit referent of the Act. Indeed, the Act is largely a strengthening of the Regulatory Act 1998, but it includes a major element, where (i) transfer of "property or rights" is no longer a taboo, and where "open access" is to be promoted in a "phased manner" (Article 42). In that framework, vertical integration is still allowed (implicitly re-integration once privatised, i.e. transferred to a private licensee), but at the condition that unbundled accounts are evolved (Article 51). The accounting normalisation of distribution is therefore engaged through this article of the Act. Further, and at the core of our argument, the Article 131 is illustrative of the whole part of the Act relative to "transformation of Boards". *Article 131 specifies that, from a Board, a transfer scheme may "provide for the formation of subsidiaries, joint venture companies, or other schemes of division, amalgamation, merger, reconstruction or arrangements which shall promote the profitability and viability of the resulting entity, ensure economic efficiency, encourage competition, and protect consumer interests"*. In other words, and as far as a management contract does provide all these conditions, an management contract as an "arrangement" falling under this category is quite feasible.

Further, far from necessarily involving a full transfer, the Act details that this transfer can be limited to "specifying or describing the property rights and liabilities in question". Now, if we focus on specific rights, if property in the classical sense (the way lawyers define them) and rights (the property rights the way economists define them) can be separated as the Acts allows, then Management Contract totally falls under the possibilities offered by the Act. In practice, the implicit logic of the Act revolves around a long term horizon of a large private sector, where commission are also to promote competition, and, among all, open access. In open access, any company can wheel its power through the distribution network and sell it to its clients. Paradoxically, this truly corresponds to a logic where distribution becomes a business of optimising a network, of reducing its costs, and where integration with a generator is merely a provision allowed by the Act, but not necessarily the norm (for, actually, distribution is a local monopoly and different energy providers can compete through it). This in turn really normalises the function of electricity distribution and totally aligns it with the logic and advantages of the management contracts, earlier amply described.

7.4. The Supporting Role of the Centre: Changing the Paradigm

The book exemplifies and demonstrates that the Government as an administration is no longer legitimate in operating the power sector. The essential measure to take is to enterprise the SEBs, the book has argued. Beyond this central reform, however, it does not mean that some public undertakings (especially NTPC) have no role to play as *public enterprises*. The tone of the book is also far from denying the role the Government as an administration can *have in supporting the emergence of power markets and power regulation for fostering cost-efficiency.* For there are at present unfortunately very few rules based on incentives for generators, transmitters and distributors to increase the supply at competitive efficiency, let us briefly present how the Government should support competitiveness in the short run, though in a less detailed manner compared to the SEBs. These constitute as many directions to deepen the reflection on accompanying measures.

7.4.1. Supporting the Enterprisation of SEBs

Once agreed that the SEBs are destined to be enterprised, most of the administrative coordination that kept busy the Ministry of Power,

Government of India, disappears, for a part of it is left to the enterprised heir entities of the SEBs themselves, and another part is transferred to the Regulatory Commissions. In a span of few years, from now, the Ministry of Power will be left free doing something else.

Supporting the Enterprisation of SEBs

The political economy model previously presented has suggested enough that enterprisation might not be feasible everywhere with an equal support of the private sector. Since a crucial role of the private is to ensure the creation of informational mechanisms, the correlative role of the Central government will be two-fold. It should not only try to bring the private sector under a different form, but also to replicate under a form or another, an informational mechanism. In fact, this is in this case that, rather than waiting the reform process of the entire Electricity Board to be completed, project level lending and investment can begin as described in Chapter 5 of the book. A private bank focusing on issue-specific project may bring the stimulating impetus for reform. It needs not being necessarily private and, as a funding agency is concerned, PFC for instance can usefully complete this scheme.

The role of the Regulatory Commission, to serve this purpose should then be specifically reinforced in this sense, with the full support of the Central level, either directly or channelled through the CERC, to help in bettering the governance levels and monitoring the progress of the SEB.

Lastly, recent schemes for pilot distribution Circles have been initiated by the Ministry of Power. The "Accelerated Power Development Programme" has been initiated in the financial year 2000-01, under which a "focused investment programme has been initiated in 63 identified distribution circles" the Ministry of Power (2002) reports. These projects still need being evaluated, but these help in the right way, and should be specially strengthened for those States which go towards a non-private reform.

Supporting the Capacity Building of Regulatory Commissions

As far as regulation is concerned, the system of cost plus pricing is built into the Electricity Act, 1948 and its newer versions, integrating the Electricity Regulatory Commission Act, 1998. Tariffs work out a rate of return on the cost of electricity to serve. Let us take an example on how regulatory commissions can be instrumental in evolving this paradigm. Alagh, Shah & Shah (1998) had shown that if unplanned shutdowns at the generation unit level could be reduced, substantial savings would emerge. Examining the record of each generator, they found that the major hours of shutdown were on account of tube failures. If the GEB could improve the maintenance of tubes, the cost of production of electricity would go down on account of three reasons: reduction in energy input per unit of output, overhead costs distributed over larger volumes of production and larger revenue sales from the same capacity.

Alagh *et al.* estimate this saving at 40 paise per unit if GEB could achieve the maintenance norms set by the NTPC. This example goes with the margins of improvement already discussed in distribution transformers repair and many others. The key issue will be the competency-building in SERCs and the availability of resources for them to carry counter studies to push for change of procedures. That way, the recently issued tariff orders show a progress in the SERCs mastering technical and financial data provided by the Boards. For instance in Uttar Pradesh, the Commission has been able to differentiate short run and long run margins in losses reduction, by taking into account the ratio between low voltage lines and high voltage lines, or to mathematically model the minimisation of network costs (see UPERC, 2002). The role of the Government of India should be to further support this capacity building.

In this respect, we believe the N.K. Singh Committee has proposed steps leading to the right direction, since in the preamble of the report it is underlined that some States have not yet enforced an SERC, while some others have already unbundled their utilities. While the committee is optimistic on the effect of unbundling, we have earlier underlined the limits of such a process towards enterprisation, but we agree that this constitutes an enabling factor if management contracts are thought of.

7.4.2. Supporting the Emergence of a Market to Save on Social Costs

At a second level, the Central Undertakings may be similarly enterprised and corporations like NTPC, which already have a reasonably cost-effective functioning, should be fully allowed to participate the redefined power sector, including in joint public-private partnerships in both generation and distribution. In a sense, and, without much demonstration, we can consider that NTPC is closer to an enterprise in nature. Indeed, though it is ultimately subjected to the political decisions of the Government of India, it has introduced a better cost *versus* benefit analysis assessment system in its planning after it started participating the bulk power market.

Further, the activity of power generation, in the Indian demand profile, can comparatively better rely on a mono-technique model than transmission or distribution would. Procedures can find a better justification. The Power Trading Corporation (PTC), which has started trading in 2001, though it presently trades a mere 2 per cent of the Indian total generation (over 4,000 million units in 2002-03, according to Powerline, 2003a), is to become a key institution in this activity. PTC, by its trader nature, has higher opportunities to evolve in an enterprise-like manner. Before NTPC, PTC and others gradually take-off on their own, the Ministry of Power, will have an accompanying role.

Again, transition is the key word, when the N.K. Singh committee underlines the fact that "complete migration to a tariff based regime may not be possible universally in the short and medium term due to lack of depth and absence of other conditions facilitating competition" (GoI, 2004). The committee had been set-up with the particular assignement to propose a framework for fostering investment as a principal task, but also "suggest roadmap for effective functioning of the State Electricity Utilities, including reduction in the cost of delivered power, in the context of the Electricity Act, 2003", and recommend both Tariff and National Electricity Policies (GoI, 2004). It has actually proposed measures pertaining to fiscal regime as well as import duty on equipment, fuel, distribution tax. It is also proposed extension of deduction measures in income tax from 2006 to 2012. These are in the nature of favouring a market development, of which limited size but essential accompanying role we have largely stressed. The principal financial measures include:

- relaxing the exposure norms on financial institutions, to allow them to invest in bonds raised by reasonably rated power companies,
- including power bonds in the list of items associated to statutory liquidity ratio,
- giving access to external commercial borrowings as well as access to capital market, both debt and equity.

These measures, we believe, should be in the nature of making understood that (i) the financial problem is not *the* crux of the matter; managerial issues remain once this is solved, (ii) in such a framework, potential private partners (in both cases of management contracts and privatisation) can better secure their financial position and focus on management, and (iii) in the case of high governance and low income, the State can all the more confidently go for a management contract that it no longer has to expect the private to give an investment which it is not willing to provide. We see then these proposals as being in close complementarity to the framework we propose.

Adding Reactive Capacity

A large scope for technical improvements in capacity utilisation and cost reduction, resides in the creation of a market for reactive capacity creation. This aspect is far more technical, we mention it for the sake of exhaustivity, but do not run into the details. Chitkara, Kalra, and Shekhar (2002) give these, and isolate the analysis of Auxiliary Services within SEBs. They stand that "the natural choice of initiating privatisation is to start with privatisation of auxiliary services". They quote the following reasons: "total investment made by the private investor would have been minimum, improvement of voltage profile and increased power availability can build customers confidence for privatisation, transition of SEBs to the market environment would be gradual". According to the authors, "these services can easily enhance system capability up to 20 to 30 percent". They argue all the more that benchmarking of auxiliary services is not a difficult task, since "auxiliary services can be treated in a manner similar to generation". They propose to outsource them. It is indeed not out of reach for any Regulatory Commission to regulate the provision of these.

Creating Energy Markets

The example of the power supply to the Southern Grid based on availability tariff is interesting. The Ministry should gradually entrust and empower PTC to expand the experiment throughout the country. The finalisation of the tariffs should be fully given to the respective competencies of the CEA and the CERC, to further enable PTC to actually trade energy and become the initial institution of a bulk power market for India, leading to optimising and savings on generation costs and volumes. Interviews show that this experiment is now accepted by the public sector (both by the SEBs and the concerned Regional Electricity Board). A transitory mechanism will be to keep the private sector under 'cost-plus' and 'pass-through' tariff principles. In a later stage, and under some conditions that the Government should fix, they could marginally join this market, to make it a non-restricted market (Alagh, 1996 and also Coelho Committee – Government of India, 1998b).

Beyond the mere question of supplying the demand, what is the economic stake associated to the proper monitoring of a 'merit-order' (starting first the cheapest units) principle in the field of generation? Alagh (1996) has estimated that the average cost of generation varied from 19 to 115 paise per kWh for hydro-electric stations, and from 79 to 288 paise per kWh for thermal stations. Average costs for thermal and hydro-electricity was of 187 paise in 1996-97, that is, 45 per cent more expensive than in 1992-93. These costs do take into account the practical functioning of plants, including a low PLF and therefore high share of fixed costs. On the other hand, the Planning Commission estimates for normative costs for Indian coal *versus* imported naphtha were as indicated in Table 7.4.

Table 7.4

Normative Generation Costs as Considered by the Planning Commission in 1996-97 in Paise/kWh

Fuel Type/Location	*Delhi*	*Gandhar*	*Vizag*	*Cuddalore*	*Ib Valley*
Indian Coal	199	209	177	213	158
Imported Naphtha	246	219	219	223	229

Source: Alagh, 1996.

Normative costs, as they refer, are only normative. As Alagh (1996) mentions, "it is quite obvious that normative costs of new plants can compare favourably with the actual cost of electricity to serve, even when their capital charges are much higher". Therefore, not only efficiency pricing has serious implications for the economy, but also, in order to achieve this, one has to rather rely on transparent and regulated market mechanisms than on normative centrally planned figures, which are only administered figures. In other words, here as well the paradigm has to be changed.

As Alagh discusses, opposition from power producers who want to stick to guaranteed returns has to be faced. Earlier described mechanisms involving PTC may be instrumental in this (this stands true for transmission). Alagh (1996) further suggests that transitory strategies involving "command type" (administered) have to be developed. However, we believe that they should be complemented with some more structural elements. Though they can be successful for some time, the example of the PAGER program, discussed in Chapter 3, shows that they can always be terminated overnight, as is in the nature of the administration. This book rather favours institutionally secured measures with in-built economic mechanisms, which is the only way to prevent administrative go-and-backs. Let us for this discuss the question of the private generators. At the macro-economic level, the necessity to guarantee working conditions to the private generators, has conducted the Government to ensure payments in case of 'deemed generation', that is, if the contracted load is not met by the concerned SEB. These amount to important social costs that can be later avoided by designing a tariff structure that would also benefit the private sector compared to keeping recourse to benefits of not producing power.[15]

---

15. The implicitly suggested system amounts to a very similar logic as the one which has presided the constitution of the Southern Grid power transfers. The indemnities for deemed generation do not cover the 'complete costs' (fixed plus variable) of the private generators. If paid little more, and if the increase compares positively to the variable costs, they will be ready to produce for any other SEB than the SEB with which they had initially contracted out. From the public side, the amount of money to be given is higher than in the case of deemed generation penalty of course, but this allows to get some energy, which the deemed generation penalty did not bring. Ultimately, the difference in cost between the two scenarios will ultimately amount to the cost for the public of the decision to propose this scheme to the private generator. If the tariff is well-fixed enough, this differential cost can be cheaper than energy produced elsewhere on the network. Then, imagine an additional financial measure where the SEB which initially contracted out the private power, is allowed to pay the equivalent of the 'deemed generation' penalty to PTC. If this is allowed, then PTC only has to pay the differential cost to the private generator, and the situation is neutral for the initial SEB. The situation becomes as follows: the social cost is no longer borne, since existing capacity is used instead of a more costly somewhere else, the private generator has a higher profit, PTC gets cheaper power to be sold to other SEBs, and the initial SEB is not affected. The ultimate stage of the system is of course when an additional financial transfer happens: PTC pays back a part of benefit it derives to the initial SEB which has now a way to lower its financial payment compared to the 'deemed generation' scenario. One can even imagine that some money is also transferred to the plant of the system that would have been operated otherwise, to help covering the fixed costs of this latter plant. Again, rules have to be fixed for that and the legitimate body should be the CERC, but, though they look complex, they can actually be easily made operational and lead to substantial savings in the power sector.

Parallel to this wider scope for NTPC and other Central Undertakings, an actual enterprisation of these entities would save time for the Ministry of Power to focus on long-term issues. To fully conclude on these latter elements (reactive capacity, energy markets), these are the actions that an administrative SEB cannot undertake, for they assume to officially distinguish between types of users. An enterprise, and thus a private company would do it, because it is at the core of its functioning to adjust to its clients. Likewise, a private contractor could carry these tasks.

Again, there is some scope for even the Government simulating a market: the N.K. Singh committee proposes that "the unallocated share of NTPC stations should be made available for trading over a period to allow the beneficiaries to align themselves" (GoI 2004). In the same line, the Electricity Act (2003) had proposed an open access for all the loads superior to 1 MW by 2008; the Planning Commission is now suggesting to speed-up the process, if necessary through an interim higher threshold (as is currently taking place in the EU). This measure, analysed in terms of creation of property rights, definitely goes in the direction of enterprisation of the sector seen as a whole.

7.4.3. Focusing on the Energy Choices

Under this framework, the Central Government should ultimately focus on long-term energy choices and serve as a facilitator for the enterprisation process, including the creation of the key institutions linked with the various power markets to come. The Central Government may focus for instance on large scale generation, for scale advantages lead to large cost advantages. Besides coal-based power generation, this role of the State stands true for balancing the costs and advantages of HVDC (High Voltage Direct Current) transmission or (costly) recondensation of imported gas. The role of the Government should be to really prioritise projects and ensure a proper timetable monitoring for the projects. This time-consuming activity would become possible with the Ministry of Power being discharged from the present day-to-day aspects of the administrative functioning of the power sector. In the long term, the natural interlocutors of the Ministry of Power will become the Ministries of Coal, and Renewable Energy Sources, more than power utilities, companies, or corporations.

7.4.4. The Shift in Paradigms

To conclude, the core argument of the book is that the long neglect for maintenance, quality of service, cost-efficiency and conservation measures has come from an administrative paradigm. The book really proposes another one. Shifting from one paradigm to another always requires a catalytic element, as well as, bridging the political lock-ins. We are confident that the public debate in India is progressing towards clarification of analysis and evaluation of past experience, that the technological innovations may serve a catalytic purpose, and that political lock-ins may be overcome.

As foreseen and analysed by Joskow and Schmalensee (1983), and as confirmed since then, technical change has brought the ability to decentralise technological improvement to the user end. This has broken the long-time paradigmatic vision of the power sector as a naturally vertically integrated sector. The ancient argument was that transmission is a natural monopoly, and leads to the integration of the whole sector because of the coordination needs and the many externalities the transmission network has on distribution and generation.

Technological change has introduced innovative coordination forms (Finon & Glachant, 2000) and changed the ancient paradigm into a trade-off between the coordinative pros and cons of integration (Glachant, 2002). True, the problems of the power sector in administered economies are radically different (Ruet 2002) and any reform in India has to integrate the issues described here. Only then, technology can be fully made use of. Enterprisation may fix the targets and the milestones for catching such sources of improvement. At this degree of complexity (including in policy formulation), neither the administrative paradigm, nor the 'full-private' paradigm can succeed. As Phadke & Rajan (2003) put it, using at par examples of developed and developing countries, and relating these to India, "ownership change must be looked as one among several options for changing incentives and not as an end goal". The reduction of the debate to mere ideology at the turn of the nineties has produced nothing but the worst capacity addition in the recent five-year plans.

In this highly sensitive field, a sound political debate focusing on genuine arguments matter. Political lock-ins are getting progressively overcome in India. Regulatory Commissions have been given birth through an Ordinance, soon changed as an Act. Though they were not compulsory, they have gained most of the States and might become compulsory if the new Bill is passed. Minimal tariffs for agriculture could not be centrally imposed, neither in 1996, nor in 1998, nor any time later on. Today, nearly all the States have adopted their own minimal tariff for agricultural consumption[16], and a legal minimal national tariff might finally come.

A transmission bill opening the field to private investment could be accepted by a Parliamentary Committee, after objections of the left run States were answered and they got convinced that grid operation would be in public control, even with private investment. Availability tariffs, which had suffered from a pause because of judicial cases filed by NTPC, are soon to be back. The case has been rejected by the Supreme Court in November 2002, therefore subjecting all the public generators to the economically sound system of availability tariffs.

Finally, the energy efficiency legislation still faces hurdles from the private sector. Working conditions for the private sector to join are still to be found, but this is no longer considered as out of reach. This provides a positive context, but this is not sufficient, the book has all along underlined, and the shift in paradigm must take place at the organisations level, at the consumer-end level, at the local project level if they are to sustain. The political power has a crucial role in making these policies start, prove that it sometimes knows how to overcome its own lock-ins. *If well-designed and legally enforced, all-levels enterprisation will then sustain, because it has a sound economic basis, and is no longer limited to a mere administrative measure.*

7.5. Conclusion

For State Governments, committing to reforms under the public supervision can be seen as a way to access conditional loans and allow the system to go on for some time, whether this commitment is expected to last or not. It is then all the more imperative that funding agencies, if concerned with the social welfare, design a phased mechanism to cope with this. On the other hand, even a well-designed privatisation faces the problem of valuating the so-called and nowhere to be found 'assets'.

16. The August 2004 untargeted free agricultural power in post-electoral Andhra Pradesh is unfortunately a dwart in the face of a State which already cannot seriously fund targeted social programmes.

To solve both drawbacks, funding agencies as well as the Central Government should support schemes that would plan a first attempt on management contract basis, to be followed by privatisation in case of failure, but not necessarily in case of success. Indeed, put in other words, the only way to separate the earlier social functions of administrations and the new cost-efficient productive role assigned to them, is to separate the subsidies from the *operation* of the sector and directly allocate them. Administrative and productive functions should not be mixed. For this, only one tool exists, management contracts. In order to solve the issues of (i) the credibility in of the setting up of property rights, and (ii) the measure of efficiency, we suggest to design the management contracts such as to:

- give provisions to administratively sanction the faults, at least by posting different people in place of corrupt officers,
- give the right and means to add private-financed posts in the hierarchy, with the right to invite the public officers to join this privately financed type of posts,
- give a full discretion over a certain amount of investment (still financed by the public),
- base the fee both on a fixed part and on a success based part linked with the operating surplus to sales in current prices.

Such a scheme based on management contracts has the advantage of establishing not only control rights whose credibility will rely on a reputation game, but also proper incentives once these rights are set. It also creates cash flow rights, at least for the contractor, if not for the organisation itself. This hence helps the management to also benefit from the setting up of cash flow rights. Under this framework, nobody has an interest in a break-out of the contract. As long as it lasts, its very continuation gives the external signal that the enterprisation is progressing. Looked at that way, the management contract is a mighty way to produce information in a continuous manner, since a break-up is an instant signal of problem. Thus, for the supporting agency, this provides valuable data as well as information on the commitment of the State. If the State Government makes clear that it will support a management contract scheme implemented that way, then the bias for an opportunistic behaviour of the State is partly suppressed, at the benefit of welfare. In that respect, the management contract also offers a tool for a close and reactive monitoring, thus opening space for a phased disbursement of loans.

Conversely, if the choice to privatise is made, 'selling shares' or 'divesting' might be desirable, but is far less feasible or credible given the radical uncertainty in bidding. Here again, an initial management contract turns out to be the most credible way to ultimately achieve the goal of privatisation in many configurations.

This proposed 'theoretical optimal solution', a deeper enterprisation through public reform under the form of a management contract, also better shows the economic status of privatisation. Indeed, only once the enterprisation is achieved, the questions of the de-integration and of the privatisation can be discussed on their natural and usual ground, that is the increasing of (actual & comparative) efficiency through competition.

And only then theories and concept developed in a different framework and context can be fully used as far as the Indian power sector is concerned.

8

General Conclusion: Reform and Theory of the Indian State

The economic debate on privatisation as a tool for the reforming of the public sector is alive in India, as well as evolving. This debate takes place within a specific Indian political economy of reforms. Let us subsequently detail how the conclusions of this book practically relate to these, as well as the analytical perspectives it opens up.

8.1 Theoretical and Practical Impacts

The analytical framework we propose allows reformulating the debate on the inefficiency of the Indian power sector by endogenising and setting out structural elements of the internal organisation of the State Electricity Boards (SEBs). It discusses and goes beyond the explanations usually given. Our thesis is that the inefficiency of SEBs structurally derives from their organisational nature itself. Indeed, independently of their legal status, the SEBs are administrations, and not, as they are usually analysed, public enterprises. Accordingly, we:

(i) characterise the internal structure of SEBs and its influence over the decision-making process,

(ii) discuss the non-pertinacity of analytical tools based on the concepts of costs, with the strong belief that this can be generalised to other emerging countries,

(iii) as well as we assess the (in)-effectivity of reforms based on these models, and

(iv) we make practical recommendations for the reform of SEBs, taking a view on the opportunity and political and economic conditions for success of privatisation.

SEBs as Administrations

The SEBs are subjected to the executive instructions of the State. These executive instructions are different from political directives of a share-holding State that are usually analysed by the economic theory. In fact, the 'principle' of the agency theory restrains itself to setting-up general rules. It then leaves its 'agent' with the discretionary power and the accountability to reach the objectives the way it considers to be the best. In its relationships to the SEBs, the Indian State does not, at all behave in such a way. Far from only fixing the general objectives to attain while allowing discretionary power to the SEB, the State also haphazardly specifies time-bound and spatially-specific measures to be implemented. From then on, a hierarchic relation is in place and the statutory autonomy of the SEB *de facto* does no longer exist. This has both short term and long-term implications on their activity.

The objectives of the State are numerous, non-hierarchised and variable in time. This situation does not even correspond to relation of an agency with multi-principal, due to both the unstable and discretionary character of the State intervention. These latter models simply do not describe the reality of the functioning of SEBs. In fact, this functioning corresponds to the definition of an administration. *The SEBs are an integral part of the State administration. They cannot be analysed out of the State, nor in isolation from it.*

The logic of the State is in-built in the structure of the SEBs, just the same way the SEBs are part of the State apparatus. The administrative nature of the SEBs translates in a structural way into their internal organisation. This restricts and orients the decision-making. The book is structuralist in that sense, and the internal organisation of SEBs can be stylised by three characteristics:

- *The decisions are based on the respect of techno-administrative procedures and not on cost-benefit comparison*: The systemic possibility of executive instructions renders cost-benefit calculation impossible because, for any decision, the conditions can *ex-post* be considerably modified. In this situation of uncertainty it becomes logical to rely on stable administrative procedures (standard actions are carried out if certain simple parameters present given characteristics and are sanctioned by an internal bureaucracy). In parallel to these procedures, the internal organisation of the SEB revolves what the book calls paper work. This consists in making the work of identification/ sanction of parameters from one administrative phase to the following. Once processed and sanctioned, the paper work is considered as complete. Its actual implementation hardly matters.

- *The reporting system is designed to administratively control that procedures have been followed, and not to evaluate the cost-efficiency of coordination of actions*: In particular, the reporting system is non-integrated, that is to say, that the figures related to physical data and the accounting data are written out separately. The latter are often substituted by statistical values or simple 'guestimates'. This reporting system thus does not allow the evaluation of the productive efficiency of any SEB or its units or divisions. Similarly, at the level of SEB units there is no concern for comparing the incoming quantities of energy or money (when the figures exist) to the outgoing quantities (here too, when the figures exist). Thus there is neither any measure of the technical efficiency (link between incoming and outgoing energy) nor of the cost-efficiency of any sub-unit (revenue – expenditure link), nor of commercial efficiency (link between energy supplied and collection of revenues). The interest of cost-benefit analysis is already limited by the executive instructions. The non-integrated information system ultimately makes cost-based decision-making technically impossible.
- *The subjecting of the SEB to the discretionary power of the State is transmitted to each level of the hierarchy and materialises into an absence of local discretionary power*: Each level in the hierarchical chain must refer in everything to higher levels. Every decision goes through a procedure involving at least three hierarchical levels. In particular, there is no real budgetary allocation. The most simple and repetitive tasks cannot be decided by the concerned officers.

All these characteristics of the SEBs show that neither the cost nor the productive-efficiency are sought after by SEBs and the book specifies how these different characteristics mutually strengthen each other. They are, in fact, rationally articulated to the willingness of the State to arbitrate on a discretionary basis between objectives that cannot be reconciled through sole monetary parameters. This makes up the specificity of the SEB-organisation. More accurately, the procedures are oriented towards the short term quantitative extension of the generation capacity and of the network. In other words, they respond to a mono-technical vision of the sector (a single input: the planned expenditure, as well as, a single product: the additional MW of generation capacity). This model suited to a non-electrified country where human capital exists but is limited, such as the newly decolonised India of 1947. It is now, by and large, inefficient in tackling more subtle short run operational issues that are characteristic of a mature power industry. The short run inefficiencies have accumulated in such a way to impede the long run development of the system. The present organisation is unsuitable to modern India.

To sum up, this book brings out the weight of the structural causes in the inefficiency of the SEBs. Therefore, we give relativity to the situational explanations put forth by certain proponents of the debate in India. Moreover, through the *détour* of the organisational analysis, we explain the functioning of the inside of the SEB 'black box'. Questions such as the organisational nature of the SEB, its mode of rationality are taken up. This leads, to document and organise the presentation of the mode of functioning of the SEBs. The latter is at the same time not known to the public. But also often little known in its details and practical problems by the Power Secretaries or even the Chairmen of the SEBs, who are high ranking, non-specialised, officers, at times posted for very short periods. Similarly the politicians know the problems of the SEB only through their interactions with the public but are not familiar with their internal problems.

This concern of documentation and stylisation thus allows on these three accounts to provide material for the political economy debate on the role of SEBs in the Indian economy and society; we shall come back to this. But further, the analysis in terms of opposition between administration and enterprise presents the advantage of recalling, or even bringing out the organisational specificity of the SEBs for external consultants not much used to this kind of institutions or seldom available for extended stays in the field. From this point of view, the concern of stylising the procedures allows at the same time a synthetic presentation and thus a better dissemination of ideas, but also to make operative the opposition between administration and enterprise.

Finally, but not the least important in the eyes of the author, this work makes it possible to bring an external insight and a distance for the public officers themselves.

Analytical Consequences: India as Exemplifying the Debate on Socialism and Property Rights

This characterisation then calls for the study of the pertinacity of economic concepts and theories based on cost. The concept of cost presents two characteristics in economy: of *ex-post* access to the reconstruction of parameters of a decision, but also of explanatory and choice variable *ex-ante* to the decision. In the case of SEBs, none of these is available.

Indeed, a cost is the price of an opportunity, associated to a differential of financial consequences, between a decision and a reference pattern. These consequences are negative or positive (the 'benefits') and their combination does constitute the cost of the decision. By nature, the reference pattern, but also the decisional pattern are inaccessible in the SEBs, the place of the discretionary power of the State. Therefore, the cost is not used *ex-ante* in the decision-making process. As well, *ex-post*, even if it is possible, at an aggregated level, to calculate proxies for average expenses, this does not constitute a cost, in the sense that no expense can directly relate to any identifiable decision. The first function is not available at the level of an elementary operation, that is to say, not inside the administrative sphere. Thus, one can neither express nor measure any cost that is linked with any decision, that is to say which explains it or reveals it.

The concept of cost is not operative for the analysis of the decision in a SEB. That is to say that not only the cost does not influence the decision *ex-ante* but also it does not reveal the decision *ex-post*. In other words, it is not a *cognitive structure* at all. Similarly, the concepts of investment, or of assets refer back to the concepts of costs. In enterprises, the link between costs and profits that they convey forms such a cognitive structure of the organisation. This evidently is not the case in the SEB, where these concepts have no reality. *In SEBs, these are the concepts of planned expenditure and new equipment that constitute the reference variables. These variables are alien to such concepts as an investment or an asset. The concept of cost is alien to SEBs, and the radical difference between the administration and the enterprise is thus directly consubstantial with the non-integration of information and the recourse to procedural rationality*. That is to say, not only the administrative nature precludes integrating the information, and legitimises the recourse to procedural rationality, but also on the reverse, these two characteristics legitimise the discretionary practices at stake in the administrative nature.

As regards the validity of explanations for the inefficiency of the SEB in terms of soft budget constraints or non-incentive allocation of property rights, they are based on a substantive rationality faced with monetary criteria. This suffices to disqualify their pertinence in the analysis of SEBs. They don't allow the decisional analysis, neither *ex-post* nor *ex-ante*.

Furthermore, the decisional structure implies that there is no allocation of residual control rights, therefore no property rights in the sense of Grossman & Hart (1986). In fact, at the level of the decision itself, the concepts of soft budget constraint, or of property rights, are founded on the hypotheses of behaviour where the agents: (i) identify costs (ii) have the discretionary power to base their decision on these costs, and (iii) use this power to indeed adopt a behaviour based on them. Soft Budget constraint theory and mis-allocation of Property Rights explanation are consequently not applicable in the SEBs, respectively because the decisions are not based on budgets but on techno-administrative procedures linked to physical or political objectives and expressed in physical variables, and because there are no property rights *stricto sensu* (in the sense of residual control rights of Grossman & Hart) in or on the SEBs.

This last point deserves to be explained in detail and articulated to the organisational characteristics of the SEBs. Due to the absence of internal allocation of discretionary power, the Field units do not have residual control rights. True, they can use the non-integration of the information system to hide facts or delay the execution of decisions, but in a locally restricted manner, only being able to follow the natural slope of the system. The Field has no real power to actively influence the system. Therefore this cannot translate into a residual control right. Similarly, neither the Headquarters nor the State have the residual control right, and this despite the discretionary power of the State. In fact, taking into account the information system and its consequences, the concrete application of instructions is all but guaranteed. There is thus no place in the SEB or 'outside' (the SEB being a part of the State administration) where any property right exists.

One of the contributions of the book is therefore also analytical, on the concepts used in economics. Indeed, when the pertinence of theories founded on the soft budget constraints or property rights or still the explicative capacity of concepts such as those of cost, budget, decision, are discussed for the analysis of the SEBs, this work leads to specifying their respective fields of application. Thus, it allows extending to India the academic debate on the specific forms or the absence of property in socialism, post-socialism or countries such as China.

Evaluation and Political Economy of Reforms: 'transfer' of Ownership is not the Point

In India, there exists a growing rejection of the inefficiency of the SEBs. From then on, taking into account the alien character of the concept of efficiency in the SEBs, if one wants to deal with this problem, one must come out of the administrative logic of the SEB and substitute it with the functioning of an enterprise, the natural framework for this kind of preoccupations. *The reforms based on an analysis in terms of soft budget constraints (proposal of 'hardening of the constraint') or on the reallocation of (supposedly badly allocated) property rights miss in fact the essential, which is to change the nature of the SEBs.* The reforms aiming at introducing productive efficiency as a central dimension of the functioning of the SEBs must rest on a radical change of the organisational nature itself of the SEBs, which we call 'enterprisation'. SEBs will thus have to be 'enterprised', that is to say transformed from an administration into an enterprise. Enterprisation is a concept that emerged from the study of reforms in the post-socialist East European countries. The enterprisation can be defined for the SEBs from their preceding stylisation. Enterprisation is achieved when executive instructions are substituted with policy directions, when an internal allocation of discretionary power is put in place, with an integrated information system, and especially when the concept of cost becomes central in the decisions. One indication of this enterprisation is the creation and the allocation of property rights at the level of the SEB and in the SEB.

From this point of view, the structural reforms (corporatisation, de-integration, setting up of Regulatory Commissions) do not lead to an enterprisation. Corporatisation is only a judicial change of status, which in itself does not affect the organisational nature of the SEBs, as their current status of Board already guarantees them a *de jure* autonomy that they do not exercise *de facto*. Setting up Regulatory Commissions is only an external incentive mechanism, to which the SEB will not be *a priori* sensitive. Worse, SEBs will even be powerless in facing the regulator's decisions if they are not enterprised. The facts are that de-integration neither leads to the changing of the internal structure of each new sub-entity, nor to making the relations between sub-units clearer (it does not create control rights and, in certain States, nor even on the cash flow between sub-entities), nor even making the relations between the former SEB and the State clearer. The analysis in terms of enterprisation contributes thus to indicating what is missing in the current reforms proposed by the Government of India. The detailed study of the creation of property rights shows that only the de-integration has effects – still in a very limited way – in this regard.

Further, the privatisation of the distribution activity of the SEBs, proposed by the World Bank, can be discussed on a sound basis. The privatisation that took place in Orissa in fact shows that (i) the targeted investors withdrew in large numbers from the investment tender and (ii) the remaining are highly pessimistic about the possibilities of improvement in the short term. The classical explanation in terms of absence of guarantees is conceptually poor and at the same time non-operative. The analysis in terms of enterprisation allows to relativise the privatisation/non-privatisation problematic which is presently central to the political economy of the reforms of the Indian power sector.

Our argument is that the uncertainties in privatisation are structurally linked to the nature of non-enterprised SEBs. Indeed, *privatisation goes through a process of bidding, which implies monetary evaluation of the SEB or one of its parts. This is technically impossible in a SEB not enterprised beforehand.* As a matter of fact, the preparatory phase of the privatisation ought to focus on the creation of property rights (among others by giving guarantees in limiting the discretionary intervention of the State). But still, on the one hand, the evaluation of the credibility of these rights is not easy and on the other hand, the information on the value that the use of these rights can generate does not exist. The privatisation of a SEB not enterprised beforehand can thus lead to an under-bidding, with each investor making a depreciated offer. This is the reason for shifting the emphasis from the problematic of privatisation to the wider and more preliminary analysis of the modalities of enterprisation. The question of enterprisation thus takes precedence over that of privatisation.

Formally, the enterprisation can thus be carried out either in a public framework or in a private manner. The former gives rise to notable problems of credibility/sustainability of reforms in the Indian case, while the latter involves technical and economic drawbacks due to the difficulty in valuating an administrative structure which by nature does not possess property rights. It is in this context that the advantages of an enterprisation 'short of cash-flow rights transfer' are shown. That is, a public enterprisation before privatisation. Its benefits include a higher sale value, progressive redistributive effects, as well as, a higher efficiency in bringing the potential investors.

To get round the risk of an opportunistic behaviour of the State, an hybrid mechanism of enterprisation via a management contract with a private entrepreneur is proposed. It allows specifying (i) the control rights to the private contractor as well as to the organisation itself, (ii) the financial rights (and the related incentives) to the contractor. The key element of this mechanism is that it produces external information on the level of intervention of the State. In fact, in last analysis, the credibility/sustainability of this mechanism resides in a game of threats between the State and the contractor. If the State intervenes through executive instructions, it exposes itself to breach of contract by the private contractor, thereby indicating that the attempt of enterprisation has failed due to the State. Reciprocally, a private company concerned with its reputation must avoid unilateral breaking of the contract by the State upon fault of the contractor. From this point of view, the management contract, if it is supervised by a financial organisation, can be a strong source of information. It is thus an hybrid mechanism that is proposed, without resorting to private investment, but to its management capacities. *Besides, whereas enterprisation, as an economic tool, focuses on cash-flow rights, management contracts, focus on control rights, that is more central to the problem, we argue.*

Whatever be the political choice made later, the path of enterprisation through management contracts should be given importance to. In fact, it makes it possible to reform really and efficiently without selling the assets to the private sector if such is the choice of the State or the constraint imposed by the market (in a privatisation there must undoubtedly be offerers but also takers, which is far from ensured in India). In terms of feasibility, this measure provides a large framework of application since it takes into account the political constraints. Beyond, even if, ultimately, the political choice of the State is to privatise, this mechanism is the only one which really provides the information necessary for privatisation. Thus enterprisation through management contracts is the only mechanism which allows later privatisation in both conditions of economic efficiency and with a satisfactory speed.

To sum up, the administrative characterisation of the SEBs and the derived concept of enterprisation makes it possible to settle in a radical way the debate on structural reforms currently underway. In terms of propositions, the analysis shows that the thinkability itself of the concept of cost is not ensured in a SEB. Any reform must therefore preliminary ensure that the concept itself of cost becomes thinkable. This should take precedence over non-realistic setting-up of incentive systems. The concept of enterprisation then shifts the level of analysis of reforms to the inside of the SEB 'black box', and provides an assessment criterion for the proposed reforms.

In short, in the analytical framework of the book, privatisation is subordinated to enterprisation. This can contribute towards renewing the debate of political economy of reforms in India. In that respect, here is the place to specify the current situation. During ten years of reforms of the power sector (in reality already preceded by fore runner signs right from mid 80s) several successive strategies have been proposed by the Government of India. The entire political class is now convinced that the SEBs are the weak links and, within the complex Centre-State game, the Government of India has succeeded in bringing most of the States round to its structural reforms (corporatisation, de-integration, regulation). Also, a large number of States are, at least off the record, showing interest in privatisation (though often more out of concern for getting rid of the problem than for looking for economic efficiency). The political debates are structured around two stakes:

- the political acceptability of these reforms and, in particular, of privatisation,

- and unfortunately in a lesser way, the efficiency of the reforms, since the preliminary results in certain pilot States brought to the fore the numerous limits of this approach.

The first question calls for, above all, considerations of timetable, taking into account the negative redistributive effects on certain categories of players considered as electorate. The second is used in fact as a scarecrow by those who do not have an interest in reforming (these same players organised into interest groups, a part of the political class). In a 'benevolent' approach (the State is looking for the most economically efficient reform), the results presented here can therefore be used to analyse the current failures and to improve the reforms propositions by correcting the shortcomings of the so-called structural reforms in a perspective of productive efficiency. Moreover, more specific calculations carried out by Ruet (2002) also allow to nourish debates on the possibility of setting up of targeted subsidies in the transitory phase to limit the redistributive shocks. This however must take along the support of development agencies and States. By promoting the management contract, the book suggests especially to strongly relativise the question of privatisation which is one of the most politically sensitive one. In terms of feasibility of the reform, it thus makes it possible to enhance its acceptability, an argument perhaps politically stronger than the economic ones proposed in the model (sale price, efficient selection and increasing the chances of success of privatisation).

In fact, an opportunistic use of the results of this book is also probable. From that point of view, a number of players could insist only on the fact that structural reforms are not efficient and can propose much lighter solutions (simple cost centres). Similarly, they could limit themselves to or on the fact that reform must remain public and as a result distort the discussion on privatisation. These two distortions of the analysis are not the view of the author. A careful reading of the book negates them as too narrow-minded. More fundamentally, the politicians of the States who are sufficiently strong politically actually wish to get rid of the problem in the short term. Therefore, a low sale price (but paid in short term), even with an increased risk of default of the private investor in the mid-term, may not be sufficiently discouraging against a not well enough timely phased privatisation. Finally, so far as the Government of India is concerned, it is in many ways the last resort financier of the power sector, for instance through the mechanisms of federal budgetary transfers but also through its power generation units. However, it does not reap any direct political dividends from it which rest with the States. Consequently, it has an interest in a speedy disengagement of the States. This constitutes for it a relative power climb-up in the Centre-State game. On these questions, the work in this book has limited itself in giving elements of analysis and debate to those who support search for efficiency and sustainability of reforms.

8.2 Domain of Validity and Extensions

Let us finally discuss the retained hypothesis and the choices made in terms of method and field.

The Stylisation of SEBs

Let us underline the advantages as well as the methodological limits of the retained approach. The behaviourist analytic framework proposed by James March[1] has been followed. This method offers the advantage of entering the 'black box', but also of studying an organisation that is not an enterprise, by using the internal parameters and mechanisms specific to this organisation. In relation to usual economic concepts, this method thus does not necessarily make the implicit – and wrong in the case of SEBs - hypothesis of a behavioural sensitivity to monetary incentives. It allows identifying and articulating in a proper rationality some lines of regularity. For this reason, it allows *ex-post* explanatory analysis but also a certain forecasting analysis (reason for blockage in setting up of certain economic tools). Beyond this however, the concept of incentive becomes by definition pertinent after the enterprisation.

In terms of fields, choices were necessary. In fact, certain micro-local fine balancing in the decision-making process, could not be studied (local power of delaying/accelerating a file, local parameters of choice), which would probably allow to refine the explanation of the actual implementation of decisions beyond the paper work. However, this kind of analysis would imply recourse to the sociology of organisations, a vast field extending beyond the present economic

1. Following his works with Simon (March & Simon, 1958) and those with Cyert (Cyert & March, 1963).

framework. A second concerns corruption; difficult to identify, difficult to stylise in sole monetary terms (without sociological referents). The choice was made to focus on the systemic factors of lock-in, that constitute limiting factors in themselves. Corruption is a reinforcing but not a structural element in the problem of the SEBs (we have shown that the corruption opens up a space of discretionary power only within a limit forced by the organisation and does not constitute property rights).

On sociological aspects, an apparently important dichotomy came up during the investigation, that between 'bureaucrats' and 'technocrats', or between the body of IAS officers and the body of SEB engineers. Coupled with a heightened sense of hierarchy and seniority, the study of this caesura would merit the contribution of a sociologist (the multi-disciplinary approach of Dorin, Flamant, Lachaier, Vaugier-Chatterjee (2000) has shown the relevance of this type of study). This would not question or challenge the stylisation but would ultimately specify it in order to envisage reforms. In fact, whatever be the degree of hierarchisation of a society, the difference between an administration and an enterprise can be maintained and the analysis remains intact.

To conclude on the representativity of the stylisation of the SEBs, the investigation work revolved around about 200 meetings and interviews in seven States. Also, some investigations conducted in other sectors (water, mines, public manufacturing enterprises, cf. Ruet, 2001a) show the presence of an administered system of co-ordination within the public sphere. Finally, variations between different SEBs of different States do exist, but the stylisation explains a common inefficiency and functioning. There are several studies, which consider their relative inefficiency. They include parameters exogenous to the framework retained here (public financing, development level etc.). By doing so, these studies try to quantify the inefficiency or the scale of financial deficits but, we believe, without explaining their origin. The stylisation presented here allows doing so.

The Proposed Measures

The concept of enterprisation must feed on experiments carried out and a learning process has to crystallise. In implementation, the following issues will be stringent.

A specification of the enterprisation process in terms (i) of initial distribution – after enterprisation – of property rights, (ii) of future evolution of this distribution under, for example, the development of the regulatory framework, (iii) of feasibility of this evolution, will be an important theoretical guide in the implementation of the enterprisation. At this particular level, the questions of corruption and hierarchy are important (for example, in order to know how to entrust a discretionary power, if one has to set up a parallel hierarchy etc.). However, at the present stage of practical experiments (only a few States having a sufficient degree of 'learning by doing', but in the absence of an enterprisation attempt as such), this analysis will certainly depend on hypotheses demanding a practical validation that will require a close monitoring.

A field of related questions also opens up: the enterprisation can go through the creation and contribution of a real market, that is to say, by establishing supplier-client relations. Thus, a study of various forms of subsidiarity in the distribution (associations, single point village entry, inset appointments or private development etc.) and their evolution are needed along the practical implementation. This will open up a very prospective field of relatively new organisational forms for the power sector in general. In this book, stress has been given as much as possible on indicating these paths and the attempted experiments.

Future will show the emerging institutional arrangements and practical ways of enterprising. The concept and the practice of enterprisation may provide guidelines for the study and monitoring of this institutional change. The latter may be new to India, but might as well provide something new from India.

Annexure

Annexure: Status of Reform in the Indian States, by September 2002 & April 2004

Table

Completed Steps in Each State

State	*Decision to Set up SERC*	*SERC Operational*		*Number of Tariff Orders*	*Studies for Unbundling*	*Creation of Distribution Circles/unbundling*		*Decision to Privatise(X)/ Date of Completion*
		2002	*2004*	*2002*	*2002*	*2002*	*2004*	
Arunachal Pradesh	X				X			
Andhra Pradesh	X	X	X	3	X	Feb. 99	X	X, Postponed
Assam	X	X	X		X			
Bihar			X		X			
Chhattisgarh			X				X	
Delhi	X	X	X	2	X	X	X	May 02
Gujarat	X	X	X	1	X	X	X	
Goa					X			
Haryana	X	X	X	3	X	Aug. 98	X	
Himachal Pradesh	X	X	X	1				
Jammu & Kashmir					X			
Jharkand			X					
Karnataka	X	X	X	2	X	X	X	X, Postponed

Contd...

...Contd...

State	*Decision to Set up SERC*	*SERC Operational*		*Number of Tariff Orders*	*Studies for Unbundling*	*Creation of Distribution Circles/unbundling*		*Decision to Privatise(X) /Date of Completion*
		2002	*2004*	*2002*	*2002*	*2002*	*2004*	
Kerala	X	X	X	1				
Meghalaya								
Madhya Pradesh	X	X	X	1	X			
Maharashtra	X	X	X	2	X			
Manipur	X							
Mizoram	X		X					
Nagaland	X		X					
Orissa	X	X	X	4	X	X	X	Sep. 99
Punjab	X	X	X		X		X	
Rajasthan	X	X	X	1	X	X	X	
Sikkim								
Tamil Nadu	X	X	X					
Tripura								
Uttaranchal	X	X	X					
Uttar Pradesh	X	X	X		X	X	X	
West Bengal	X	X	X		X			

Note: X shows that the measure has been completed.

Sources: Powerline, New Delhi (Vol. 4 No. 12 September 2000, Vol. 5 No. 2 November 2000, Vol. 5 No. 3 December 2000, & Vol. 6 No. 12 September 2002), GoI 2004.

In Kerala, profit Centres have been set up without unbundling, while Tamil Nadu contemplates the same approach. Nagaland, Meghalaya, Mizoram, Manipur, Tripura, Sikkim, show a willingness to constitute a Joint Electricity Regulatory Commission.

Appendices

Assessing Income Level

Net State Domestic Product and Electric Consumption

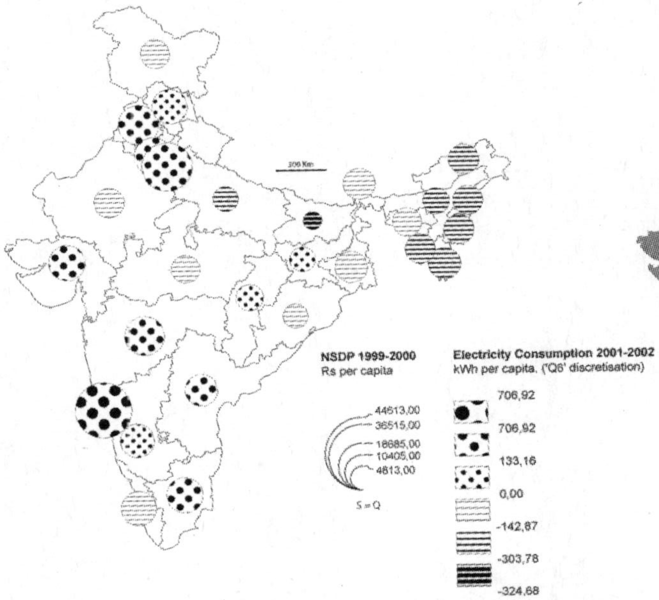

Assessing Governance

SEBs Rating and Funding Agencies for Reforms

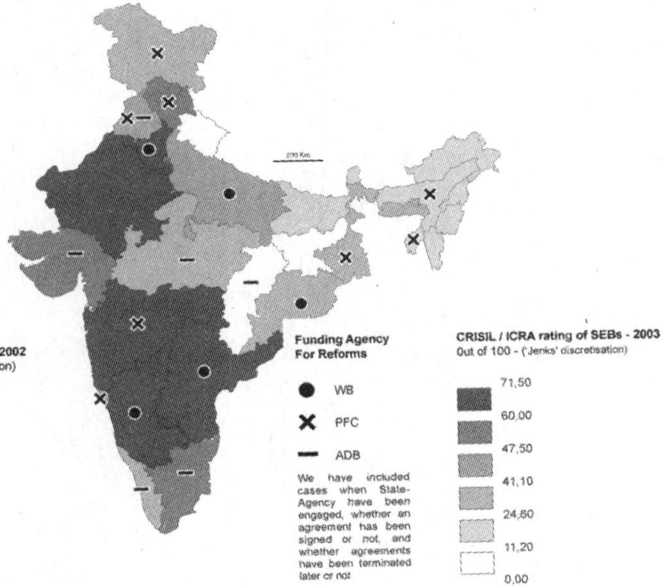

Source: Net State Domestic Product, source: *www.indiastat.com*, Rajya Sabha Unstarred Question No. 2028, dated 11.03.2003; Electricity Consumption, source: *www.indiastat.com*, Lok Sabha, Unstarred Question No. 288, dated 17.8.2004; State-wise Rating Score of State Electricity Boards/Utilities by CRISIL (Credit Rating Information Services of India Ltd)/ICRA (Investment Information and Credit Rating Agency Ltd.), source: *www.indiastat.com*, Lok Sabha Starred Question No. 330, dated 13.03.2003; Funding Agency, source: interviews, *www.adb.org*, *www.worldbank.org*, *www.pfcindia.com*.

The Feasibility Domain of Management Contracts and Privatisation

GOVERNANCE		INCOME: **LOW** *(Low interest for the investor)*	INCOME: **HIGH** *(Interest in catching the cash-flow rights)*
	LOW *(Relative support to privatisation)*	Problematic Situation but, ultimately, at most a management contract is feasible (**MC**) /	● Privatisation (**P**)
	HIGH *(Relative push for Management Contract)*	Management Contract is preferable (**MC+**) ✖	⊗ Both are feasible: the State can decide on a economic trade-off basis (**MC+ or P**)

	INCOME*	GOVERNANCE**	Preferable Reforms	
Delhi, Haryana, Maharashtra, Goa, Punjab	HIGH	HIGH	MC+ or P	⊗
		LOW	P	●
Andhra Pradesh, Gujarat, Karnataka, Rajasthan, Arunachal Pradesh, Himachal Pradesh, Kerala, Mizoram, Sikkim, Tamil Nadu, Tripura, West Bengal	INTERMEDIATE	HIGH	MC+	✖
		LOW	MC	/
Assam, Bihar, Jammu & Kashmir, Madhya Pradesh, Manipur, Meghalaya, Nagaland, Orissa, Uttar Pradesh, Chhatisgarh, Jharkhand	LOW	LOW	MC	/
		NA	MC	/
Uttaranchal	NA	NA	NA	NA

* Income: Thresholds separating low, intermediate and high are 13,000 and 20,000 Rs per capita.

** Governance: Rating of SEBs is taken as a proxy ; threshold is fixed at 50 up to 100.

Typology of Indian States According to their Level of Income and Governance

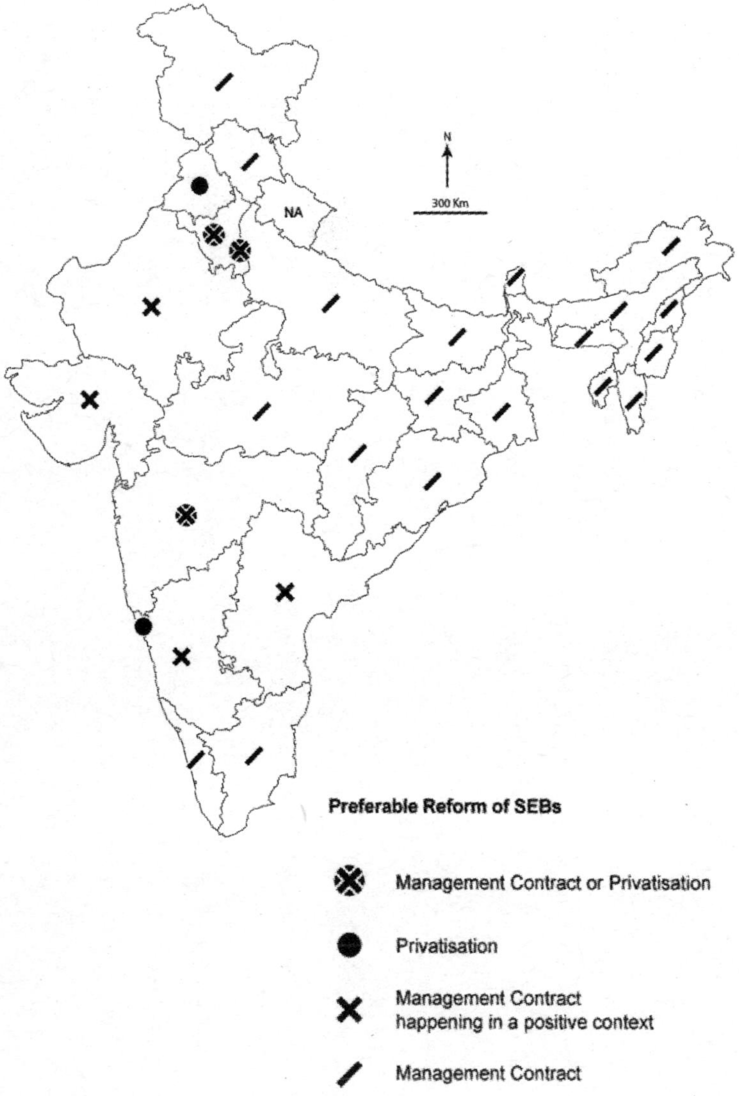

References

Ahrens, Joachim (1997). "Prospects of Institutional and Policy Reform in India: Toward a Model of the Developmental State?", Asian Development Bank, *Asian Development Review*, Vol. 15 No. 1, pp. 111-146.

Alagh, Y.K. (1996). "Fuel for Power", Lovraj Kumar Memorial Lecture, in *Current Science*, November 1996, Bangalore.

————. (2001). "Community & Cooperative Action", Keynote Address on Development and Governance, in Ginkel & Thakur, *UNU Millenium Series, 2001*, United Nations University, Tokyo, pp. 73-82.

————. (2001a). *Technology Policies and Investment Strategies*, OECD-ADB Asia Forum, OECD Paris, 165-180.

Alagh, Y.K., Jayatri Shah, & V.K. Shah (1998). *Power Economics in Gujarat*, Har-Anand Publications, New Delhi, 176 p.

Alchian, Armen & Demsetz, Harold (1973). "The Property Rights Paradigm", *Journal of Economic History*, March 1973, 33:17, pp. 16-27.

Bai, Chong-en & Wang, Yijiang (1995). *A Theory of Soft Budget Constraint*, Boston College and University of Minnesota, mimeo.

Banfield E.C. (1976). "Corruption as a Feature of Governmental Organisation", *Journal of Law & Economics*, December 1976, pp. 587-605.

Bhaduri, Amit (1990). "Optimal Price Adjustment under Imperfect Information", *European Economic Review*, Vol. 34, 1990, pp. 941-952.

Bhambhri, C.P. (1997). "The Indian State: Journey from Intervention to Liberalisation", *Indian Journal of Public Administration*, Vol. XIII No. 3, pp. 293-304.

Bomsel, Olivier (1995). "Enjeux industriels du post-socialisme: Capitalisation et Entreprisation", *Revue d 'Economie Industrielle* No. 72, pp. 31-46.

Boycko, Maxim; Shleifer, Andrei and Vishny, Robert (1996). "Theory of Privatisation", *Economic Journal*, 106: pp. 309-319.

Brousseau, Eric & Fares, M'hand (1998). "Incomplete Contracts and Governance Structures", Presented in 2nd Conference of the ISNIE, September 1998, Paris, *www.isnie.org/ISNIE98/Brousseou-Fares.doc.*

Burns, Phil and Estache, Antonio (1999). "Information, Accounting and the Regulation of Concessioned Infrastructure Monopolies", Policy Research Working Paper No. 2034, World Bank, 23 p.

Campbell-White, Oliver and Anita Bhatia (1998). *Privatisation in Africa*, World Bank, 1998, Washington DC.

CEA (1998). *Financial Performance of the SEBs During 1991-92 to 1994-95*, March 1998, New Delhi.

Chakravarty, Lata (2004). "Contracting for Power Purchase-Ensuring A Fair Deal For The Private Investor As Well As The Power Purchaser", in Ruet (ed). *Against the Current III*, Manohar Publishers, New Delhi.

Chakravarty, Shukhamoy (1987). *India: The Planing Experience*, Oxford University Press, New Delhi, 137 p., French Translation: *La planification du développement*, L'expérience indienne, Ed. De la Maison des Sciences de l'Homme, Paris, 1994, 151 p.

Chandran, T.R. Satish (1998). "Electricity Sector in India, Organisation and Financing of Development", Presented at the Seminar 'L'énergie en Inde', Centre de Géopolitique de l'Energie et des Matières Premières de l'Université de Paris-Dauphine, 15-16 janvier, 16 p.

Chitkara, Kalra, and Shekhar (2002). "Preparedness of State Electricity Board for Privatisation", Chapter 7, in Joël Ruet, ed, *Against the Current: Organisational Improvement of the SEBs*, Manohar Publishers, Delhi.

Cohen, Michael, March, James, & Olsen, Johann (1972). "A Garbage Can Model of Organisational Choice", *Administrative Science Quarterly*, 17: pp. 1-25.

Cyert, Richard & March, James (1963). *A Behavioral Theory of the Firm*, Prentice-Hall 1963, 264 p.

Demsetz, Harold (1967). "Toward A Theory of Property Rights", *American Economic Review*, May 1967, 57:2, pp. 347-359.

Dewatripont & Maskin (1995). "Credit & Efficiency in Centralised and Decentralised Economies", *Review of Economic Studies*, Vol. 62, pp. 541-555.

Dhameja, Nand (1997). "Public Sector Growth and Finance: Emerging Trends", *Indian Journal of Public Administration*, Vol. XIII No. 3, pp. 527-538.

Djankov, Simeon & Classens, Stijn (1998). "Politicians and Firms in Seven Central and Eastern European Countries", *Policy Research Working Paper No. 1954*, World Bank.

Djankov, Simeon (1998). "Enterprise Isolation in Transition Economies: Evidence from Romania", *Policy Research Working Paper No. 1952*, World Bank.

Dossani, Rafiq and V. Ranganathan (2004). "Farmer's Willingness to Pay for Power in India: Conceptual Issues, Survey Results and Implications for Pricing", in Ruet (ed), *Against the Current III*, Manohar Publishers, New Delhi.

Dubhashi, P.R. (1997). "Restructuring and Reform of Indian Political, Administrative and Economic System", *Indian Journal of Public Administration*, Vol XIII No. 3, pp. 362-368.

Eckstein, H. (1958). *The English Health Service*, Cambridge: Harvard University Press, 178 p.

Edwards, W. (1968). "Conservatism in Human Information Processing", in B. Kleinmutz (ed), *Formal Representation of Human Judgement*, pp. 17-52.

Electricity Act (2003). Act No. 36, 72 p., *The Gazette of India*, New Delhi.

Estache, Antonio & Martimort, David (1998). "Transaction Costs Politics, Regulatory Institutions and Regulatory Outcomes", presented in the conference *Regulacion post-privatizacion, la experiencia de America Latina*, Buenos Aires, May.

————. (1999). "Politics, Transaction Costs, and the Design of Regulatory Institutions", *Policy Research Working Paper No. 2073*, World Bank.

Fama E. (1980). "Agency Problems and the Theory of the Firm", *Journal of Political Economy*, 88: pp. 288-307.

Feldman, J. (1963). "Simulation of Behavior in the Binary Choice Experiment", in E.A. Feigenbaum & J. Feldman (eds). *Computers and Thought*, pp. 329-346.

Figueiredo Rui, Spiller Pablo & Urbiztondo Santiago (1999). "An Informational Perspective on Administrative Procedures", *Journal of Law Economics & Organisation*, Vol 15 No. 1, pp. 283-305.

Finon, Dominique, & Jean-Michel Glachant (2000). "Why do the European Union's Electricity Industry Continue to Differ? A New Institutional Analysis", pp. 313-334, in Claude Ménard, ed., *Institution, Contracts, and Organisations: Perspectives from New Institutional Economics*, Edward Elgar, London.

Galal, Ahmed & Shirley, Mary *et al* (1995). "Bureaucrats in Business", *World Bank Policy Research Report*, xix + pp. 347, Oxford University Press, New York.

Garibaldi, Alberto (1999). "The Institutions of Corruption: A Governance Approach to Administrative Corruption and its Control", Presented in 3rd Conference of the ISNIE, September, Washington D.C, *www.isnie.org/ISNIE99/ISNIEPanels913.pdf.*

Geng, Xiao (1999). The Role of Firm Ownership in Transitional Economies: Recent Evidence from China, Presented in 3rd Conference of the ISNIE, September, Washington D.C, *www.isnie.org/ISNIE99/Payers/Xiao.pdf.*

Giraud, Pierre-Noël (1996). L'inégalité Du Monde, Coll. Folio, Gallimard, Paris, 352 p.

————. (1998). Economie le grand satan, coll. Textuels, Gallimard, Paris, 142 p.

————. (2000). Economie et propriété dans les socialismes, présenté au Colloque de Cerisy, 1999, unpublished working document, CERNA, Paris, *www.cerna-ensmp.fr/ Documents/PNG-Cerisy.pdf.*, 13 p.

Girod, Jacques (1993). Les industries électriques du Burkina Faso, de la Côte d'Ivoire, du Mali et du Sénégal: performances et modèles organisationnels", revue de l'énergie, No. 448.

Glachant, Jean-Michel (1994). Le marché et le hors-marché; une analyse économique des entreprises publiques françaises, Publications de la Sorbonne, Paris, 250 p.

————. (1997). Le pool d'électricité en Grande-Bretagne: un marché incomplet sous administration privée et publique, Université Paris I, ATOM.

————. (2002). L'approche néo-institutionnelle de la réforme des industries de réseaux, pp 425-436, Revue Economique Vol. 53 No. 3, May 2002, Paris.

Glachant, J. M., Finon, D. eds. (2003). "Competition in European Electricity Markets : A Cross-country Comparison", Cheltenham: Edward Elgar, 367 p.

Godbole, Madhav (2003). "Electricity Act, 2003: Questionable Wisdom", pp. 4104-4110, *Economic and Political Weekly*, Vol XXXVIII No. 39, Bombay.

————. (2003a). "Power Sector Woes: No Easy Answer", *Economic and Political Weekly*, pp. 3781-3784, September 6, Bombay.

Gordon, R.A. (1948) "Short Period Price Determination", *American Economic Review* 38: pp. 265-288.

Government of Haryana (1998). "The Haryana Electricity Reform Act", *The Haryana Government Gazette*, 10th March.

Government of India (1995). *Government Policy & Rules for Private Sector Participation in Power Industry*, p. 86, Centre of Publications, New Delhi.

————. (1998). "An Ordinance to Provide the Establishment of a CERC and SERCs, Rationalisation of Electricity Tariffs, Transparent Polices Regarding Subsidies, Promotion of Efficient & Environmentally Benign Policies", *Gazette of India*, 25th April.

————. (1998a). "Electricity Sector in India, Organisation and Financing of Development", by T.R. Satish Chandran, presented by Dr. M.R. Srinivasan, Planning Commission, in January 1998 in Paris, p. 16.

————. (1998b). "Managing Distribution Reforms", Ministry of Power, *Committee on Distribution*, Chaired by Coelho, S.J., Working Document.

————. (2004). *Report of the Task Force on Power Sector Investment and Reforms* , Vol. I, p. 358, February, Government of India, New Delhi.

Government of Orissa (1995). *The Orissa Electricity Reform Bill*, The Orissa Legislative Assembly.

GRIDCO (1998). "Reform in GRIDCO – Revenue Improvement Action Programme", Document issued by the GRIDCO Information Cell, Bhubaneshwar, Orissa.

Grossman, Sanford & Hart, Oliver (1986). "The Costs & Benefits of Ownership: A Theory of Vertical and Lateral Integration", *Journal of Political Economics*, XCIV (86) pp. 691-719.

Haldea, Gajendra (2001). "Whither Electricity Reforms?", *Economic and Political Weekly*, Reprint in Ruet (ed), Against the Current: Organizational Restructuring of State Electricity Boards, p. 226, 2003, Manohar, New Delhi.

————. (2003). "Salvage Reforms", in *India 2002*, Seminar No. 521, January, New Delhi.

————. (2003a). Interview, in *Business Line, Financial Daily*, Friday, Jun 20.

————. (2003b). Interview, *Business Standard*, Thursday, October 16.

Hart, Oliver and John Moore (1990). "Property Rights and the Nature of the Firm", *Journal of Political Economy*, Vol. 98, Issue 6, pp. 1119-58

Haryana SEB (HSEB) (1991). *HSEB Notification No. 130*, dated 18th December, on "Revised Financial Powers".

———. (1998). Circulars and Notifications Issued by the Board, 1997-98.

———. (1999). Detail of requisition of funds for the month of 5/99, Memo 8350-S-3, & Memo 4652-FA.

———. (1999b). Circulars and Notifications Issued by HVPN, 1998-99.

———. (2000). Circulars and Notifications Issued by HVPN, 1999-00.

Hayek, Friedrich (1935). "Introduction and Concluding Essay", in *Collectivist Economic Planning*, Ed. Hayek, George Routledge & Sons Ltd, London.

———. (1945). "The Use of Knowledge in Society", *American Economic Review*, Vol. 35, pp. 519-530, in French: (1986). L'utilisation de l'information dans la société, Revue française d'économie, Vol. 1 No. 2.

Heiner, Ronald A. (1983). "The Origin of Predictable Behavior", *The American Economic Review*, Vol. 73 No. 4, pp. 560-595.

Hirschhausen (von). Christian (1995). "From Privatisation to Capitalisation: Industrial Restructuring in Post-socialist Central and Eastern Europe", in *Industrial Transformation in Europe: Process and Context*, Sage, London.

———. (1996). Du combinat socialiste à l'entreprise capitaliste – une analyse des réformes industrielles en Europe de l'Est, L'Harmattan, Paris.

Hocquart, Claire & Oury, Jean-Marc (1987). Vers une nouvelle économie de l'entreprise, Annales des Mines, juin 1987.

Holmstrom Bengt & Tirole, Jean (1989). "The Theory of the Firm", in *Handbook of Industial Organization*, chapter 2, Ed. Schmalensee & Willig.

Huchet, Jean-François & Xavier Richet (2000). "Entre bureaucratie et marché : Les groupes industriels chinois à la recherche d'un nouveau gouvernement d'entreprise", Working Paper No. 2 Centre d'Etudes Français sur la Chine Contemporaine (CEFC), Hong Kong, October 2000,

IMI (1999). *A Study on Financial Management of the State Electricity Boards*, a three volume report for the Finance Wing of the Ministry of Power, 3 × 250 pp, International Management Institute, New Delhi.

Iyer, Ramaswamy R. (1992). "Past Experiences with Public Enterprise Performance Evaluation System in India, Lessons for MoU's", pp. 762-772, in *Memorandum of Understanding, An Approach for Improving Public Enterprise Performance*, Ed. by Prajapati Trivedi, International Management Publishers, New Delhi, p. 896.

Jain, R.B., (1998). "Political Control of Bureaucracy in India", *Indian Journal of Public Administration*, Vol XIV No. 1 pp. 1-16.

Jefferson, Gary H. & Rawski, Thomas G. (1995). "How Industrial Reform Worked in China: The Role of Innovation, Competition, and Property Rights", Proceedings of the Annual World Bank Conference on Development Economics 1994.

Jensen, Michael. C. & Meckling, William.H. (1976). "Theory of the Firm: Managerial Behavior, Agency Costs and Ownership Structure", *Journal of Financial Economics*, 3 (1976) pp. 305-360.

Jiahua, Che & Yingyi, Qian (1998). "Insecure Property Rights and Government Ownership of Firms", *Quarterly Journal of Economics*, CXIII Issue 2 pp. 467-496.

Jian, Sun (1999). "State-owned Enterprises in China: Soft Budget Constraints and Competition", presented in 3rd conference of the ISNIE, September 1999, Washington D.C.

Jones, Leroy (1991). "Performance Evaluation for State owned Entreprises", pp.179-205, in Ramamurti, Ravi, & Vernon, Raymond, ed., *Privatisation and Control of State-owned Enterprises*, p. 332, *EDI Development Studies*, World Bank, Washington.

Jones, Leroy; Tandon, Pankaj; and Vogelsang, Ingo (1991). "Selling State-Owned Enterprises: A Cost-benefit Approach", pp. 28-53, in Ramamurti, Ravi, and Vernon, Raymond, ed., *Privatisation and Control of State-owned Enterprises*, p. 332, *EDI Development Studies*, World Bank, Washington.

Joskow, Paul, & Schmalensee, Richard (1983). *Markets for Power, An Analysis of Electrical Utility Deregulation*, MIT Press.

Joskow, Paul (1996). "Introducing Competition into Regulated Network Industries: From Hierarchies to Markets in Electricity", *Journal of Corporate Change*, Vol 5 No. 2.

Khilnani, Sunil (1997). *The Idea of India*, Penguin, UK, 263 p.

Kikeri Sunita, Nellis John. & Shirley Mary (1992). *Privatisation: The Lessons of Experience*, World Bank, Washington D.C..

Kornai, Janos (1986). "The Soft Budget Constraint", *Kyklos*, Vol. 39 pp. 3-30.

Kornai, Janos (1990). "The Affinity between Ownership forms and Coordination Mechanisms: The Common Experience of Reform in Socialist Countries", *Journal of Economic Perspectives*, Vol. 4, No. 3, pp. 131-147.

Kornai, Janos (1992). *The Socialist System: The Political Economy of Communism*, Clarendon Press, Oxford, 644 p.

Kumar, Suresh (1997). "Public Sector in Independent India", *Indian Journal of Public Administration*, Vol. XIII No. 3 pp. 510-516.

Latsis, Spiro J. (1972). "Situational Determinism in Economics", *The British Journal for the Philosophy of Science*, 23, pp. 207-245.

Laville, Frédéric (1998). "Modélisation de la rationalité limitée: de quels outils dispose-t-on?", *Revue Economique*, Vol. 49, no. 2, pp. 335-365.

Levy, Brian & Spiller, Pablo (1994). "The Institutional Foundations of Regulatory Commitment: A Comparative Analysis of Telecommunications Regulation", *The Journal of Law Economics and Organisation*, Vol. 10 No. 2.

Lotter, Françoise (1995). "Efficacité transactionnelle vs. efficacité parétienne: How and why regulate utilities?", Communication au colloque international d'économie publique ENST de Bretagne, Département d'économie, 7-8 Septembre, p. 33.

March, James & Olsen, Johan (1986). "Garbage can models of decision-making in organizations", in Ambiguity and command: organizational perspectives on military decision-making, March, James and Weissinger-Baylon, eds., Cambridge, MA: Ballinger, pp. 11-35.

March, James G. (1962). "The Business Firm as a Political Coalition", *Journal of Politics*, 24: pp. 662-678.

——————. (1978). "Bounded Rationality, Ambiguity, and the Engineering of Choice", *Bell Journal of Economics*, 9: pp. 587-608.

——————. (1987). "Ambiguity and Accounting: The Elusive Link between Information and decision-making", Accounting, Organisations and Society No. 12, pp. 153-168, reprinted in Decision-making under ambiguity,

——————. (1991). "Exploration and Exploitation in Organisational Learning", *Organisation Science*, 2, pp. 71-87.

——————. (1994). *A Primer on Decision-making: How Decisions Happen*, (Chapter 5, on 'Ambiguity and Interpretation' pp. 175-220), Macmillan Free Press, NY.

March, James, & Simon, Herbert (1958). *Organisations*, Wiley, New York.

Martimort (1996). "The Multiprincipal Nature of Government", *European Economic Review*, 40: pp. 673-685.

Mathur, B.P. (1997). "Public Audit and Financial Control", *Indian Journal of Public Administration*, Vol XIII No. 3 pp. 464-472.

Mayer, Colin (1998). "Financial Systems and Corporate Governance: A Review of International Evidence", *Journal of Institutional and Theoretical Economics*, Vol. 154, pp. 144-165.

Ménard, Claude & Shirley, Mary (1999) "Reforming Contractual Arrangements: Lessons from Urban Water Systems in Six Developing Countries", Working Paper, p. 40.

Ménard, Claude & George Clarke (2000). "A Transitory Regime Water Supply in Conakry", *Guinea Policy Research Working Paper 2362*. World Bank, Development Research Group, Washington, D.C., June.

Milgrom, Paul & Roberts, J. (1990). "Bargaining Costs and the Organization of Economic Activity", Chapter 3 in James E. Alt. & K.A. Shepsle, Eds. *Perspectives on Positive Political Economy*, Cambridge University Press.

Ministry of Power, Government of India (1985). "Commercial Accounting System for SEBs", *Electricity Supply Annual Accounts Rules*.

————. (1993). "Proceedings of the Conference on Power Sector Reforms in India", Co-sponsored by the Government of India and the World Bank, held in Jaipur on October 29-31, p. 243 New Delhi.

————. (1997). *Annual Report 1996-97*, New Delhi.

————. (2000). *Conference of the Power Ministers*, 26 February, "Agenda Notes", p. 41 New Delhi.

————. (2001). *Blueprint for the Power Sector Development*, New Delhi.

————. (2002). *Annual Report 2001-02*, New Delhi.

Minocha, O.P. (1997). *Public Sector in India: From Commanding Heights to the Present Status*, pp. 517-526.

Mishra, Ram Kumar (2000). "Public Enterprises: Performance, Problems and Challenges", p. 8 Working Paper, Institute for Public Enterprise, Hyderabad.

Mohan, Rakesh (1997). *The India Infrastructure Report*, Spécial Supplement of 1997 to the JMJ Book Info, New Delhi.

Morris, Sebastian (2003). "The Electricity Act 2003, Implications for the Development of the Sector", Presentation made at *The Seminar of Power Sector Reforms: Technological Aspects*, co-organised by IIT-Kanpur & CSH-Delhi, September, to be published in Kalra & Ruet (ed), Manohar Publishers, New Delhi.

MPSEB (2003). *Sankalp*, Sambhaag Burhampur, Madhya Pradesh Raja Vidhyut Mandal, p. 42.

Naughton, B. (1985). "False Starts and Second Winds: Financial Reforms in China's Industrial System", in E.J. Peng & C. Wong (eds) *The Political Economy of Reform in Post-Mao China*, Cambridge MA: Harvard University Press, pp. 223-252.

Nee, Victor (1999). "The Role of the State in Making Markets", presented in 3rd conference of the ISNIE, September 1999, Washington D.C.

Nellis, John (1991). "Contract Plans: A Review of International Experience", pp. 278-324, in Ramamurti, Ravi, & Vernon, Raymond, ed., *Privatization and Control of State-owned enterprises*, 332 pp, EDI Development studies, World Bank, Washington.

Niskanen, W.J. (1975). "Bureaucrats and Politicians", *Journal of Law & Economics*, December Vol. 18, Issue 3, pp. 617-643.

NPC (1995, 1996, 1997, 1998). *Annual Reports of Noida Power Company Ltd, 1994-95 to 1997-98.*

NTPC (1997). *Annual Report 1996-97*, New Delhi.

Oi, Jean (1994). *Rural China Take off: Incentives for Reform*, Cbook manuscript, Harvard University.

Orissa Electricity Regulatory Commission (1997). Order No. 9 dated 12th March, Bhubaneshwar.

Oury, Jean-Marc (1981). L'économie du déséquilibre, mimeo, Ecole des Mines de Paris.

————. (1981). La tyrannie de la sédentarité, mimeo, Ecole des Mines de Paris.

————. (1983). Economie politique de la vigilance, Calmann-Lévy.

————. (1995). Cours d'économie de l'entreprise, polycopié, Ecole des Mines de Paris.

Phadke, Amol and Sudhir Chella Rajan (2003). "Electricity Reforms in India: Not too late to go back to the drawing board", pp. 3061-3072, *Economic and Political Weekly*, Vol XXXVIII No. 29, Bombay.

Planning Commission (1997). *Annual Report on the Working of SEBs for the Year 1996-97*, Government of India.

————. (1998). *Annual Report on the Working of SEBs for the Year 1997-98*, Government of India.

————. (1998a). *Report on the Financial Performance of SEBs from 1991-92 to 1994-95*, New Delhi, March 1998.

————. (1999). *Annual Report on the Working of SEBs for the Year 1998-99*, Government of India.

————. (2001). *Annual Report on the Working of SEBs for the Year 2000-01*, Government of India.

————. (2002). *Annual Report on the Working of SEBs for the Year 2001-02*, Government of India, 199p.

Powerline (2003a). *Powerline Magazine*, Vol. 7 No. 6, March, New Delhi.

————. (2003b). *Powerline Magazine*, Vol. 7 No. 10, July, New Delhi.

Prayas (2003). "A good beginning but challenges galore: A survey based study of resources, transparency and public participation in electricity regulatory commissions in India", p. 78, Prayas Energy Group, February, Pune.

Quraishi, S.Y. (1998). "Power Sector Regulation and Restructuring: Haryana's Experience", Paper presented at the International forum on Power Sector and Restructuring, New Delhi.

Raghavulu, C.V. (1997). "Economic Policy in India: From Centralised Planning to Liberalisation", *Indian Journal of Public Administration*, Vol XIII No. 3 pp.473-490.

Rajan Raghuram and Zingales Luigi (1998). "Power in a Theory of the Firm", *Quarterly Journal of Economics*, CXIII Issue 2, pp. 387-432.

Rajan, Thillai (2000). "Restructuring of a Vertically Integrated Electric Utility: A Process Study", dissertation, Fellow Programme in Management, p. 247, Indian Institue of Management, Bangalore.

Ramamurti, Ravi (1991). "The Search for Remedies", pp.7-28, in Ramamurti, Ravi, & Vernon, Raymond, ed., *Privatization and Control of State-owned Enterprises*, p. 332, *EDI Development Studies*, World Bank, Washington.

Ramamurti, Ravi, and Vernon, Raymond, ed. (1991). "Privatisation and Control of State-owned Enterprises", p. 332, *EDI Development Studies*, World Bank, Washington.

Ranganathan, V. (1997). "Commercialization of Nepal Electricity Authority", *Report for the Nepal Administrative Staff College*, p. 50, Indian Institue of Management, Bangalore.

Ranganathan, V., and Gupta, Sanjay (2000). "SEB Performance: Lessons from Thailand", *The Hindu Business Line*, 1st February.

Ruet, Joël (1999a). *Administrations for Sale: The State Electricity Boards; Private vs. Public 'enterprisation'*, Cahiers du CERNA, 99-C1, Paris.

————. (1999b). "Investment Needs and Possible Iincomes in Indian Power Sector to Bridge the Energy Gap", to be published in *The Pacific-Asia Journal of Energy*, Tata Energy Research Institute, New Delhi.

————. (1999c). "Why and How Decentralising Financial Responsibility to Circles in UHBVN", *Report to the Power Secretary, Government of Haryana and to the Managing Director, UHBVN*, October, p.10, CERNA, Paris.

————. (2000). "La mondialisation limitée du secteur électrique : de la prééminence des états au retour relatif du centre", in 'Questions d'échelle: du mondial au local', ed. Chaudhuri, Basudeb & Landy, Frédéric, collection Sciences Sociales, CNRS, Paris.

————. (2001). "Winners and Losers of the Reform of SEBs", An Organisational Study, p. 85, Occasional paper, CSH, New Delhi.

————. (2001a). "Le secteur électrique en Inde: réforme libérale ou persistance d'un modèle de développement à l'indienne?", pp. 83-104, *revue Tiers-Monde No. 165*, January-March, Paris.

————. (2002). "A New Paradigm for the Indian Power Sector", chapter 12, p 220-262, in *Privatisation of Public Enterprises*, editors R.K.Mishra & G. de Bernis, Manak, New Delhi.

————. (2002a). "L'Inde réinvente l'économie mixte", *Revue Sociétal*, September 2002, Paris.

———. (2002b). "Investment Profitability in Bridging the Power Gap in India", Vol. 49 No. 2, *Indian Economic Journal*, October-December 2001-2002, Bombay.

———. (2004). "Investment Profitability in Bridging the Power Gap in India", updated version from Vol. 49 No. 2, *Indian Economic Journal*, October-December 2001-2002, Bombay, in Ruet & Kalra (eds), Against the Current II, Manohar Publishers, Delhi.

———. (2004a). "The Future of State-owned Companies: Is Privatisation the Answer?", Vol. 51, No. 1, *Indian Economic Journal*.

Sagar, Jagdish (2003). "The Unbundling and Privatization of DVB", Paper Presented at the *Brainstorming Workshop on Power Sector Reforms*, IIM Bangalore, April 11-12, 2003.

Schroeder, Gertrude E. (1988). "Property Rights Issues in Economic Reform in Socialist Countries", *Studies in Comparative Communism*, summer, 21:2, pp. 175-188

Schwank, Stokar and North (2000). "Long-term Carbon Emission Targets Aiming Towards Convergence: A Comparative Investigation on Carbon Emission Path Options for Switzerland and India", in Audinet, Shukla and Grare, ed., *India's Energy, Essays on Sustainable Development*, Manohar Publishers, New Delhi.

Segal, Ilya R. (1998). "Monopoly and Soft Budget Constraint", *RAND Journal of Economics*, Vol. 29, No. 3 pp. 596-609.

Shahi (2003). Interview, *http://www.renewingindia.org/news1_june3_elecact.html*

Sharma, R.D. (1998). "Goals Theory as an Analytical Frame of Reference for an Administrative System", *Indian Journal of Public Administration*, Vol. XIV No. 4 pp. 78-787.

Shirley, Mary & Colin Xu, L. (1997). "Information, Incentives and Commitment: An Empirical Analysis of Contracts between Governments and State Entreprises", *Policy Research Working Paper No. 1769*, World Bank.

Shleifer, Andrei (1995). "Establishing Property Rights", Proceedings of the Annual World Bank Conference on Development Economics 1994.

Shleifer, Andrei and Vishny, Robert (1994). "Politicians and Firms", *Quarterly Journal of Economics*, 109: pp. 995-1024.

Shukla (2000). *Developing Countries and Global Climate Change, Electric Power Options in India*, Report prepared for the Pew Center on Global Climate Change, Ahmedabad, Gujarat, p. 31.

Shunglu V.K. (1997). "Role of Comptroller and Auditor General in India", *Indian Journal of Public Administration*, Vol XIII No. 3 pp. 458-463.

Simon, Herbert (1947). "Administration et processus de décision", Paris, Economica 1983, translated from *Administrative Behavior: A Study of Decision-Making Processes in Administrative Organisations*, Free Press, Macmillan, New York.

———. (1952). "A Behavioral Model of Rational Choice", *Quarterly Journal of Economics*, 69: pp. 99-118.

———. (1976). "From Procedural to Substantive Rationality", in Latsis S. (Ed), *Methods and Appraisals in Economics*, Cambridge University Press, pp. 129-148.

———. (1978). "Rationality as Process and as Product of Thought", 68 *American Economic Review* pp. 1-16.

———. (1982). *Models of Bounded Rationality*, MIT Press.

Singh, Daljit (2004). "What it takes to Improve the Performance of Distribution Companies: The Experience of Andhra Pradesh and Delhi", in Ruet (ed), *Against the Current III*, Manohar Publishers, New Delhi.

Sinha, Sidharth (2004). "Management of Power Supply to Agriculture", in Ruet (ed), *Against the Current III*, Manohar Publishers, New Delhi.

Spiller, Pablo (1991). "Politicians, Interest Groups and Regulators: A Multiple-principals Agency Theory of Regulation, or let them be bribed", *Journal of Law & Economics* 33, pp. 65-101.

Subba Rao, G. (2003). "Issue in Electricity Bill 2003", Keynote Address, 15p, IIT-CSH *Workshop on Power Reforms: Technological and Financial*, September 4-5, IIT Kanpur, to be published in Kalra & Ruet (ed), Manohar Publishers, New Delhi.

TERI (1999). *Report on Consumer's Willingness to Pay for Electricity in Orissa*, TERI, New Delhi.

__________. (2002). "Editorial", *Regulateri*, Issue 12, March 2002, TERI, New Delhi.

Trivedi, Prajapati (1990). *A Critique of Public Enterprise Policy*, International Management Publishers, New Delhi, p. 475.

__________. (1992). (Ed.) *Memorandum of Understanding, An Approach for Improving Public Enterprise Performance*, International Management Publishers, New Delhi, p. 896.

Trivedi, Prajapati and Gopal, V. (1992). "Memorandum of Understanding and Other Performance Improvement Systems, A Comparison", pp. 843-870, in *Memorandum of Understanding, An Approach for Improving Public Enterprise Performance*, Ed. by Prajapati Trivedi, International Management Publishers, New Delhi, p. 896.

UHBVN (1999). "Questions Raised by the Potential Investors", Pre-bid Meeting Working Document, Uttar Haryana Bijli Vitran Nigam, Panchkula.

UPERC (2001). *Power Diary*, August, p. 5, Lucknow.

__________. (2002). *Tariff Order 2002-03* for U.P. Power Corporation Limited, Uttar Pradesh Electricity Regulatory Commission, Petition No. 7, p. 289, Lucknow.

Vate, Madhu Danda (1997). "Ethos of Planning and Plan Administration in India", *Indian Journal of Public Administration*, Vol XIII No. 4, pp. 867-873.

Vaugier-Chatterjee, Anne (1997). "Administration et politique dans l'Inde contemporaine", *Historiens et Géographes No. 356*.

Veljanovski, C. (1987). *Selling the State*, Widenfeld and Nicholson, London.

Vernon, Raymond (1991). "A Technical Approach to Privatization Issues: Coupling Project Analysis with Rules of Thumb", pp. 54-72, in Ramamurti, Ravi, & Vernon, Raymond, ed., *Privatization and Control of State-owned Enterprises*, p. 332, *EDI Development Studies*, World Bank, Washington.

__________. (1992). "Linking Managers with Ministers, Dilemmas of the State Owed Enterprise", pp. 31-51, in *Memorandum of Understanding, An Approach for Improving Public Enterprise Performance*, Ed. by Prajapati Trivedi, International Management Publishers, New Delhi, 896 p.

Weil, Thierry (2000). "Invitation à la lecture de James March", Presses de l'Ecole des Mines, Paris, 180 p.

Williamson, Oliver E. (1994). "Efficiency, Power, Authority and Economic Organization", Colloque Economie des coûts de transaction: développements récents, Paris, mai.

_____. (1999). "Public and Private Bureaucraties: A Transaction Cost Economics Perspective", *Journal of Law Economics & Organisation*, Vol. 15 No. 1 pp. 306-342.

World Bank (1996). "Staff Appraisal Report", Orissa Power Sector Restructuring Project, Report No. 14298-IN

__________. (1997). "Project Appraisal Document", *Haryana Power Sector Restructuring Project, Report* 17234-IN

__________. (1998). "Power Sector Reform and the Privatization of Distribution in India", Main Author H. Salgo, Internal Working Document, March 98, 17 p.

__________. (1999). "Staff Appraisal Document," Andhra Pradesh Power Sector Restructuring Project.

World Bank Institute (1998). *Social Marketing Strategies to Fight Corruption*, by G.S. Kindra and Rick Stapenhurst, World Bank.

Index

F

G

H

I

L

R

S

T

U

V

W

List of State/Countries

List of Companies/Utilities

List of State Electricity Boards

List of Electricity Commissions/ Corporations